Robert E. Howard's

ADVENTURES IN AN AGE UNDREAMED OF

System Design
Benn Graybeaton, Nathan Dowdell & Jay Little

Line Development
Jason Durall & Chris Lites

Project Lead
Richard August

Writing
Lou Agresta (*The Red Pit*), Richard August (*Introduction, The Pact of Xiabalba, The Thousand Eyes of Aumag Bel, Seeds of Glory*), Benn Graybeaton (*The Caves of the Dero*), Jason Durall (*Introduction, The Ghost of Thunder River*), Chris Lites (*The Pact of Xiabalba*), Helena Nash (*Devils Under Green Stars*), Scott Oden (*The Red Pit*) & Kevin Ross (*The Seethers in Darkness*)

Approvals
Patrice Louinet & Jeffrey Shanks

Editing & Proofreading
Lisa Padol & T.R. Knight

Cover Artwork
Daren Bader

Interior Artwork
Michael Syrigos, Michele Frigo, Diana Martinez, André Meister, Martin Sobr, Richard Pace, Matthias Kinnigkeit, Nick Greenwood & Gunship Revolution

Cartography
Tobias Tranell

Art Direction
Mischa Thomas

Graphic Design
Michal E. Cross

Layout
Thomas Shook

Additional Graphic Design
Dan Algstrand & Malcolm Wolter

Produced by
Chris Birch

Head of RPG Development
Sam Webb

Production Manager
Steve Daldry

Social Media Manager
Salwa Azar

Operations Manager
Garry Harper

Community Support
Lloyd Gyan

With Thanks to
The Robert E. Howard Foundation, Fred & Jay at Cabinet Entertainment, Erwan Hascoët, Vincent Jamgotchian & Frederic Henry at Monolith

Published by
Modiphius Entertainment Ltd.
2nd Floor, 39 Harwood Road,
Fulham, London, SW6 4QP
United Kingdom

Legal

© 2017 Conan Properties International LLC ("CPI"). **Conan**, **Conan The Barbarian**, **Hyboria** and related logos, characters, names, and distinctive likenesses thereof are trademarks or registered trademarks of CPI. All rights reserved. **Robert E. Howard** and related logos, characters, names, and distinctive likenesses thereof are trademarks or registered trademarks of Robert E. Howard Properties Inc. All rights reserved.

The **2d20 system** and Modiphius Logos are copyright Modiphius Entertainment Ltd. 2015–2017. All **2d20 system** text is copyright Modiphius Entertainment Ltd.

Any unauthorised use of copyrighted material is illegal. Any trademarked names are used in a fictional manner; no infringement is intended.

This is a work of fiction. Any similarity with actual people and events, past or present, is purely coincidental and unintentional except for those people and events described in an historical context.

The image on page 59 uses brushes from Obsidian Dawn (www.obsidiandawn.com).

2nd Printing. Printed by Livonia Print, Ventspils iela 50, Riga, LV-1002, Latvia.

TABLE OF CONTENTS

Introduction
WELCOME, TO THESE BLOODY PAGES 2

Chapter 1
DEVILS UNDER GREEN STARS 5
- Lost Zukundu 5
- Approaching Zukundu 9
- Queen Chitaka and the Path of Skulls ... 12
- Hunting the Ape 15
- Beneath the Jade Keep of the Mekutu ... 19
- The Crawling Caves 20
- Inside the Jade Keep 22
- The Ebony Keep Burns 30
- Aftermath 34

Chapter 2
THE PACT OF XIABALBA .. 35
- Introduction 35
- Chapter One: A Private Little Maelstrom ... 38
- Chapter Two: Xeiros, the Dreaming City ... 42
- Chapter Three: The Hourglass 47
- Epilogue 52

Chapter 3
THE CAVES OF THE DERO .. 53
- Introduction 53
- Chapter One: Hybris 53
- Chapter Two: The Mines of Acheron ... 61
- Adversaries 64
- Chapter Three: What Lies Beneath ... 65
- Experience 70

Chapter 4
THE GHOST OF THUNDER RIVER 71
- Prelude: A Torch Shines Across the Aeons ... 71
- On the Red Spotted Trail 75
- Death at their Heels 78
- Council of Fear 82
- Souls Down the River 83
- Combing the Wilderness 85
- The Village of the Raven 85
- The Place of Whispering Fog 87
- Conclusion 89
- Experience and Rewards 89

Chapter 5
THE THOUSAND EYES OF AUMAG-BEL 90
- Prologue 90
- Arriving in the City 90
- A Return to the Streets 93
- The Robbery 93
- A Chase in the Market Place 94
- The Den of the Black Lotus 97
- The Forgotten Palace 101
- The Journey's End 106
- Experience 106

Chapter 6
THE RED PIT 107
- Prologue 108
- Synopsis 108
- And So It Begins 109
- Epilogue 120
- Experience 120

Chapter 7
THE SEETHERS IN DARKNESS 121
- Introduction 121
- The Devouring Storm 123
- The City Beneath the Sands 125
- The City's History 125
- Aftermath 135
- Experience 135

Chapter 8
SEEDS OF GLORY 136
- Campaigns and Jeweled Thrones ... 136
- Scattered Jewels... 140

INTRODUCTION
WELCOME, TO THESE BLOODY PAGES…

> *Hither came Conan the Cimmerian, black-haired, sullen-eyed, sword in hand, a thief, a reaver, a slayer, with gigantic melancholies and gigantic mirth, to tread the jeweled thrones of the Earth under his sandaled feet.*
>
> — The Nemedian Chronicles,
> from "The Phoenix on the Sword"

Collected within these pages are seven original adventures for **Conan**. Each is designed to be played on its own and to allow players and their characters to explore a different corner of Conan's world. Each adventure has been written to capture the spirit of Robert E. Howard's original Conan stories and to offer a sense of that same restless, relentless excitement.

These adventures were selected and written deliberately to remain episodic and distinct from one another in approximation of Howard's approach to the Conan stories; featuring his iconic barbarian in moments plucked from a lifetime rich with incident and adventure.

Has a trek across a desert been particularly long and arduous? Include an adventure from *Jeweled Thrones of the Earth* as a flashback to an earlier period in the player characters' careers. Or flash forward, to a time when they are richer and wiser… but also slower and older. Do you like the elements from one adventure but think that your players might find another too slow for their tastes? Mix them up and insert your own ideas together for something new.

Howard took real history, blended it with myth, and added elements flavored with his current enthusiasm to create foes for Conan to slay and dangers for him to evade. Approach these adventures the same way — take the parts you like the most and combine them into something new and uniquely calibrated for your players to enjoy. Just make sure it's exciting, dangerous, and filled with moments in which your player characters get the opportunity to be heroic.

Good luck, dog-brothers and sword-sisters, and may your doom not find you until your hair is grey and your sword is bloody!

Chapter 1: Devils Under Green Stars
A lost city, swallowed by the jungle. Three depraved cultures locked in a state of incessant war and, stalking occluded corridors, the hideous form of the Feathered Ape! What is this impossible creature, and what effect will the player characters' entrance have on this remainder of a vanished civilization?

Chapter 2: The Pact of Xiabalba
Wrecked on a mysterious island, the player characters are tricked into helping a mysterious sorceress. Lost on the tides of time and facing insurmountable odds, they must confront the consequences of a bargain made millennia ago if they are to secure their own survival!

INTRODUCTION

BEING AN ACCOUNT OF THE CONTENT OF THE APPENDICES ASSOCIATED WITH THE NEMEDIAN CHRONICLES

WHILE CONSIDERABLE WORK has been devoted to the contents of The Nemedian Chronicles (amongst which the interested reader might deign to consider my own contribution to said canon, *The Chronicles of Nemedia: A Proposed Chronology*, worthy of perusal), little attention has been paid to those other tales which constitute the Appendices of such a vast, unruly tome. While, quite justifiably in this author's humble opinion, most focus has been paid to that most remarkable figure, Conan of Cimmeria, there is much within the text which warrants greater attention. Perhaps chief amongst these are those fragments which I have titled "The Jeweled Thrones of the Earth".

These texts — or what remains of them — seem to have been assembled by a keen geographer, for each narrative explores a new aspect of the prevailing cultures of the Hyborian Age of our earth's forgotten history. Some of these places — Thunder River, Koth, and Zamboula — are familiar to those with even the most cursory grasp of these half-lost epochs of our earth. There are, however, stranger geographies hinted at in these remarkable stories — a city lost in time itself, a forsaken citadel swallowed by jungle, and ancient catacombs hollowed from the living rock by strange, dreadful beings fortunately consigned to the primordial past.

The Hyborian Age is still impossibly remote to us, even to those of us who have devoted their lives to its study. These texts, as strange and peculiar as any of those which have already been published, remind us that the kingdoms of the ancient world were teeming with life, danger, and what is very properly called the weird. The von Junzt translations of sections of The Nemedian Chronicles are amongst the most remarkable relics of a remarkable age, and these new chronicles render them more remarkable still; whatever fragments might remain out there, in the lost reliquaries and collapsed temples, waiting to be found, they are unlikely to be stranger and more unusual than those which can be found within these pages.

Prof. John Kirowan (PhD, FRS, FRAI, FRGS)
Guest Lecturer, Department of Anthropology
Miskatonic University
Arkham, Massachusetts

Chapter 3: The Caves of the Dero

Drawn by the lure of gold, the player characters must attempt to decipher the impenetrable secrets of a cabal of sorcerers hidden deep within the Earth. In mines below an old and abandoned villa lie the remnants of an impossible race of creatures, spawned in a time older and darker than the Hyborian Age itself!

Chapter 4: The Ghost of Thunder River

A mysterious figure known as the Ghost has drawn a horde of the bloodthirsty Picts to his side, and is threatening settlers and Aquilonian border forts. The player characters must find out who or what this figure is and stop him, before civilization itself is swept away on a tide of red vengeance!

Chapter 5: The Thousand Eyes of Aumag-Bel

Beneath a bustling, thriving metropolis lurks something ancient and evil. As the player characters hunt for an item of great value which was stolen from them by child thieves, they inadvertently stumble upon something far darker — can they prevent a grisly ritual from taking place once again?

Chapter 6: The Red Pit

Enslaved within the mine known simply as "The Red Pit", the player characters face a terrifying fight for their freedom. Can they inspire a general uprising to help them escape this dreadful prison, or will they be forced to break their chains alone?

Chapter 7: The Seethers in Darkness

A mysterious scholar secures the player characters' services as guides and bodyguards on an expedition to mysterious ruins, deep in the desert. What they discover will require all their skill, cunning, and resourcefulness to survive!

Chapter 8: Seeds of Glory

These short adventure seeds and potential campaign outlines are presented here for the gamemaster to develop further, or to inspire additional adventures.

> *"Then the man Conan seemed suddenly to grow up in my mind without much labor on my part and immediately a stream of stories flowed off my pen — or rather off my typewriter — almost without effort on my part. I did not seem to be creating, but rather relating events that had occurred. Episode crowded on episode so fast that I could scarcely keep up with them."*
>
> — Robert E. Howard,
> letter to Clark Ashton Smith

CHAPTER 1
DEVILS UNDER GREEN STARS

> "Five dead dogs" exclaimed Techotl, his flaming eyes reflecting a ghastly exultation. "Five slain! Five crimson nails for the black pillar! The gods of blood be thanked!"
>
> He lifted quivering hands on high, and then, with the face of a fiend, he spat on the corpses and stamped on their faces, dancing in his ghoulish glee. His recent allies eyed him in amazement, and Conan asked, in the Aquilonian tongue: "Who is this madman?"
>
> — "Red Nails"

The player characters are outsiders who stumble across the forgotten city-palace of Zukundu, where an uneasy peace between the degenerating tribes that inhabit its darkened, overgrown halls and chambers threatens to turn into bloody war, amid the mysterious and savage attacks of the "Feathered Ape". Falling in with the vengeful Xhotatse tribe, the player characters must seek the terrible creature that is taking the heads of the tribe. Their hunt takes them across the city-palace, encountering the hostile, degenerate Mekutu tribe and their monstrous pets. Will the Xhotatse have their bloody revenge or will the jade fountain of Mekutu bear more grisly fruit?

LOST ZUKUNDU

The lost civilization of Zukundu is located in the Southern Kingdoms beyond Stygia, in the uncharted jungles past Kush, Darfar, and Keshan. The high-walled city-palace occupies every inch of an island in a vast lake deep in the jungle, fed by several sluggish rivers. Titanic crocodiles, or the prehistoric ancestors of such reptiles (see *Great Reptiles*, page 9), populate the dark lake, making entering and escaping from Zukundu quite perilous.

Tall stone walls are completely overgrown with vines, lending the complex a rambling, semi-organic appearance. Glittering roofs, towers, and minarets lie beneath a great canopy of verdant green. Under the profusion of greenery from this distance, one can only discern the site as a man-made structure.

ALTERNATE LOCATIONS FOR ZUKUNDU

The gamemaster may move Zukundu to another location in the Kingdoms of the South as desired. Zukundu itself should remain geographically remote, largely hidden from the world of men. Suggested alternate locations follow below.

- **VALLEY:** Zukundu sits within a deep valley hidden in the mountains. The crags surrounding the valley are home to flying reptiles of impressive size, perhaps pterosaurs from ages gone. The mouth of the valley has long been choked and overgrown with trees.
- **HILLTOP:** Zukundu lurks deep in the jungle, sprawling atop several hills. The lower slopes of the hills are home to lumbering, sharp-toothed reptiles of considerable size.

THE ENVIRONMENT OF ZUKUNDU

The strange folk who built Zukundu did so more than a century ago. The labyrinthine construction of interconnecting chambers and galleries, the use of semi-precious stones and metals in the building work and, more ominously, the madness and death that seem to permeate its very foundations are all reminiscent of other storied ruins hidden across the continent. Large open squares, once exposed to the sky, suggest gardens and arboretums where the people of Zukundu would lounge or dream among the heady blossom of exotic flowers.

Formerly a sprawling, luxurious pleasure palace, Zukundu is now overgrown by a century or so of rampant, untended plant life. The city-palace is verdant, moist and dark, lit only by bunches of phosphorescent green "star-fruit" that grow in clumps throughout the structure. No glimpse of open sky penetrates ground level. Former open spaces are now hidden from all but the most tenacious light. The lofty towers and minarets are choked with plant life and dangerously unsteady.

In this perpetual gloom, night and day are forgotten concepts, with the inhabitants resting and waking as they choose. No rain reaches the ground, but pools, fountains, and springs serve to provide water for the inhabitants. Various fruits provide food. As one moves through Zukundu, sound is muted — absorbed by the vegetation. There are few animals loose here, save for birds, insects, and the odd small monkey and snake.

Anyone moving through Zukundu without a local guide risks getting lost, turned around, or simply taking far too long to reach their destination. In addition, there are traps and natural obstacles which could prove deadly to unwary newcomers: concealed pits, hidden vine snares, darts triggered by trip wires, small venomous snakes, slippery slopes, and crumbling masonry. See *The Dangers of Zukundu* (next page) for details.

Certain shunned structures within the city-palace are home to queer beasts like the moon lion and the Red Creeper. Below Zukundu sit subterranean caves where the crawlers lurk in the foreboding dark.

THE DANGERS OF ZUKUNDU

When prompted by the adventure, or wherever extra random peril is desired, the gamemaster should roll a d20 and consult the *Dangers of Zukundu* table below, or can introduce these hazards via Doom spends. Allow player characters to make a Challenging (D2) Survival test to spot the danger before it strikes and, optionally, a Challenging (D2) Agility test to minimize the effect of the danger if they fail to spot it.

DEVILS UNDER GREEN STARS

DANGERS OF ZUKUNDU

Roll	Event	Doom Spend	Effect
1–3	Concealed Pit	2	Concealed pit opens up beneath your feet, dropping you onto vicious fire-hardened spears. This trap deals 6 damage but a Simple (D0) Acrobatics test can be made to reduce this damage. Every point of Momentum rolled will reduce damage by 1. Each rank of the *Nimble as a Cat* talent grants 2 Momentum for this test.
4–6	Vine Snare	1	Hidden vine snare drops a net of thorns over your head and strikes a hidden chime above you. This trap causes 5 Nonlethal grappling damage. For every round that the characters remain trapped, the gamemaster gains 1 Doom.
7–9	Poison Dart	1	Poison dart shoots out of a hollow tree trunk. You are paralyzed until another player character succeeds on an Average (D1) Alchemy or Challenging (D2) Medicine test and concocts an antidote. On an Average (D1) Awareness test, you find where the trap was concealed (and can use the unlaunched dart venom to concoct an antidote). For each round that the characters remain trapped, the gamemaster gains 1 Doom.
10–12	Snake	1	Small venomous snake darts out to bite your foot. Succeed in a Challenging (D2) Resistance test or suffer 1 Fatigue.
13–16	Slippery Slope	1	Slippery slope gives way beneath your feet. Unless you pay 2 Doom, you are knocked prone and separated from the others by a considerable climb. The climb is a Challenging (D2) Athletics test.
17–20	Falling Masonry	4	Crumbling masonry falls from above. Take 4 damage.

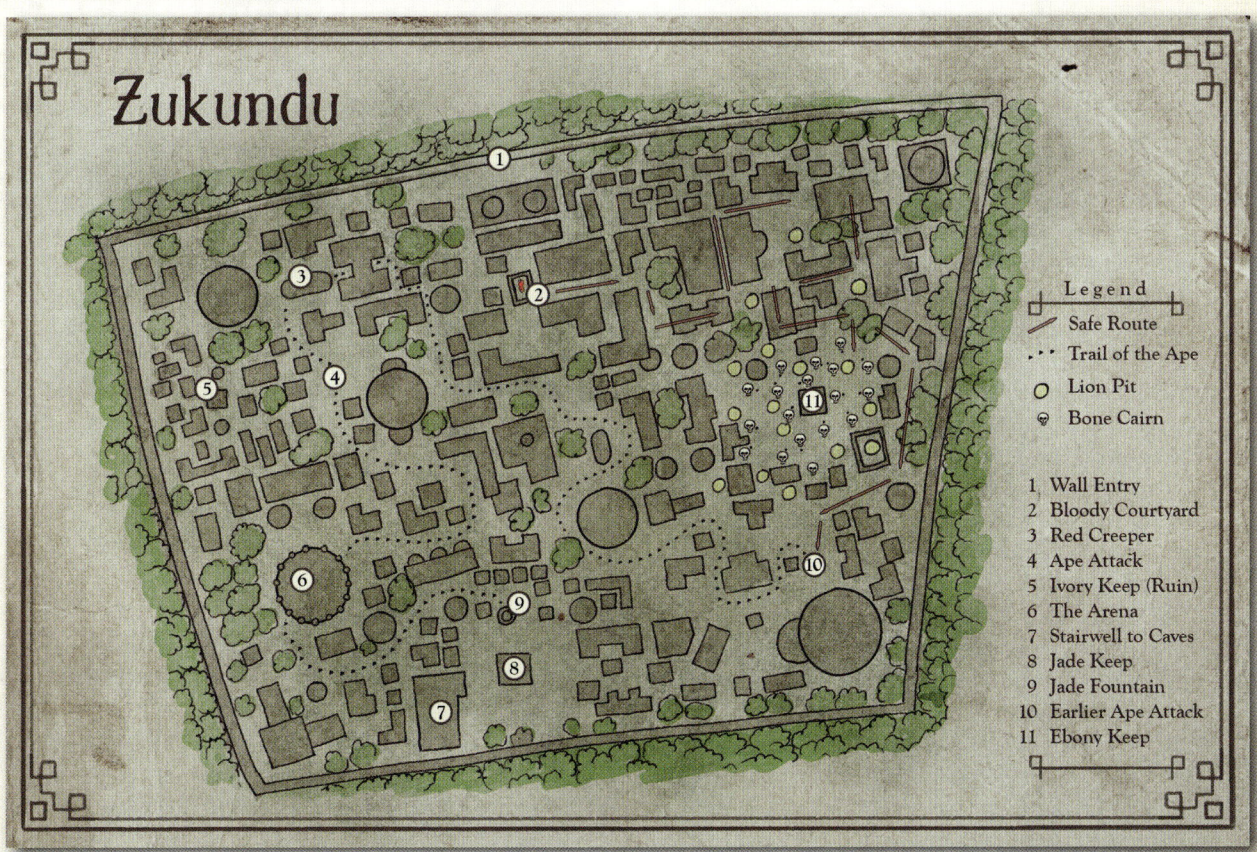

Increase the difficulty of the tests to Daunting (D3) if they are moving faster than a walking pace and to Dire (D4) if running for their lives.

THE TRIBES OF ZUKUNDU

The people who built Zukundu fell far from their original glory, and those who remain are a mere shadow of their forebears in both numbers and wisdom. Much of what was once known of the city-palace was forgotten over generations or reduced to little more than folklore. Likewise, the outside world has long since forgotten that this place, so far from inhabited lands, ever existed.

Both the natural obstacles surrounding Zukundu and the giant reptiles that prowl outside (see *Lost Zukundu*, page 5) make leaving or escaping the city-palace a challenge that none of its inhabitants have managed in many years. The seemingly unnatural power of the place breeds clannishness and territoriality, resulting in a population that barely thinks of the outside world, let alone considers leaving Zukundu.

Zukundu's green jade, the interior denizens are a degenerate lot, plagued by inbreeding and madness; the result of their isolation and, perhaps, the strange construction of the city-palace itself. Isolated from the rest of the world for so long, they intermarried many times over, breeding certain traits among their offspring. Congenital defects among the inhabitants are not uncommon and range from severe abnormalities of the mind to strange deformities of the body. Few reach old age. In general, the people are a gaunt, wiry breed, short and pale from lack of sunlight. Left undisturbed, the entire population may survive only a few generations more before dying out. All these unfortunate folk have a touch of vengefulness and madness about them.

The city-palace is home to three tribes of people who reside in different parts of Zukundu. These tribes currently exist in an uneasy truce, with no one tribe eager to attack another for fear of retribution. So great is the paranoia in Zukundu that no one tribe trusts any other enough to ally with so as to destroy the third.

The tribes are known as the Xhotatse, the Mekutu, and the Tangani. They speak a tongue similar to Stygian, and any player character fluent in that tongue will be able to understand them easily enough, though the gamemaster may also allow anyone speaking Kushite, Darfari, or Keshani to also be understood by the denizens of Zukundu.

The Xhotatse

The Xhotatse are the "glittering" tribe. They hold much of Zukundu's treasure — gold, jewels, and ivory though it is of little use to them save for decoration. Ruling the Xhotatse is beautiful Queen Chitaka. Serene and silent, she speaks through her advisor, old Inokwu. Other Xhotatse include the warriors Zyanya and Tenbo, as well as the youth Jambi.

All Xhotatse evidence slightly protuberant eyes and wear winking trinkets of precious gold. They are savage warriors who rarely take living captives. The other tribes fear the Xhotatse's fondness for stripping an enemy corpse down to its bones.

Their keep is largely constructed from beautiful, smooth ebony. The approach to said keep is littered with camouflaged lion pits. A series of small white cairns made of human bones also dot the path (see *Queen Chitaka and the Path of Skulls*, page 12). Notable locations within the keep include the treasure hoard of the Xhotatse, the throne room of Queen Chitaka, and an ornamental pond which is home to a shoal of deadly saber fish.

The Mekutu

The Mekutu are the "unholy" tribe, possessing strange artifacts and monstrous creatures. The androgynous Khenaton and his degenerate children (Badazeko, Enok, Ntombi, and Khenaton son of Khenaton) rule the Mekutu. All adults have distinctive "long smiles" — eerily broad mouths which are ritually sliced wide upon reaching adulthood.

They are as savage in battle as the Xhotatse, but more inclined to torture captives to death rather than simply executing them. This tribe is more inbred than the others, as can

---

JULLAH'S BLOOD

This drug comes from the wicked red creeper, a plant that feeds on the juices of humans. If extracted by someone with the knowledge and skill to do so (without being caught by the tendrils of the red creeper themselves), it can be distilled into a syrupy substance and used to coat sharp objects such as darts. Piercing the skin with an object coated in Jullah's Blood causes someone to transform into a fearless, frothing berserker, oblivious to reason and pain within mere seconds. The effects last one scene.

SPECIAL ABILITIES

- **Inured to Pain:** This creature suffers no penalties from Wounds.
- **Rage:** Increase all Awareness, Intelligence, and Personality tests by one step of Difficulty. Gain Inhuman Brawn 1, and Courage Soak 2.
- **Reckless Assault:** A berserker hurls himself into battle without regard for his own safety. When he makes a close combat attack, he may choose to gain 1, 2, or 3 bonus Momentum on the attack. However, until the start of his next turn, all enemies gain the same amount of bonus Momentum on their attacks against the berserker.

DEVILS UNDER GREEN STARS

be seen from Khenaton and his strange sons and daughters. He may even have sired grandchildren with his daughters.

The keep of the Mekutu is largely constructed from eerie, glittering slabs of jade. The approach to the Mekutu keep lies not across the obvious killing ground and (false) main door, but actually via the Crawling Caves underground (see *The Crawling Caves*, page 20. Notable locations within the Jade Keep include the torture chamber, the sarcophagi-lined Hall of Khenaton, and the harem.

The Tangani

The Tangani are the "dreaming" tribe. They grow many herbs and plants from which they extract drugs and poisons. Ruled by Prince Azar and his sister Princess Anepor, all Tangani have subtly elongated skulls, the result of tribal head-binding during childhood. They move and speak in a peaceful, dreamlike manner — a consequence of their habitual intoxication. But, at a command from their prince or princess, they happily jab themselves with the drugged darts worn on cords about their necks. This then transforms them into fearless, berserker madmen (see Jullah's Blood sidebar).

The once-fabulous Ivory Keep of the Tangani has long since fallen into ruin, destroyed by time and by the other, envious tribes of Zukundu. Though landless for generations, the prince and princess of the Tangani have not forgotten this great humiliation of their people nor the heights they once reached.

APPROACHING ZUKUNDU

The player characters find themselves in the Kingdoms of the South, far from Hyborian civilization. Perhaps they drifted this far south because they enraged a great tribe to the north, fled the employ of a mercenary band, or simply journeyed south following rumors of lost cities and plunder.

Taking a riverboat deep into the verdant jungle, a flash-flood washes them and their craft down a forgotten tributary. The strong current eventually ejects them and their battered craft into a vast jungle lake encircling a single great island upon which squats the vine-covered bulk of lost Zukundu. The player characters see glints from roofs, towers, and minarets, finished in metal, above the tops of the overgrown, vine-encrusted stone walls.

Oversized reptiles from prehistory (see *Great Reptiles*, page 9) soon erupt from the waters of the lake to attack the player characters. Barely evading the scaly giants, the player characters then reach the overgrown island, clambering up the vine-draped stone walls to escape the cavernous snapping maws below.

> ### GREAT REPTILES (NEMESIS)
> The over-large reptiles surrounding Zukundu were conjured from the bones of long-dead creatures from pre-history. If Zukundu is set on an island in a lake, these great reptiles resemble enormous crocodiles. If set in a mountain valley, they resemble soaring pterosaurs. If set in the jungle, they resemble lumbering tyrannosaurs.
>
> What they lack in numbers and maneuverability they more than make up for in size, strength, and endurance. A single great reptile is more than a match for even the greatest warrior.
>
> Use the *Crocodile (Toughened)* in the CONAN corebook, page 325.

PRINCESS ANEPOR'S SCHEME

An uneasy, precarious stalemate exists between the three hostile tribes. The forces of each are evenly matched, so that if any one faction were to strike at another, the third would doubtless emerge the strongest for having been uninvolved.

Thus, the cunning Princess Anepor — sister of Prince Azar of the landless and humiliated Tangani — devised a scheme to pit the Xhotatse tribe against the Mekutu and so engineer a bloody confrontation between the two rivals. The ensuing war would leave the Tangani as the dominant power in Zukundu. They would then be free to plunder the treasures and strange artifacts of the other tribes.

She shared her plan with her brother Azar — and between them they constructed the costume of the Feathered Ape, an unnatural, nightmarish monster. Made from fur, lacquered wood, and sinew, the costume boasts gaudily colored feathers.

Azar, a large, athletically built man, dons the costume then ambushes and savagely beheads several lone Xhotatse in the disputed regions of the city-palace. He takes the victims' heads with him, but leaves the decapitated bodies to be found, sometimes allowing himself to be seen as the Feathered Ape, at a distance. Azar plans to display the severed heads later, provocatively outside the Mekutu's Jade Keep, as if the ape's attacks come at the behest of foul Khenaton himself.

This spurs vengeful Xhotatse to retaliate against the hated Mekutu. The inevitable war will weaken both tribes and leave the Tangani in a dominant position. They would stand unopposed.

Unfortunately for the scheming Anepor and Azar, the unexpected arrival of the player characters at the Ebony Keep means that it is they who attack the Jade Keep of the Mekutu, rather than the hoodwinked Xhotatse. So, the vengeful sister and brother must take less cunning, more direct measures to claim their tribe's dominance, By using Anepor's knowledge of herbs and drugs, they transform their own people from peaceful dreamers to frothing berserkers who attack the Ebony Keep of the Xhotatse themselves (see *Jullah's Blood*, page 8).

The player characters easily scale the walls into the enclosed space of the city-palace, down through the canopy of trees on the other side, and into the darkened levels of Zukundu proper. Wet, hungry, and battered, they find themselves in a section of the Zyanya city-palace unclaimed by any of the resident tribes. The only light comes from the ever-present green star-fruit. An old vine trap, triggered by their footsteps, goes off and narrowly misses the player characters as it drops a ton of masonry behind them.

They quickly notice the fine — if aged — construction of the labyrinthine halls and chambers beneath the rampant plant growth and the amount of semi-precious stones and metals used in the site's construction. If only they had the wherewithal to pry the valuable materials free and cart them off in great quantities, they could live like royalty.

THE HEADLESS CORPSE

In a courtyard choked with succulent creepers and dark overhanging trees, a beheaded female corpse lands wetly at the feet of the player characters. Across the courtyard a great shaggy, colorful shape, more beast than man, bellows balefully and lopes into the undergrowth. The creature grips something head-shaped in one mighty claw. Player characters may give chase, but they cannot match the beast's head-start and speed. Should they persist, roll on the *Dangers of Zukundu* table (see page 6) to determine which trap they trigger in their headlong pursuit.

The body wears a number of small golden trinkets. The player characters may make a Challenging (D2) Observation test to determine that the head was torn off by something large, curved, and sharp such as the beast's claws. Unknown to the player characters, this is Dako, a hapless scout of the Xhotatse and the latest victim of the Feathered Ape.

"Aiiee! Outsiders! They have slain sweet Dako!"

Suddenly, the rest of the victim's patrol arrives and draw the conclusion that the player characters are the killers. This patrol of excitable, nervous Xhotatse warriors (equal in number to the player characters, plus two) includes the fearful Tenbo (see *Tenbo,* page 12). The patrol continues to accuse the player characters of the foul murder, alternating between waving their spears at the newcomers and unconsciously edging away from them, fearful of whatever strange powers these outlanders may possess.

The gamemaster should allow the player characters to make a Dire (D4) Persuade test to calm the frayed nerves of the patrol. If the player characters manage to persuade the patrol of their innocence, the Xhotatse warrior Zyanya (see *Zyanya,* page 11) soon appears and confirms their story.

If the patrol cannot be calmed, they reluctantly make ready to attack the player characters with a collective shriek of vengeance, though Tenbo hangs back and quivers nervously. But, before any blood is shed (or immediately

DEVILS UNDER GREEN STARS

after conflict begins), the bold Zyanya bursts through the undergrowth and calls off the patrol's attack with a barked command.

"Hold, fools! These strangers had nothing to do with Dako's death. It was… the Feathered Ape!"

The vengeful Xhotatse warriors immediately cease their attack and begin to curse and wail fearfully at the name of the legendary beast. They cast their eyes nervously around the greenery.

XHOTATSE WARRIOR (MINION)

ATTRIBUTES

Awareness	Intelligence	Personality	Willpower
9	8	8	8
Agility	Brawn		Coordination
9	9		9

FIELDS OF EXPERTISE

Combat	1	Movement	1
Fortitude	—	Senses	1
Knowledge	—	Social	1

STRESS AND SOAK

- **Stress:** Vigor 5, Resolve 4
- **Soak:** Armor 2 (Crude Wicker and Hide Armor), Courage 2

ATTACKS

- **Spear (M):** Reach 3, 5 🔥, Unbalanced, Piercing 1
- **Dagger (M):** Reach 1, 4 🔥 1H, Hidden 1, Parrying, Thrown, Unforgiving
- **Sling (R):** Range M, 4 🔥, Stun, Volley

SPECIAL ABILITIES

- **Animal Handling (Saber Fish):** When a target is within Close Range of the saber fish ponds, the Xhotatse warriors can spend 2 Doom to gain the Knockdown special ability. Should a character be knocked down, he lands in the water and is attacked by the fish.

ZYANYA (TOUGHENED)

A brave Xhotatse warrior and guide, Zyanya leads patrols into the disputed areas of Zukundu. She prefers not to speak overmuch and is more levelheaded than most of her tribe.

ATTRIBUTES

Awareness	Intelligence	Personality	Willpower
11	8	8	10
Agility	Brawn		Coordination
9	9		9

FIELDS OF EXPERTISE

Combat	3	Movement	2
Fortitude	2	Senses	3
Knowledge	1	Social	1

STRESS AND SOAK

- **Stress:** Vigor 9, Resolve 10
- **Soak:** Armor 2 (Crude Wicker and Hide Armor), Courage 2

ATTACKS

- **Spear (M):** Reach 3, 5 🔥 Unbalanced, Piercing 1
- **Dagger (M):** Reach 1, 4 🔥, 1H, Hidden 1, Parrying, Thrown, Unforgiving

SPECIAL ABILITIES

- **Leadership:** Zyanya is a skilled tactician, when leading a pair of warriors in battle. Each warrior can contribute +2d20 to Zyanya's spear attack, to the normal maximum.
- **Whirling Spear Defense:** Zyanya can change the Reach of her spear to 2 or 1 at will.

What Zyanya Saw

Zyanya, scout for the patrol, explains that she came upon the Feathered Ape carrying the bloody head of their comrade and gave chase, but soon lost sight of it in the branches of the trees some chambers distant. She is willing to make peace with the player characters, though she stops short of surrendering to them.

A brief parlay with Zyanya and the patrol reveals that this is the city-palace of Zukundu, home to the Xhotatse tribe and *"others"* (at this, the warriors spit with disdain). They also learn a little of recent events, that some of their tribe folk were killed in this gruesome fashion, evidently by the fabled Feathered Ape. Zyanya can offer only a fleeting description:

"It is a nightmarish beast. Larger than any man, with gaudy feathers sprouting among its fur."

CHAPTER 1

FIELDS OF EXPERTISE			
Combat	1	Movement	2
Fortitude	1	Senses	1
Knowledge	1	Social	2

STRESS AND SOAK

- **Stress:** Vigor 8, Resolve 7
- **Soak:** Armor 2 (Crude Wicker and Hide Armor), Courage 1

ATTACKS

- **Spear (M):** Reach 3, 4 ⚡, Unbalanced, Piercing 1
- **Dagger (M):** Reach 1, 3 ⚡ 1H, Hidden 1, Parrying, Thrown, Unforgiving

SPECIAL ABILITIES

- **Sneak Attack:** An ally within reach of Tenbo that makes a successful attack may add 2 ⚡ as Tenbo exploits the attack and causes additional damage.

QUEEN CHITAKA AND THE PATH OF SKULLS

Suddenly, the patrol and the player characters come under fire from arrows! From the relative safety of a balcony overlooking the courtyard, three opportunistic Mekutu warriors, drawn by the noise of the patrol, seek to kill a few of the hated Xhotatse and their strange allies. If the player characters come into close combat, they notice the Mekutus' disturbing long smiles for the first time. The Xhotatse retaliate savagely and gleefully execute the Mekutu, if not restrained. This short combat may prove the player character's prowess to the Xhotatse.

The Xhotatse patrol recognizes what an advantage these outsiders could provide them. The tribe swiftly invites, hustles, or begs the player characters to accompany them back to the safety of the Ebony Keep of the Xhotatse to meet their ruler, "wise" Queen Chitaka.

TENBO (TOUGHENED)

A nervous Xhotatse warrior and guide, Tenbo talks too much and is as likely to run as he is to fight.

ATTRIBUTES			
Awareness	Intelligence	Personality	Willpower
8	8	10	7
Agility		Brawn	Coordination
9		8	9

The Xhotatse patrol leads the player characters along darkened, crumbling corridors and overgrown gardens, occasionally stepping over, or ducking warily under, trip wires for dart traps and vine snares. Soon, they are carefully picking their way through the camouflaged lion pits guarding the approach to the Ebony Keep of the Xhotatse.

"Tread carefully. Do not stray from our path."

The patrol does not willingly explain to the player characters why they are being directed on a strangely winding path, often ignoring what appears to be the most obvious and direct path. The surface of each lion pit is lightly covered with vegetation, leaves, and twigs, concealing a deep hole with sharpened wooden stakes at the bottom.

The player characters may make a Challenging (D2) Survival test to spot the traps as they pass, or else a Daunting (D3) Persuade test to get a tight-lipped Xhotatse warrior to point them out. Falling into a lion pit requires a Challenging (D2) Agility test to grab onto the lip and avoid taking 3 ⚡ from the wooden stakes at the bottom.

A series of small white cairns also surround the immediate approach to the keep. These are made of the piled, whitened bones of intruders who trespassed on Xhotatse territory, as the patrol freely explains. Player characters making a Daunting (D3) Insight test deduce that the patrol steers the group on a winding path from cairn to nearest

DEVILS UNDER GREEN STARS

cairn, always passing on the side of the piles of bones where a single grinning skull faces them. This is the secret "Path of Skulls" which denotes a safe path through the littered lion pits.

Passing through the keep's sturdy and well-guarded bronze Door of the Elephant, the player characters enter the Ebony Keep of the Xhotatse. A small crowd of young and old Xhotatse gather around them, nervous but curious. The returning patrol proclaims the player characters new allies from beyond the walls of Zukundu.

"See the mighty outsiders, come to aid us!"

The Ebony Keep is much too large for the small crowd that has gathered there. An Average (D1) Insight test suggests that the numbers of the Xhotatse dwindled from what they once were.

THE POND AND THE MONKEY

Zyanya, or another member of the patrol, lets the queen know of the outsiders' arrival, leaving the player characters and the rest of the patrol to wait briefly in a wide, shady chamber overshadowed by a variety of thick, looping vines.

A large ornamental pond stretches completely across one side of the shady chamber. A small dark archway, the only entrance to the Xhotatse treasure hoard, stands in the wall beyond the pond. The pond is not deep, and attractive lily pads float on the surface. It looks quite beautiful and peaceful, but is, in fact, home to a shoal of pretty, yet voracious, saber fish, which the Xhotatse keep as decorative pets, as well as a means of stripping bodies of dead enemies down to skeletons in seconds.

The thick vines stretching overhead provide a relatively safe route across the pond, but only certain vines — those with white blooms — are firm enough to climb along. The vines with yellow blooms exude a slippery sap so that nothing can grip them.

A group of small Xhotatse children race into the shady chamber, chasing a small monkey. They shout that they have *"caught the Feathered Ape!"* The monkey scampers up a vine and skitters over the pond but quickly falls from a slippery yellow-bloom vine and, with a squeak, falls into the water. In seconds the pond froths with unseen fury as the saber fish swarm around the hapless monkey and strip it down to a tiny skeleton before the player character's eyes. The children shriek with distress at the creature's horrific fate.

Player characters making a Daunting (D3) Observation test or Challenging (D2) Survival test notice that the white-bloom vines were safe for the monkey to cross, while the yellow-blooms were not.

SABER FISH SWARM (MINION)

Bred by the people of Zukundu long ago, these small, attractive fish resemble piranhas crossed with lionfish. Attracted to movement and the scent of blood in the water, they are voracious and swarm around anything moving, stripping it to the bone in minutes.

ATTRIBUTES

Awareness	Intelligence	Personality	Willpower
6	4	4	6

Agility	Brawn	Coordination
8	7	5

FIELDS OF EXPERTISE

Combat	2	Movement	2
Fortitude	1	Senses	1
Knowledge	—	Social	—

STRESS AND SOAK

- **Stress:** Vigor 4, Resolve 3
- **Soak:** Armor 2 (Incorporeal), Courage —

ATTACKS

- **Savage Bloody Bites (M):** Reach 1, 3 🜂, Vicious 1, Persistent 2

SPECIAL ABILITIES

- **Aquatic**
- **Incorporeal 2:** Though not truly incorporeal, the saber fish swarm is made of so many fish that attacks against individuals are fairly inconsequential.
- **Keen Senses (Scent)**
- **Swarm:** The swarm can take the Disengage action as a Free Action.

DOOM SPENDS

- **Always More Where That Came From:** For each Doom spent on reinforcements, two additional saber fish swarms arrive as reinforcements at the end of the turn. These may join any existing Mob or Gang, each of which is made up of multiple saber fish swarms.
- **Swarm Attacks:** For each Doom spent, the swarm may make one additional attack when it makes a standard action close combat attack. Each attack must be targeted at a different enemy.

THE THRONE ROOM

Led into a richly furnished throne room in the heart of the keep, the player characters find themselves in a grand room decorated with golden mirrors, carved ivory, and exotic potted flowers. Before them sits beautiful, serene Queen Chitaka, bedecked in many fine jewels and golden trinkets. Her aged advisor, Inokwu, stands to one side, whispering in her ear from behind a feathered fan. Speaking on behalf of the queen, who remains silent but smiling throughout, Inokwu greets the player characters.

"Queen Chitaka welcomes you to the Ebony Keep, honored visitors. Lifetimes have passed since outsiders have come to great Zukundu."

Inokwu relates a little of the layout, wildlife, and ecology of Zukundu (see *The Environment of Zukundu*, page 6), though he knows little of the city's true origin, and nothing of the secrets of other folk living in the city-palace. A Challenging (D3) Persuade test can get him to also admit that nobody has ventured beyond the walls of the city-palace in generations. He also freely relates that the Feathered Ape was thought to be a legend until these recent attacks upon the Xhotatse.

He implores them to help the embattled (and undermanned) Xhotatse track and destroy the terrible Feathered Ape that has taken the heads of their people:

"Our queen bids you hunt this beast. Find it and slay it. And bring back its corpse that we may stack its monstrous bones atop the walls of the Ebony Keep for all to see!"

Zyanya and the other Xhotatse in the throne room stamp their feet and cry out at this with glee, the fires of vengeance flickering in their eyes. The queen herself begins to clap daintily with girlish excitement before Inokwu motions for her to maintain her composure.

The player characters can either accept the mission out of the goodness of their hearts, or if they are reluctant to do so for free, Inokwu offers them payment for their trouble. He instructs a Xhotatse tribesman to *"Fetch some trinkets from across the pond"*. The tribesman duly races off to the treasure hoard and returns minutes later with a few small items of precious gold and ivory jewelry about his neck, which Inokwu casually but sincerely offers to the player characters.

"Please take these. There is more if you do this service for the Xhotatse."

Speaking for the queen, Inokwu insists that the player characters are accompanied by Xhotatse guides. The guides will be able to show them how to get to any part of the city-palace without falling prey to traps or natural obstacles (see *The Environment of Zukundu*, page 6). The guides are also a useful source of local information and rumors, can carry messages back to the Ebony Keep, and fight by the player character's side when needed. Either Zyanya or

The Ebony Keep of the Xhotatse

1. Elephant Gate
2. Cistern
3. Guard Room
4. Privies
5. Bone Room
6. Food Store
7. Living Quarters
8. Stairs to Wall
9. Stairs to Wall
10. Wall
11. Guard Barracks
12. Wide Chamber
13. Treasure Hoard
14. Throne Room
15. Courtiers Room
16. Queen's Chamber

DEVILS UNDER GREEN STARS

Tenbo can go with them, or both if the player characters do not have many warriors in their group. The guides do not know about the chamber of the Red Creeper, the moon lion in the arena, the Crawling Caves, or anything of the interior of the Jade Keep of the Mekutu.

Perhaps an enthusiastic youth like Jambi (see page 15) may also attempt to accompany the exotic outsiders, but is told that he is too young to venture beyond the walls of the Ebony Keep.

The player characters may make a Daunting (D3) Insight test to notice that Inokwu does not always remember to lean in close and whisper with the queen before speaking. This is a clue to the true nature of their relationship.

QUEEN CHITAKA

Unknown to her subjects, Chitaka is simple of mind, little more than a child in a woman's body. She is no more than a beautiful, though beloved, figurehead. If attacked or startled, Chitaka wails and cries like a child. She trusts her aged advisor, Inokwu, implicitly and is happy to do as he says, even pretending to give him whispered commands from her throne, though she quickly tires of such boring grown-up games.

INOKWU

As advisor to the queen, it is the loyal old Inokwu who truly rules the Xhotatse. Taking "whispered commands" from his queen from behind a feathered fan, he secretly makes all the decisions for the good of the people of Xhotatse. He is not a bad man, but perhaps a little unhinged, and certainly unwilling to let the rest of the tribe discover that their queen has the mind of a child.

JAMBI (TOUGHENED)

An eager youngster not yet old enough to leave the safety of the Ebony Keep, Jambi secretly dreams of one day seeing the world beyond Zukundu.

ATTRIBUTES

Awareness	Intelligence	Personality	Willpower
8	11	8	8
Agility	Brawn		Coordination
8	8		8

FIELDS OF EXPERTISE

Combat	—	Movement	1
Fortitude	1	Senses	1
Knowledge	—	Social	1

STRESS AND SOAK

- **Stress:** Vigor 8, Resolve 8
- **Soak:** Armor 2 (Crude Wicker and Hide Armor), Courage 1

ATTACKS

- **Dagger (M):** Reach 1, 3 💀, Hidden 1, Parrying, Thrown, Unforgiving
- **Sling (R):** Range M, 3 💀, Stun, Volley

SPECIAL ABILITIES

- **Warning Shout:** Jambi has a loud voice and is practiced at summoning aid. While in the Ebony Keep he can pay 1 Doom to summon a mob of five Xhotatse warriors or pay 3 Doom to summon 4 Mobs of warriors.

HUNTING THE APE

Searching outside the Ebony Keep and the green corridors of Zukundu, it is hard at first to find any tracks of the Feathered Ape, but a smart player character might ask their guides to lead them to scenes of earlier attacks. There, with a Challenging (D2) Observation test, they spot the telltale marks made by its (metallic) claws in the soil, on trees, and even on flagstones. If not, a Xhotatse guide picks up the Ape's trail as needed for the adventure to proceed.

RUMORS IN THE EBONY KEEP

The player characters can find out a little about the feared Feathered Ape from a Xhotatse guide, if they decide to ask. The gamemaster can pick a rumor from the following list, or roll a d20. Rumors include:

1–3	The Ape is strong enough to tear the head off a grown man. (True)
4–6	The Ape has metal claws. (True)
7–9	The Ape is a mythical demon, a spawn of Jullah, that crawled up from the caves under the city-palace. (False)
10–12	The Ape can command lesser beasts such as monkeys to do its bidding. (False)
13–15	The Ape prefers women victims. (False)
16–20	The Ape can pass through locked doors as smoke. (False)

THE CHAMBER OF THE RED CREEPER

The trail of the Feathered Ape leads the player characters to an area their guides have not visited in years. Through a greenhouse-like area with a particularly rich, musky scent they come upon a chamber where a single type of plant grows, covering the walls and floor quite thickly. A lone narrow path twists and undulates across from one door to the next. The plant is red creeper (see page 16) from which the Tangani extract a powerful drug (see *Jullah's Blood*, page 8). The blooming plants are a rich, deep red, fat with moisture. The Xhotatse guides know nothing of this plant, stating only that is was not here when they last passed through years ago.

Indistinct shapes bulging out under the creeper on the walls and floor are actually human victims who were fed to the Red Creeper over the years. Some are dry, long-dead husks, while others are skeletal near-mummies whose sunken eyes move so slowly it is hard to tell that they are still conscious. If examined, the Xhotatse guides can identify the victims by their distinctive elongated skulls as landless, "dreaming" Tangani.

Unknown to the player characters and their guides, the Tangani were sent here by their own Princess Anepor to feed the red creeper, which requires human juices to produce Jullah's Blood. Tiny red tendrils burrowed into every open orifice of the victims. The tendrils hold them tight to the ground and walls, and must be cut or pulled free, or neutralized by some esoteric means. The victims struggle feebly, unable to make more than tiny gasps.

But the red creeper does not give up its food easily. As soon as any embedded tendrils are disturbed, the red creeper begins to writhe and defend itself!

Once the sinister plant is subdued, a player character making a Dire (D4) Alchemy test can examine an inert red creeper and identify its succulent red blooms as the key component of the drug known as Jullah's Blood. When extracted and distilled, the syrupy liquid induces a berserker-like state in those mixing it with their own blood.

The captive Tangani, if they are freed, are incredibly feeble and near death, but could be saved by determined player characters making an Epic (D5) Healing test. They are all but incapable of speech and terrified of both their Xhotatse enemies and the strange player characters. Driven to the point of insanity, one pathetically attempts to draw his rusting dagger and stab weakly at a player character. Unless restrained, the practical and ruthless Xhotatse guides quickly slit the throats of any Tangani. If the Tangani are allowed to live, the Xhotatse will ignore them so long as they are unable to cause trouble.

RED CREEPER (TOUGHENED)

This plant covers every surface of an area if left untended. It feeds exclusively on the juices of living beings, humans being its preferred source. If well fed, the blooms of the red creeper turn a rich crimson and grow fat with moisture. A powerful drug can be extracted from the blooms (see *Jullah's Blood*, page 8).

If disturbed, the red creeper begins to writhe and defend itself. Tiny red tendrils reach out to ensnare and trip anyone in the area. If the tendrils touch bare flesh, they latch on tightly, exuding a sap which makes the victim weaker and more sluggish with each successive tendril. They also burrow into every open orifice of the creeper's victims. Victims are conscious but unable to do anything more than struggle feebly and make tiny gasps. They may last months in that state, gradually desiccating into mummy-like husks before eventually dying.

DEVILS UNDER GREEN STARS

ATTRIBUTES

Awareness	Intelligence	Personality	Willpower
10	—	—	—
Agility	Brawn		Coordination
7	11 (3)		6

FIELDS OF EXPERTISE

Combat	1	Movement	—
Fortitude	2	Senses	1
Knowledge	—	Social	—

STRESS AND SOAK

- **Stress:** Vigor 14, Resolve —
- **Soak:** Armor —, Courage —

ATTACKS

- **Lashing Thorny Tendrils (M):** Reach 3, 5 🎲, Grappling, Stun

SPECIAL ABILITIES

- **Brain Dead:** These plants have no brain and are driven purely by instinct. They mindlessly attack the nearest living creature. They cannot attempt Reactions, are immune to any mind-influencing effects, and cannot suffer mental damage.
- **Inhuman Brawn 3**

DOOM SPENDS

- **Soporific Sap:** When it has successfully grappled a victim, the red creeper can pay X Doom to inject the victim with a sedative sap which forces the victim to make an Average or higher (D1+X) Resistance test or suffer 2 🎲 Fatigue.
- **Many Tendriled:** For each Doom spent, the creeper may make one additional attack when it makes a Standard Action close combat attack. Each attack must be targeted at a different enemy. The creeper cannot use the Swift Strike Momentum spend.

THE APE AND THE ARENA

The bellow of the Feathered Ape leads the player characters through the lush, dark chambers and thickets of Zukundu. At last they spy the bestial killer at a distance — the fearsome Feathered Ape! It just murdered and beheaded a Xhotatse fruit gatherer who wandered too far from the protective walls of the Ebony Keep. The gamemaster should describe the Ape to the player characters, as this is the first time they see it in full.

RUMORS FROM THE XHOTATSE GUIDES

This scene is an opportunity for the Xhotatse guides to provide the player characters with a little information about the reclusive Tangani tribe. The gamemaster can pick a rumor or roll a d20 to determine which one the player characters receive. Rumors include:

1–4	The Tangani are known as the "dreaming" tribe because of their fondness for certain strange herbs and drugs which they grow and consume in great quantities. (True)
5–8	The Tangani were once the third great tribe of Zukundu, but their Ivory Keep was destroyed and sacked by a brief alliance of the other tribes long ago, reducing them to a handful of landless nomads. (True)
9–12	The Tangani are a secretive lot. (True)
13–16	The Tangani are ruled by a brother and sister. (True)
17–20	The Tangani's elongated skulls are the result of their ancestors having mated with serpents. (False)

This scene ends with a distant bellow — which the Xhotatse guides identify as that of the Feathered Ape — further along the trail, drawing the eager Xhotatse and the player characters to the next encounter.

> "The Feathered Ape is an unnatural, nightmarish monster. Far larger than a man, its posture is stooped, like a gorilla making mock of a man. From its powerful chest protrude thick, overlong arms. Both its hands and feet are tipped with gleaming red claws. Most strikingly, its hairy simian hide is interspersed with gaudy colored feathers. Small, cunning eyes gleam from sockets set deep within a great brutish head."

Taking the severed, dripping head with it, the Ape bounds off into the undergrowth, leading the player characters on a chase across the city-palace. The player characters make Dire (D4) Athletics tests to close the distance between them and the elusive Ape. This leads to the more athletic player characters reaching the arena ahead of their fellows.

Their pursuit takes them into forbidden Mekutu territory, which their Xhotatse guides mention nervously as they race along. The Feathered Ape leads the player characters into the ruins of a great stone arena, constructed of pillars and arches circling a large dark pit. The pit looks deep and cluttered with collapsed masonry and vines. A great fallen tree spans its length. It is too dark to see the bottom from the edge.

The Ape nimbly skips along the great fallen tree, using its sharp claws to provide a sure footing, though player characters find it more difficult to move along the fallen tree as it wobbles precariously. Using its great strength, the Ape does its best to tip any pursuing player characters off the tree and into the dark pit below. A Daunting (D3) Agility test or Challenging (D2) Acrobatics test is required to cross the shaking tree without falling. If no player characters fall, a Xhotatse guide tumbles into the pit instead.

The fall into the pit isn't fatal — dazing the victim and causing 2 ◈ damage, but a confrontation with the moon lion that prowls down there might be. The moon lion is the last of its kind, the others having either died of old age or disease, or been eaten by this one. It survives on scraps thrown down by the nearby Mekutu and eagerly hunts down and attacks anyone unlucky enough to fall noisily into the pit (see *Moon Lion*, below).

The Feathered Ape takes advantage of the moon lion encounter to make good its escape, leaving a trail that leads to the nearby Jade Keep of the Mekutu. It will remain at such a range to prevent missile weapons from having much effect, and will spend as much Doom as possible in its escape.

> *In the splotches of shadow between them, the green jewels winked like the eyes of angry cats. Beneath their feet the dully lurid floor smoldered with changing hues and colors of flame. It was like treading the floors of hell with evil stars blinking overhead.*
>
> — "Red Nails"

MOON LION (TOUGHENED)

Moon lions originate from a specially bred pride that the people of Zukundu once used in gladiatorial spectacles. Huge, lean, snow-white and all but blind with great black eyes, they navigate by sound and can locate anyone that strays into their hunting ground by the noises they make.

PRINCESS ANEPOR

If the gamemaster chooses, they can use the chamber of the Red Creeper as a sly way to introduce one of the two ultimate villains of the adventure, the cunning Princess Anepor. This additional encounter requires skillful roleplaying on the part of the gamemaster to portray Anepor as nothing more than a harmless minor character passing through.

Having learnt of Zukundu's new arrivals — the player characters — from her spying, she places herself in their path to learn more of the strange newcomers, lurking near the Red Creeper chamber until they approach.

Using her skills as an actress, she appears before the player characters once they successfully pass through the chamber. She appears alone, unarmed, and completely harmless, carrying only a pouch of simple berries. Moving and speaking in a dreamlike, possibly drugged, manner, Anepor nonetheless flees at speed if attacked. But, if the players show restraint, she languidly introduces herself as a simple forager from the lowly, landless Tangani.

She claims to know nothing of the Feathered Ape, but does supply, far too late to be of any use, a warning not to disturb the deadly Red Creeper. The player characters only have a minute or two to talk to her before hearing the distant bellow of the Feathered Ape. Anepor immediately flees with a fearful cry in the opposite direction and does everything in her power to elude any player character trying to chase after her. The gamemaster should spend as much Doom as is necessary to keep her from being caught, including interposing a group of Tangani into the player characters' path.

After she flees, the gamemaster may choose to allow the player characters to make a Dire (D4) Insight test to suspect that the woman was not all she appeared to be.

Having learned a little of the player characters, she returns to the Tangani and considers how these outsiders affect her plan (see *Princess Anepor's Scheme*, page 10). If any of the player characters accepted Inokwu's trinkets earlier (see *The Throne Room*, page 14), Anepor spots the ivory about their person and quietly notes that they wear the long-ago looted treasure of the Tangani (see *The Feathered Ape Revealed*, page 31).

ATTRIBUTES

Awareness	Intelligence	Personality	Willpower
9	5	6	8

Agility	Brawn	Coordination
10	10	5

FIELDS OF EXPERTISE

Combat	3	Movement	2
Fortitude	1	Senses	2
Knowledge	—	Social	1

STRESS AND SOAK

- **Stress:** Vigor 10, Resolve 8
- **Soak:** Armor 2 (Toughened Hide), Courage 1

ATTACKS

- **Bite (M):** Reach 1, 4⚡, Grappling, Unforgiving 2
- **Claws (M):** Reach 2, 5⚡, Vicious 1
- **Savage Growl (T):** Range M, 3⚡ mental, Vicious 1

SPECIAL ABILITIES

- **Pack Hunter:** Moon lions are fearsome pack hunters. A moon lion gains 1 bonus Momentum on any attack roll against a foe already attacked by an ally this round, and on Stealth tests where the enemy can see one or more of the moon lion's allies.
- **Pounce:** If a moon lion makes the Movement Minor Action before attempting a close combat attack, the moon lion may add the Knockdown quality to its Claws attack. If the target is knocked prone, then the moon lion may spend 1 Momentum to make a Bite attack against the same target.
- **Keen Senses (Hearing)**
- **Night Vision:** Note that this is gained from hearing and not sight.
- **Vulnerable to bright light:** Daylight terrifies the moon lion, and it avoids it at all costs. Exposure to daylight forces the moon lion to make a Challenging (D2) Fortitude test or suffer 4⚡ mental damage. Once a moon lion suffers a trauma from daylight, further exposure causes it no harm.

DOOM SPENDS

- **Bellowing Roar:** The roar of a moon lion is terrifying to hear, and few creatures can stand firm in the face of such a dreadful noise. By spending 2 Doom when it attempts a Threaten action, the moon lion gains the Bellowing Roar Display (T), Range M, 4⚡ mental, Area, Vicious 1.

BENEATH THE JADE KEEP OF THE MEKUTU

The player characters follow the trail of the Feathered Ape to the Jade Keep of the Mekutu. The approach to the keep is uneventful, but eerily quiet.

RUMORS FROM THE GUIDE

The player characters learn a little about the hated "unholy" Mekutu from a Xhotatse guide, if they decide to ask. The gamemaster may roll a d20 or pick an appropriate rumor. These include:

1–3	The Mekutu are ruled by the "man-woman" Khenaton. (True)
4–6	The Mekutu have "strange beasts" at their command. (True)
7–10	A green-eyed "demon" lives among the Mekutu. (True)
11–15	Khenaton sacrifices his own children to dark gods. (False)
16–20	Khenaton is immortal; he is centuries old. (False)

THE JADE FOUNTAIN

On the edge of the killing ground before the Jade Keep of the Mekutu, the player characters discover the Xhotatse victims' severed heads displayed ominously. The heads bob and jerk in a large jade ornamental fountain fed by a natural spring. The fountain has carvings of a strange androgynous face, repeated around the basin. Above this face are the ornate words: "For the Pleasure of Khenaton" in the language of Zukundu, readable to anyone who can read Stygian.

The disembodied heads and rictus grins whirl and careen in a hideous, blackly comic fashion. They were recently deposited here by the Feathered Ape to deliberately insult and provoke the Xhotatse against the Mekutu. The Xhotatse guides spit with rage.

"The insult is plain! We must revenge ourselves on the foul Mekutu!"

The guides urge the player characters to find a way into the Jade Keep immediately and take their revenge on the vile Mekutu.

CHAPTER 1

THE KILLING GROUND

A flat, open killing ground around the keep is clear of vegetation, though littered with the rotting, arrow-stuck skeletons of past attackers. Crude arrow holes adorn the high, jade walls high of the fortification. Anyone crossing the killing ground and approaching the (false) door to the keep becomes visible to the keep's defenders.

Barely-glimpsed Mekutu guards, safely ensconced up high behind the keep's jade arrow holes, can easily fire down at anyone venturing into the killing ground and approaching the door. Mobs of Mekutu warriors equal to twice the number of player characters are stationed behind killing holes. Each Mob consists of five guards who count as having Soak 4 while behind the holes. The Mobs automatically act first when player characters approach, unleashing massed arrow fire. If the player characters have particularly high Acrobatics skills, the gamemaster is encouraged to spend Doom and use the Volley ability.

A player character making a Challenging (D2) Observation test or Average (D1) Warfare test deduces that, as the jade walls of the keep are both high and smooth, save for the small arrow holes and securely-shuttered windows several floors up, there is no way to climb in here. The keep's walls are too far from any trees to cross over, and there is no access within from the smoothly sloping roof.

The large door to the keep is but a façade of wood behind which stands a solid wall of jade — it was sealed long ago. A player character making a Daunting (D3) Insight test notices that the earth before the door is quite undisturbed by footprints or the scuff marks that a door in regular use might make.

The player characters have to find another way inside.

THE CRAWLING CAVES

To enter the keep, the player characters can search the side chambers outside the killing ground and find a darkened stairwell leading down into the Jade Keep. Footprints reveal regular traffic in the area. The stairwell leads straight down for some distance and then levels off, continuing as a stone passage. Clumps of rotting star-fruit — left by passing Mekutu — hang from crude iron hooks at irregular intervals, lighting the passageway with patches of faltering, eerie green luminescence interspersed by long expanses of darkness. The passage ends

---

"STOP, YOU FOOL!"

If the gamemaster would like to demonstrate the folly of trying to enter the Jade Keep via the door or walls, they may include this incident.

A particularly hot-headed Xhotatse guide declares that they will cross the killing ground and scale the walls of the Jade Keep. Unless physically restrained by the player characters, the guide charges out into the killing ground with grim determination. This foolhardy action is doomed to failure, as the cruelly barbed arrows from hidden Mekutu archers slay him. The dying guide reaches the large door of the Jade Keep, only to exclaim that it is nothing but a façade.

"The door... it is not... "

The body, shot through with arrows, slumps bloodily to the ground at the base of the door. Derisive, hooting laughter from unseen Mekutu is heard. Unless the player characters make themselves visible, the crazed Mekutu dismiss this incident as a random foray by a lone Xhotatse fool.

DEVILS UNDER GREEN STARS

at an iron-barred gate with a latch that is easily unlocked by humans. An unpleasant stench wafts from beyond, a mixture of meat and dung. An Average (D1) Animal Handling test or a Challenging (D2) Survival test also indicates a strong reptilian odor among the other foul smells. It is strangely chilly down here too, a feature of the creatures that dwell beyond the gate.

These extensive caves beyond the gate are home to a small pack of crawlers. The Mekutu keep them down here as pets and guards. They use their *bone pipes* (see page 22) to soothe the crawlers, enabling them to pass uninjured to and from the Jade Keep. In the darkness of the caves, the crawlers lie coiled in great heaps, still but not slumbering. The gamemaster may choose to forewarn the player characters by adding the sound of something large and heavy sliding and rasping across the stone floor, just out of sight.

Humans picking their way through the chill, serpentine bodies must make a Challenging (D2) Animal Handling test or an Average (D1) Stealth test to avoid rousing the creatures. The player characters must find a way of getting past or face a nasty battle with these reptilian horrors.

Soon, the solution is demonstrated. A strange piping sound ululates from somewhere deep in the Crawling Caves and a single Mekutu woman slowly emerges out of the darkness, a clump of star-fruit strung from her neck. She plays her bone pipes to pass the crawlers unscathed. She spies the player characters unless they choose to hide by making a Daunting (D3) Stealth test. She may be ambushed as she approaches the stone passage on her way out, or else the players characters may choose to hide from her and let her pass. If startled or attacked, she uses her bone pipes to rouse the nearest crawlers and drives them to attack the player characters.

If the player characters do not manage to take the bone pipes from the Mekutu woman, they must find some other way to emulate its soothing sounds, perhaps with sorcery, singing, or their own musical instrument.

If the player characters negotiate the Crawling Caves, they find another iron-barred gate, as easily unlatched as the earlier one. Beyond the gate is a stairwell leading up into the Jade Keep itself.

CRAWLERS (TOUGHENED)

These sinuous, writhing reptiles are from the same stock as the kind found in haunted Xuchotl. Monstrous and serpentine, their two great fangs protrude from the upper jaw. Strangely, they also exude an unnatural chill noticeable to anyone in close proximity. They are semi-tamed with proper feeding, training, and the use of special pipes to control them (see Bone Pipes, page 22). Their scaly hide is an iridescent, ever-changing hue.

ATTRIBUTES

Awareness	Intelligence	Personality	Willpower
8	3	8	8
Agility	Brawn		Coordination
10	11		3

FIELDS OF EXPERTISE

Combat	1	Movement	2
Fortitude	—	Senses	1
Knowledge	—	Social	—

STRESS AND SOAK

- **Stress:** Vigor 11, Resolve 8
- **Soak:** Armor 2 (Scaly Skin), Courage 2

ATTACKS

- **Bite (M):** Reach 2, 5 ⚔
- **Envelop (M):** Reach 1, 5 ⚔, Grappling
- **Constrict (M):** Reach 1, 5 ⚔, Unforgiving 2, only on grabbed targets.
- **Ungodly Screech (T):** Range C, 5 ⚔ mental

SPECIAL ABILITIES

- **Chilling Aura:** Characters within Reach suffer 1 ⚔ Fatigue from the cold every round.
- **Monstrous Creature**
- **Night Vision**

DOOM SPENDS

- **Hypnotic Hide:** The shimmering hues of the crawler's iridescent hide lulls its victims into a trance-like state, causing the victim to stand motionless, their eyes fixed on the crawler. The crawler may spend 3 Doom to use the *Enthrall* spell, as if it were a sorcerer.
- **Swallow Whole:** Foes wounded by the crawler's envelop attack are swallowed whole. While swallowed, a character counts as Staggered, and whenever the crawler takes damage, the swallowed character suffers the same damage which is soaked as normal. Every time the crawler takes damage, the crawler can spend 1 Doom to inflict an additional 3 ⚔ to the swallowed victim.

BONE PIPES

Carved from slender forearm bones, these panpipes emit sounds at a pitch designed to bring the reptilian horrors known as "crawlers" under the user's control. Most often, the pipes sole function is calming the crawlers by anyone needing to pass through their lair, but they can also be used to drive the reptiles forward to attack those before them. They may also be used on the great reptiles outside Zukundu, though they are less effective. Calming the crawlers is accomplished as a Threaten action with the pipes dealing 4 ⚔ mental damage, with Traumas caused by the pipes causing the crawlers to calm themselves. If other Threaten actions are attempted while calming the crawlers, the crawlers instantly heal any damage caused by the pipes.

STAR-FRUIT

Green phosphorescent fruit grown exclusively in Zukundu, this food gives off an eerie emerald light day and night. If plucked, the fruit remains glowing for several days before rotting and dimming. The fruit may be eaten with no ill effects, save for one's body waste briefly retaining a slight luminescence.

SPECIAL ABILITIES

- **Phosphorescence:** The character gains Night Vision (see page 310 of the **Conan** corebook), but Stealth tests are made one step more difficult.

INSIDE THE JADE KEEP

Constructed largely of a sickly green jade, the interior of the keep is polished to a smooth finish and sometimes carved in strange sinuous patterns, perhaps emulating the forms of the Mekutu's pet crawlers. Slowly rotting clumps of star-fruit deposited at intervals along the passages provide erratic light to the chamber. Filth and clutter litter the floor.

The stench from the Crawling Caves below gradually blends and then disappears under the heavy, sweet incense that burns in bowls throughout the keep. This incense is mildly disorienting and may affect the player characters' ability to sense direction and aim. Every player character must make a Challenging (D2) Resistance test when they first breathe the incense. Failing the test results in a minor one step penalty to all Awareness and Coordination tests until they get clear of the incense outside the keep. The Mekutu themselves have a built-up immunity to the ill effects of the incense.

DEVILS UNDER GREEN STARS

Withered corpses, impaled on great timber posts bolted to the walls, punctuate the halls and corridors. The corpses bear the marks of torture and mutilation. Some corpses are recognizable to the Xhotatse guides as lost beloved kinfolk, while others bear the telltale elongated skulls of the lowly Tangani. There are even a few widely-smiling Mekutu corpses on display, victims of their sadistic ruler's cruel, mercurial moods.

One body, not long dead, bears curious small bite marks all over its body. Partly healed, they look as if something repeatedly chewed on the victim while still alive. A Challenging (D2) Animal Handling test suggests that whatever creature ate the victim, it has a mouth similar to, but much smaller than, the crawlers down in the caves. In truth, this was the work of Safiki, the ghoulish Enok's pet hatchling.

Grisly furnishings — divans upholstered in strange cured hides, glass cabinets of long-mummified heads, great stuffed crawlers arranged in lifelike rearing poses — litter the passageways, chambers, and cells of the Jade Keep, lending the entire structure a gruesome, horrific air.

An Average (D1) Insight test indicates, by the number of long unused sleeping quarters and cells in the keep, that the number of the Mekutu have dwindled from what they once were.

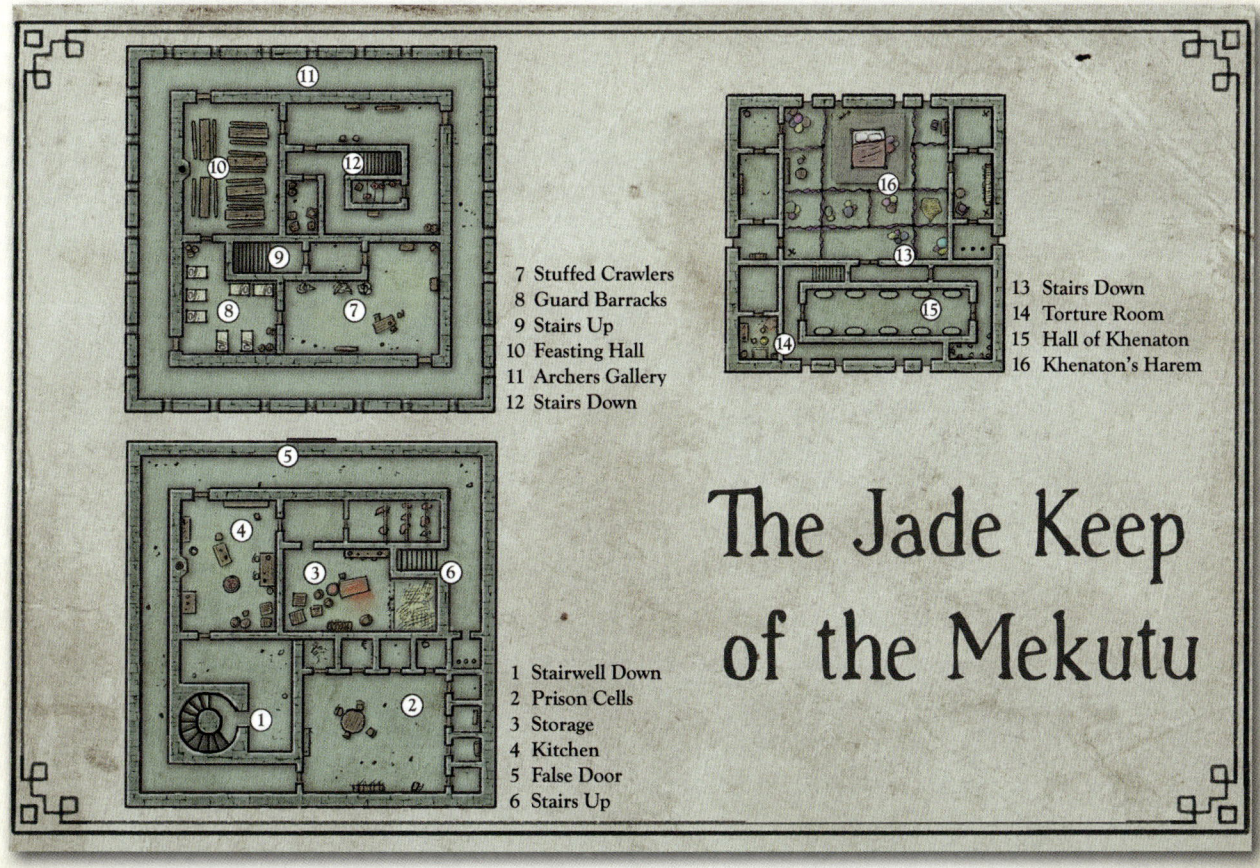

7 Stuffed Crawlers
8 Guard Barracks
9 Stairs Up
10 Feasting Hall
11 Archers Gallery
12 Stairs Down

13 Stairs Down
14 Torture Room
15 Hall of Khenaton
16 Khenaton's Harem

1 Stairwell Down
2 Prison Cells
3 Storage
4 Kitchen
5 False Door
6 Stairs Up

The Jade Keep of the Mekutu

EVIDENCE OF THE APE

Quite simply, the player characters find no evidence that the monstrous Feathered Ape has ever been inside the Jade Keep. But they are unable to fully determine that the Mekutu, foul though they may be, are innocent of the Ape murders until they confront Khenaton and his freakish family at the climax of this episode.

The gamemaster should allow player characters some simple searching and tracking time with a Daunting (D3) Observation test as they move through the Jade Keep, making it clear that they find none of the Ape's telltale tracks. Likewise, allow them to question any Mekutu that they capture with a Dire (D4) Persuade test, but the captive confesses that they know nothing of this monstrous beast, nor of the Xhotatse heads in Khenaton's jade fountain.

Ensure that the vengeful Xhotatse guides are nonetheless convinced of the Mekutu's guilt in this matter, however, and use them to draw the player characters through the Jade Keep toward the harem in search of answers.

MEKUTU WARRIOR (MINION)

ATTRIBUTES

Awareness	Intelligence	Personality	Willpower
9	8	8	8

Agility	Brawn	Coordination
9	9	9

FIELDS OF EXPERTISE

Combat	1	Movement	1
Fortitude	—	Senses	1
Knowledge	—	Social	1

STRESS AND SOAK

- **Stress:** Vigor 5, Resolve 4
- **Soak:** Armor 2 (Crude Wicker and Hide Armor), Courage 2

ATTACKS

- **Hunting Bow (R):** Range M, 4 🔥, 2H, Volley
- **Dagger (M):** Reach 1, 4 🔥, 1H, Hidden 1, Parrying, Thrown, Unforgiving
- **Long Smile (T):** Range C, 5 🔥 mental, Stun

SPECIAL ABILITIES

- **Resist Drugs and Poisons:** Mekutu warriors roll an additional +1d20 to resist any poison.

WANDERING MEKUTU

Probably, the player characters encounter — or have to avoid — small groups of Mekutu moving around the keep on several occasions before reaching their goal. An Average (D1) Awareness test by any player character is enough to forewarn them of approaching Mekutu in time to hide in a side chamber or behind some grisly furnishing until the enemy passes.

Whenever the player characters enter a new chamber or corridor, the gamemaster should roll a D20 and consult the *Wandering Mekutu* table (below).

These Mekutu may be changing guard, hauling live struggling prisoners to the torture chamber, dragging dead mutilated bodies from the torture chamber down to the Crawling Caves for disposal, or hurrying to bring sweetmeats and fruit wine to Khenaton's harem. These last servants loudly scold one another for being late, and

WANDERING MEKTUTU

Roll	Wandering Mekutu
9 or less	Nothing. All is quiet.
10	A lone drunken Mekutu approaches, armed with a knife and carrying a flask of foul wine. He's quite drunk and suffers a one step Difficulty penalty to attacks and parries
11	A lone muttering Mekutu approaches, armed with a knife and carrying meat for the crawlers.
12	Two complaining Mekutu approach, armed with bloodied knives and dragging a dead mutilated body.
13–15	Two cackling Mekutu approach, armed with knives and dragging an unconscious Tangani prisoner.
16–18	Two arguing Mekutu approach, armed with knives and carrying sweetmeats and fruit wine.
19	A tired squad of four Mekutu guards approaches, returning to their quarters, armed with bows and knives. These Mekutu have 2 Fatigue.
20	A fresh squad of four Mekutu guards approaches, on their way to their watch, armed with bows and knives.

DEVILS UNDER GREEN STARS

in doing so indicate that they are heading toward the ruler of the Mekutu:

"Hurry, fool! If your slack footedness makes us late to the harem, I will make it clear to Lord Khenaton that you are to blame for his thirst!"

One filthy, ragged prisoner being dragged past is in a near catatonic state. He has been driven mad with terror by repeated exposure to Badazeko's jade eyes. As he is dragged past, he screams over and over again in terror.

"The eyes! The jade eyes!"

Unless restrained, Xhotatse guides accompanying the player characters immediately and loudly attack any Mekutu they come across with vengeful fervor — and vice versa — which causes the alarm to be raised.

The alarm will be raised by any substantial noise of combat in the Jade Keep, or by bodies and blood left carelessly in the player characters' wake in full view of any passing Mekutu. Wise player characters can hide any such bodies behind the various items of grisly furnishing about the Jade Keep, or else in an unused cell. Spilt blood and gore may be harder to quickly deal with, though the smoky incense, general filth of the keep, and the poor lighting will lower the Difficulty by one or more steps for any Stealth tests made for concealment attempts.

If the alarm is raised, the warriors of the Mekutu, including the family of Khenaton, rush from the harem to confront the hated Xhotatse invaders and their player character allies. See *Khenaton's Harem* on page 26 for details on how Khenaton's family fights.

Following the servants bearing wine to Khenaton's harem at a discreet distance takes the player characters past the torture chamber.

THE TORTURE CHAMBER

This location provides further evidence of the Mekutu's foul habits, hints at the existence of Enok and his pet crawler Safiki, and adds extra horror.

On one side of the passage leading to Khenaton's harem, the door to a torture chamber is open. Screams come from within. A fire pit in the center lights the chamber. Within, a capering hunchbacked torturer gleefully applies a heated iron to the chest of a squealing prisoner. The smell of blood and crisped meat fills the air. The torturer urges the quivering prisoner not to flinch so much.

"Or I will be forced to hand you over to Enok... and his little pet."

At this grim warning, the cowed prisoner tries feebly not to move while the poker again touches his tortured flesh.

The torturer attacks any intruder with his heated iron.

TORTURER (TOUGHENED)

ATTRIBUTES

Awareness	Intelligence	Personality	Willpower
9	8	8	9
Agility	Brawn		Coordination
9	9		9

FIELDS OF EXPERTISE

Combat	1	Movement	1
Fortitude	—	Senses	1
Knowledge	—	Social	1

STRESS AND SOAK

- **Stress:** Vigor 9, Resolve 9
- **Soak:** Armor 2 (Crude Wicker and Hide Armor), Courage 2

ATTACKS

- **Heated Iron (M):** Reach 2, 3 ⚔, 1H, Burning, Piercing 1, Stun

SPECIAL ABILITIES

- **Torture Captive:** The anguished cries of the torture victim send shivers down the spine. All player characters must make a Challenging (D2) Discipline test each round or suffer 1 Trauma. If the gamemaster spends 1 Doom, this becomes 1 point of Despair.

NIGHTMARE DUST

This cloying powder is a powerful alchemist's compound designed to induce terrifyingly real hallucinations. It is sometimes used in small spring-loaded traps concealed within the lids of containers. Opening said lids causes the unwary to inhale the dust into their lungs.

If inhaled, the gamemaster should make a secret Challenging (D2) Resistance test on behalf of the victim. If the test fails, inform the victim that they are under attack by a suitably frightening, but plausible, horror such as the contents of the trapped chest suddenly come to life.

The effect of the Nightmare Dust wears off in a few short minutes.

SPECIAL ABILITIES

- **Nightmarish Hallucination:** The character increases the Difficulty of all tests by one step and suffers 4 ⚔ mental damage.

THE HALL OF KHENATON

The player characters must pass through this grand and ornately decorated hall before reaching Khenaton's harem. Along the walls stand a series of upright jade-inlaid sarcophagi containing the mummified remains of Khenaton's forebears. Each sarcophagus is inscribed with the name "Khenaton." A sarcophagus may be opened with a small creak, but doing so releases an unpleasant cloying powder into the face of the person opening it if they do not detect and disarm this trap first with a Daunting (D3) Thievery test.

The powder is nightmare dust (see sidebar, a powerful alchemist's compound placed in the lids of the sarcophagi to punish those who would rob the dead Mekutu nobility by inducing terrifyingly real hallucinations. If inhaled by anyone, the gamemaster should make a secret Daunting (D3) Resistance test on behalf of the victim. If the test fails, inform the victim that the long-dead mummy inside the sarcophagus has come to life and attacks them. Make them roll for combat, but this encounter should use the rules for an Undead (Minion) using wounds as per the illusory wounds effect (see page 179 of the **Conan** corebook).

If not restrained, the victim believes they must defend themselves against the "undead thing", and may set off an alarm. The effect of the nightmare dust wears off in a few short minutes. In truth the mummies are no more than long-dead corpses, though the player characters may notice how they have become increasingly deformed with each generation.

KHENATON'S HAREM

A few doors beyond the Hall of Khenaton are the doors to the harem where Khenaton, the ruler of the Mekutu, spends the majority of his waking hours with his many wives, children, and grandchildren. Two Mekutu sentries guard the door and pass the time by throwing rotting star-fruit at a small monkey tied to a perch nearby. The monkey squeaks every time it is hit, while the sentries laugh cruelly with their horribly wide grins.

If the guards at the harem doors are not bypassed quietly, the noise raises the alarm, and the warriors of the Mekutu, including the family of Khenaton, rush from the harem to confront the hated Xhotatse invaders and their player character allies.

The harem itself is a large chamber divided by tattered silk hangings which effectively partition it into smaller sections easily brushed aside. Moldering divans and cushions lie scattered, and the somewhat cleaner floor is covered in ancient animal pelts — including apes, moon lions, and crawlers. It is slightly better lit than the rest of the Jade Keep, as fresh star-fruit is decoratively arranged about the chamber. The scented incense is richer and muskier here, making the air itself shimmer slightly.

DEVILS UNDER GREEN STARS

It is possible, but difficult, to skulk unseen through the harem using the furnishings and silk hangings as cover, requiring a Dire (D4) Stealth test or else some clever ruse or sorcerous trick.

Numerous children and women live here along with Khenaton. They doubtless scream and scatter at the first sight of the player characters. His grown family members — Khenaton son of Khenaton, Badazeko, Ntombi, and Enok — are found slaking their desires in other corners of the harem, but come running at the first sounds of alarm.

At the far end of the harem lies Khenaton himself on his great bed, a high, tiered construction of dark wood measuring the length of two men in both directions. Before the bed squat two more Mekutu warriors — his bodyguards. Atop the silken bed sheets long-smiled Khenaton lounges with several of his wives. To one side stand several gaunt prisoners from various tribes. They are horribly mutilated, lacking eyelids and tongues, and bear plates of sweetmeats and goblets of fruit wines which they drop to the floor when the player characters appear. As soon as he sees the player characters, Khenaton himself shrieks in fear.

"Aiee! Demons, sent by the accursed Xhotatse to drag me down to hell! Save me, my beautiful children!"

Khenaton's wives and younger children cluster around him, screaming and wailing.

Facing the Family of Khenaton

Fear grips Khenaton, screaming that this "Xhotatse invasion" is an unprovoked declaration of war. In response, his grown family members move forward to defend him from the player characters. Khenaton son of Khenaton leads her hulking sister Ntombi and two Mekutu warriors into close combat, declaring the player characters "Outsider dogs, in the pay of the cowardly Xhotatse!". The eerie Badazeko uses his terrible jade eyes to paralyze his foes with fear before moving in for the kill. Enok and his pet crawler Safiki lurk on the edges of the battle, striking out at vulnerable foes and then retreating with a titter back into the shadows.

If the player characters and the Xhotatse look likely to emerge victorious, with the majority of the Mekutu forces dead or dying, Khenaton cravenly flees. What happens to him after that is largely up to the player characters. If not chased, Khenaton disappears into the caves beneath the city-palace or even flees Zukundu entirely, either to meet his fate at the hands of the great reptiles or else to plague the player characters again at a later date. Likewise, tittering, self-serving Enok flees if the tide of battle turns against him and his family. The gamemaster may make use of the *Dangers of Zukundu* (see page 6) table to assign a grisly end for a fleeing villain or to add a little random peril to any player character giving chase.

If the player characters emerge triumphant and defeat Khenaton and his horrid, degenerate brood, the body count among any Xhotatse guides accompanying them is high.

> ### JADE EYES
> These powerful magical items come as a pair of faceted jade stones about the size of human eyeballs. The Zukundu created the artifacts using magic now lost to memory. If placed in empty eye sockets, they restore sight to their user, though the wielder now only perceives living beings as featureless green-tinged versions of their actual selves. The eyes glow an unearthly green.
>
> The wielder sees clearly in perfect darkness. The eyes also cause unnatural fear in those who the wielder gazes upon. Prolonged use of the jade eyes causes the wielder's skull, and eventually their skeleton, to glow greenly through their increasingly thinning skin and muscle.
>
> #### ATTACKS
> - **Deathless Stare (T):** Range C, 8 🧠 mental, Intense
>
> #### SPECIAL ABILITIES
> - **Deathless Stare (T):** Range C, 8 🧠 mental, Intense
> - Special Abilities
> - Night Vision
> - Fear 2
>
> #### DOOM SPENDS
> - **Jade Gaze:** The fully focused gaze of the jade eyes is terrifying to behold, and few creatures can stand firm in the face of such a dreadful sight. When attempting a Threaten action, the wearer of the jade eyes can spend 2 Doom to gain the Jade Gaze display, which grants the Area and Vicious 1 qualities to any Threaten action. Player characters using the eyes will add Doom to the Doom pool.

Lesser Mekutu family members, wives, servants, and slaves cower in corners of the harem or have long since fled. If any Xhotatse have somehow survived the battle, they grimly begin hunting down and executing the remaining Mekutu, unless restrained. Should Badazeko be killed, a particularly bold player character may choose to pluck out his jade eyes. See *Jade Eyes* (see sidebar).

KHENATON (NEMESIS)

Khenaton has an especially "long smile", wider and more unsettling than other adult Mekutu. He is almond eyed, with androgynous wide hips and a fleshy chest. Despite his uncanny appearance, he is strangely beautiful and alluring, though something of a coward and a sadist. He is father and grandfather to many of his tribe.

ATTRIBUTES

Awareness	Intelligence	Personality	Willpower
8	10	12	10

Agility	Brawn	Coordination
9	8	8

FIELDS OF EXPERTISE

Combat	1	Movement	—
Fortitude	—	Senses	1
Knowledge	2	Social	1

STRESS AND SOAK

- **Stress:** Vigor 8, Resolve 10
- **Soak:** Armor 1 (Clothing), Courage 2

ATTACKS

- **Crawler Fang Dagger (M):** Reach 1, 4 ♦, 1H, Parrying, Thrown, Unforgiving 1
- **Long Smile (T):** Range C, 5 ♦ mental, Stun

SPECIAL ABILITIES

- **Fanatical:** Khenaton may re-roll a single d20 on any Discipline test.
- **Beloved:** Any Mekutu within reach will attempt to prevent Khenaton coming to harm.
- **Alluring Voice:** Khenaton may add an additional d20 when attempting to distract, charm, persuade, seduce, or Threaten.

BADAZEKO (NEMESIS)

Called "Beautiful One", Khenaton's once handsome son was blinded years ago. Khenaton saw fit to place the arcane jade eyes in his son's empty sockets. This restored his sight, after a fashion, though his eyes, and indeed, his skull and, increasingly, the rest of his skeleton glow greenly through his now thinning skin. He can see in perfect darkness. The eyes cause unnatural fear in those whom he gazes upon (see *Jade Eyes* on page 27).

ATTRIBUTES

Awareness	Intelligence	Personality	Willpower
11	8	7	9

Agility	Brawn	Coordination
9	11	12

FIELDS OF EXPERTISE

Combat	1	Movement	1
Fortitude	3	Senses	3
Knowledge	1	Social	1

STRESS AND SOAK

- **Stress:** Vigor 14, Resolve 12
- **Soak:** Armor 2 (Crude Wicker and Hide Armor), Courage 2

ATTACKS

- **Clawed Hands (M):** Reach 1, 4 ♦, Grappling
- **Deathless Stare (T):** See *Jade Eyes*, page 27.

SPECIAL ABILITIES

- **Fear 2:** See *Jade Eyes*, page 27.
- **Night Vision:** See *Jade Eyes*, page 27.

DOOM SPENDS

- **Jade Gaze:** See *Jade Eyes*, page 27.

DEVILS UNDER GREEN STARS

ENOK (NEMESIS)

Called "Snake", Enok is Khenaton's skeletal, ghoulish son, often given to tittering. Enok has a pet baby crawler called Safiki, who is small enough to curl about its master's shoulders or slink around his legs.

ATTRIBUTES

Awareness	Intelligence	Personality	Willpower
10	8	7	8

Agility	Brawn	Coordination
11	9	11

FIELDS OF EXPERTISE

Combat	2	Movement	3
Fortitude	1	Senses	1
Knowledge	1	Social	1

STRESS AND SOAK

- **Stress:** Vigor 10, Resolve 9
- **Soak:** Armor 2 (Crude Wicker and Hide Armor), Courage 2

ATTACKS

- **Blowpipe (R):** Range C, 4 ⚡, Piercing 2, Venom (see Venom, below)
- **Safiki's Bite (M):** Reach 1, 5 ⚡, Vicious 1
- **Tittering Dance (T):** Range C, 2 ⚡ mental, Stun

SPECIAL ABILITIES

- **Tittering Dance:** Enok can pay X Doom to increase his Tittering Dance damage by X ⚡.
- **Slithering Escape:** Enok can pay 3 Doom to immediately escape the scene.
- **Safiki:** Enok can pay 1 Doom to have Safiki attack in addition to his blowpipe or Tittering Dance (above).
- **Venom:** Characters hit by the venom suffer 1 Fatigue.

NTOMBI (NEMESIS)

Called simply "Girl", Ntombi is Khenaton's large, brutish daughter. Though strong and powerful, she defers to her smarter brothers and sisters.

ATTRIBUTES

Awareness	Intelligence	Personality	Willpower
8	7	7	8

Agility	Brawn	Coordination
11	14	8

FIELDS OF EXPERTISE

Combat	4	Movement	3
Fortitude	3	Senses	1
Knowledge	1	Social	—

STRESS AND SOAK

- **Stress:** Vigor 17, Resolve 11
- **Soak:** Armor 2 (Crude Wicker and Hide Armor), Courage 2

ATTACKS

- **Jade Sliver Studded Crawler Bone Club (M):** Reach 2, 8 ⚡, Stun, Knockdown, Vicious 1

SPECIAL ABILITIES

- **Rampage:** If Ntombi hits a character she can roll 1 ⚡. On an effect, Ntombi makes an additional attack for X Doom where X is 1 greater than the Doom paid for the Rampage attack.

KHENATON, SON OF KHENATON (NEMESIS)

Called "Favored Son", she is actually Khenaton's daughter, the least deformed or mad of his brood. She commands the warriors of Mekutu in her father's name and wears scraps of the moon lion's pelt.

ATTRIBUTES

Awareness	Intelligence	Personality	Willpower
8	9	11	12

Agility	Brawn	Coordination
9	9	9

FIELDS OF EXPERTISE

Combat	3	Movement	1
Fortitude	1	Senses	1
Knowledge	1	Social	3

STRESS AND SOAK

- **Stress:** Vigor 10, Resolve 13
- **Soak:** Armor 2 (Crude Wicker and Hide Armor), Courage 2

ATTACKS

- **Crawler Fang Dagger (M):** Reach 1, 5 ⚡ 1H, Parrying, Thrown, Unforgiving
- **Superior Bow (R):** Range M, 4 ⚡, 2H, Piercing 1, Volley

SPECIAL ABILITIES

- **Leadership:** Khenaton is a skilled tactician. When leading a pair of warriors in battle, each warrior can contribute 2d20 to Khenaton's attack.

Blood on Silk

After the battle, the player characters can make a quick search of the blood-drenched harem with a Challenging (D2) Observation test, but as before (see Evidence of the Ape on page 24), they find no evidence that the monstrous Feathered Ape was inside the Jade Keep. Likewise, they can question any captive Mekutu with a Dire (D4) Persuade test, but the captive confesses that none of the Mekutu — not even Khenaton himself — knew anything of the Ape nor of the Xhotatse heads in the jade fountain. The players may now conclude that the Mekutu, foul though they may be, are innocent of the Ape murders. But if that is the case, why did its trail lead to the Jade Keep, and why did it slay only Xhotatse? (see *Princess Anepor's Scheme*, page 10).

But the player characters have little time to ponder matters further, or revel in their victory as, suddenly, a grievously injured Xhotatsan runner stumbles into the chamber and, dying of his wounds, gasps:

"The Ebony Keep... under attack! The Ape! Save the Queen from the Feathered Ape!"

THE EBONY KEEP BURNS

The player characters race back through the vine-choked chambers of the city-palace heading straight for the territory of their Xhotatse allies. As they near the Ebony Keep, they see that the hidden lion pits have been uncovered, the concealing vegetation, leaves and twigs kicked aside. There is no need for them to carefully pick their way through the Path of Skulls.

There are fresh corpses in some of the lion pits, bearing the distinctive elongated skulls of the "dreaming" tribe, the Tangani. All are impaled on the nasty wooden stakes lining the pits, but one Tangani is incredibly still alive! Despite a huge wooden stake sticking up through his stomach, which he doesn't seem to feel, the man gnashes his teeth and coughs up a great plume of blood as he claws uselessly up at the player characters above. Then he slumps back, dead of his terrible injury. A Challenging (D2) Alchemy test or Challenging (D2) Insight test indicates he was in some sort of enraged, painless (berserk) state.

An Average (D1) Observation test shows that the fallen Tangani wear small bloodied darts on cords about their necks. A successful test also reveals a small amount of syrupy substance coating a tiny puncture wounds in their chests. This is where they jabbed themselves with Jullah's Blood at the command of Azar and Anepor.

BEYOND THE DOOR OF THE ELEPHANT

Reaching the Ebony Keep of the Xhotatse, the player characters find the bronze Door of the Elephant unbarred and thrown open, and the black walls of the keep partially aflame. A Challenging (D2) Observation test picks out a rough line of fresh, deep gouges leading up and over the ebony wall. The gouges resemble the claw marks left by the Feathered Ape. Bodies of the guards lie just within the gates, their heads torn from their bodies in the manner of the Ape's

CRAWLERS ON THE LOOSE

If the player characters need encouragement to swiftly exit the Jade Keep of the Mekutu and make haste for whatever is happening back at the Ebony Keep of the Xhotatse, use this section to chase them through the city-palace at speed.

Somehow, the crawlers have escaped from their caves! Perhaps a Mekutu fleeing from the player characters failed to secure the inner gate behind them. Now, the unmistakable rasping sound of the sinuous reptiles is heard just outside the harem. A terrifying serpentine head pokes through the doors followed by several others. Any remaining Mekutu scream and gibber at the sight of the crawlers unleashed. The creatures fall upon the nearest Mekutu while the rest bear down on the player characters who should be strongly encouraged to outrun this tide of scaly death.

Shuttered windows to the rear of the harem can be unlocked to open directly over the killing ground far below. Hastily improvised climbing ropes torn from silk hangings and bedclothes can be used to climb down the walls with little risk, or else the player characters make a Challenging (D2) Athletics test or Challenging (D2) Acrobatics test to avoid falling and injury.

Several crawlers give chase, squeezing out through the shuttered windows and clinging eerily as they scuttle down the outer wall of the Jade Keep toward the player characters. Keep up the chase until the player characters reach the Ebony Keep of the Xhotatse, and the pursuing crawlers find more than enough fresh (Tangani) corpses among the lion pits to slake their reptilian hunger.

If desired, the gamemaster can make use of the *Dangers of Zukundu* table (see page 6) during the chase to add extra peril to both player characters and the pursuing crawlers.

DEVILS UNDER GREEN STARS

victims. The player characters may correctly deduce that the Ape climbed up over the ebony walls, slew the guards, and opened the gates from within the keep.

Inside the smoking keep, bodies of the Xhotatse, old and young alike, lie everywhere, slain by spear or poisoned blowpipe darts, or beheaded like the guards at the door. A single dead Tangani warrior lies among the bodies, slain by several spears still embedded in her limbs and torso. A close examination reveals a syrupy puncture mark in her chest. Sounds of battle — screams, bestial howls, the clash of weapons and a chillingly familiar bellow — are heard deeper into the keep in the direction of the throne room of Queen Chitaka.

The gamemaster may choose to spring two berserker Tangani on the player characters at this point, charging out from a side chamber straight toward them. This encounter gives the player characters a chance to learn the berserk Tangani's strengths and weaknesses in combat.

A small figure lies in a pool of its own blood in the middle of a broad passage that leads to the throne room. It is old Inokwu, a terrible clawed wound in his side (delivered by the Feathered Ape). A thick trail of his blood glistens behind him. He looks up at the player characters with dimming eyes.

"Madmen! They came so suddenly. Led by the beast itself. That clever woman at his heels. Fighting like demons, caring nothing for their own lives. The 'dreaming' tribe. Pah!"

He coughs up a great deal of blood and makes a dying request.

"You outsiders, you must save her, my dear innocent Chitaka. She has the mind of child."

TANGANI WARRIOR (TOUGHENED)

ATTRIBUTES

Awareness	Intelligence	Personality	Willpower
7	7	9	8
Agility	Brawn		Coordination
9	10 (1)		9

FIELDS OF EXPERTISE

Combat	2	Movement	1
Fortitude	1	Senses	1
Knowledge	—	Social	—

STRESS AND SOAK

- **Stress:** Vigor 11, Resolve 8
- **Soak:** Armor 2 (Crude Wicker and Hide Armor), Courage 4

ATTACKS

- **Spear (M):** Reach 3, 7⚡, Unbalanced, Piercing 1
- **Dagger:** Reach 1, 6⚡, 1H, Hidden 1, Parrying, Thrown, Unforgiving
- **Berserk Fury (T):** Range C, 3⚡ mental, Vicious 1

SPECIAL ABILITIES

- **Reckless Assault:** A berserker hurls himself into battle without regard for his own safety. When he makes a close combat attack, he may choose to gain 1, 2, or 3 bonus Momentum on the attack. However, until the start of his next turn, all enemies gain the same amount of bonus Momentum on their attacks against the berserker.

THE FEATHERED APE REVEALED

Following the sounds of battle and the trail of Inokwu's blood, the player characters reach the large shady chamber with the pond of saber fish beyond which lies the throne room. It is much changed from before. A howling pack of berserk Tangani press hard to overwhelm a knot of embattled Xhotatse warriors who erected a makeshift barricade at the far end closest to the throne room. Bodies of slain warriors from both sides litter the bloody floor.

The player character may spot young Jambi, the eager Xhotatse youth, among the desperate defenders. He, like the others, cannot hope to hold out for long. There is no sign of Queen Chitaka who must be in the relative safety of the throne room.

At the head of the Tangani pack is the unmistakable form of the Feathered Ape. With a bellow, its great metallic claws rip a screaming Xhotatse warrior from the barricade and toss him to the baying Tangani to be torn apart. To one side of the melee, near the ornamental pond, stands a Tangani woman (who the player characters may recognize as Anepor if they met her earlier in *The Chamber of the Red Creeper*, page 16). She urges the Ape and the berserkers on to victory. Then, she spots the player characters and reveals a little of her great plan.

"See, my brother! The outsiders have come to witness our triumph! Did you slay the degenerate Khenaton and his inbred spawn for us, fools? A pity you did not take more of these Xhotatse dogs along to die."

The Feathered Ape breaks off its attack against the Xhotatse barricade and muscles back to stand protectively at the side of Anepor as she exchanges heated words with the player characters.

"Oh, these proud, glittering Xhotatse! See how they have paid for laying our forebears low. They and the filthy Mekutu! Now, Azar, my brother, my prince, send these interfering fools to hell and let us take this keep's treasures and all of Zukundu as our own!"

At this, the Feathered Ape removes his exotic simian headpiece with a mocking laugh, to reveal the handsome face of Anepor's brother Prince Azar. He sketches a warrior's bow to the player characters and speaks in a voice as educated as his sister.

"Ho, you bold fellows! I rejoice to see you yet live. I enjoyed our earlier games of hunt and hide across the city-palace, but confessed to my sister Anepor here that I feared missing my chance to pit the Claws of the Ape against you in combat. I look forward to tearing your outsider heads from your necks."

Prince Azar, the Feathered Ape, leaps forward to do battle with the player characters accompanied by a group of berserker Tangani (the berserkers should number two more than the number of player characters). He uses speed and agility to move around the combat, rarely trading blows toe to toe for long. The berserk Tangani accompanying Azar make a wild, frontal assault, fighting to the death as will proud Azar, unwilling to let his sister's carefully conceived plans fail at the last. Princess Anepor, strikes at the player characters from a distance using her blowpipe and poison darts.

If any of the player characters accepted Inokwu's trinkets earlier (see *The Throne Room*, page 14), Anepor and Azar identify the ivory about their person and loudly condemn them for wearing the long-ago looted treasure of the Tangani. Such player characters bear the brunt of the Tangani attack.

If the gamemaster chooses, Anepor can take advantage of the confusing melee between her brother and the player characters to strike down some of the Xhotatse defenders at the barricade and sneak past into the throne room, intent on taking hostage or murdering the helpless Queen Chitaka. Allow the players characters a Daunting (D3) Awareness test to see her slip into the throne room so they can take action to intercept Anepor before she murders Chitaka.

If the player characters and the remaining Xhotatse look to be victorious, Princess Anepor, more inclined to self-preservation than her brother, chooses to flee if she can, using loyal Tangani berserkers to shield her escape.

Should the player characters emerge victorious, they and any Xhotatse survivors make their way over the bodies of the slain into the throne room where they find Queen Chitaka alive and curled up on the throne crying like the child she truly is. She rushes forward to hug the nearest player character, weeping with gratitude.

PRINCE AZAR, "THE FEATHERED APE" (NEMESIS)

Azar is large, strong, and agile. In the guise of the murderous Feathered Ape, he makes the ideal "simian-looking man". His costume includes vicious metallic red claws which help him climb trees and walls with ease and deliver wicked slashing attacks (see *Claws of the Ape*, page 33).

Azar loves his sister Anepor to distraction.

ATTRIBUTES

Awareness	Intelligence	Personality	Willpower
11	8	10	9

Agility	Brawn	Coordination
13	13 (1)	11

FIELDS OF EXPERTISE

Combat	3	Movement	3
Fortitude	3	Senses	2
Knowledge	1	Social	2

STRESS AND SOAK

- **Stress:** Vigor 17, Resolve 12
- **Soak:** Armor 2 (Crude Wicker and Hide Armor), or 3 (Ape Costume), Courage 2

ATTACKS

- **Claws of the Ape (M):** Reach 2, 8 ⚡, Knockdown, Stun, Vicious 1
- **Crushing Hug (M):** Reach 1, 6 ⚡, requires a successful grapple (see below).

DEVILS UNDER GREEN STARS

SPECIAL ABILITIES

- **Master Acrobat:** Prince Azar is a master acrobat, and all acrobatics or climbing tests are at one less difficulty than normal. In addition to this, he can reroll any one d20 failing to roll a success in addition to the one d20 granted by the Claws of the Ape (see above). Ranged attacks against him are at one step of Difficulty greater than normal. He never takes damage from a fall.
- **Iron Will**
- **No Mercy**
- **Grappler**
- **Deflection**
- **Riposte**

DOOM SPENDS

- **Crushing Hug:** If the Feathered Ape grapples a character, it can spend 2 Doom to make a Crushing Hug attack (see above).

PRINCESS ANEPOR (NEMESIS)

Cunning and skilled in the use of certain drugs, Anepor arms herself with a blowpipe and poisoned darts. If pushed to make a choice, Anepor would sacrifice her brother to save her own skin. She is also an accomplished actress, skilled in deception and appearing as an innocuous character.

ATTRIBUTES

Awareness	Intelligence	Personality	Willpower
8	12	11	10
Agility	Brawn		Coordination
6	9		10

FIELDS OF EXPERTISE

Combat	1	Movement	2
Fortitude	1	Senses	2
Knowledge	3	Social	4

STRESS AND SOAK

- **Stress:** Vigor 10, Resolve 11
- **Soak:** Armor 3 (Alchemically-enhanced Clothing), Courage 3

ATTACKS

- **Blowpipe (R):** Range C, 2⚡, Piercing 2, Venom (see Venom, below)
- **Dagger (M):** Reach 1, 4⚡, 1H, Hidden 1, Parrying, Thrown, Unforgiving

CLAWS OF THE APE

The Feathered Ape costume is equipped with cunningly wrought claws that fit over the hands and feet of the wearer. Made of a strong reddish metal, they enhance the wearer's natural ability to climb and leap, enabling them to scale trees and vault distances that few normal people could manage. They may also be used as offensive weapons in close combat though they prohibit the use of any other weapon or shield.

CLAWS OF THE APE

Reach	Damage	Size	Cost	Enc
2	4⚡	—	—	—

Qualities: Knockdown, Stun, Vicious

Special Ability

- **APE CLIMB:** The Claws of the Ape enable one to re-roll any d20 that does not generate a success when making a movement-related test while climbing or moving through trees. The second result is final.

A FITTING END FOR ANEPOR

Rather than letting Anepor fall in battle, or escape to menace the players characters another day, the gamemaster may choose to make her meet a fittingly unpleasant end. Seeing the battle turn against her and the Tangani, she turns to flee, but the path she chooses is straight across the ornamental pond which holds the deadly flesh-devouring saber fish (see *The Pond and the Monkey*, page 13).

Anepor leaps up to grab hold of a white-bloom vine. She begins to swing arm over arm across the pond, feet above the deadly waters. She knows it contains saber fish, thanks to her careful spying.

"The ivory! I must reclaim it!"

If they choose to do so, a player character may also grab a vine and give chase in a perilous final fight to the death above the pond, or else they may let fate take its course.

Halfway across, Anepor foolishly grabs hold of a yellow-bloom vine which slips from her grasp. She plummets down into the pond with a splash. Then, she cries out in pain, stumbles, and drops down to her knees screaming as the saber fish swarm about her, snapping and biting. The water turns red as she slips from view.

SPECIAL ABILITIES

- **Alchemy:** Anepor has access to all petty enchantments except for blasting powder.
- **Acting:** Prior to being unveiled, Anepor always counts as if she has spent 1 Fortune point on every Social test used to disguise her identity.
- **Venom:** Characters hit by the venom suffer 1 Fatigue.

AFTERMATH

The end of the adventure varies, depending on how many members of the different tribes the player characters managed to save or slay. But the end result probably amounts to the same: a bloodbath, tribal keeps sacked or burning, the surviving population of Zukundu substantially reduced.

Should the Xhotatse and their keep survive intact, a great, savage victory feast lasts for what feels like several days. Here, the player characters are honored.

Unless restrained, the victory-maddened Xhotatse summarily execute their prisoners and feed their corpses to the saber fish. The bones of the enemy dead form a great new cairn before the Door of the Elephant. Prince Azar's bones, as promised, are stacked atop the ebony walls for all to see.

If the player characters decide to take the treasure promised to them by the Xhotatse and leave, there are probably few within Zukundu willing or able to stop them — save perhaps for some crawlers now roaming wild among the halls (see *Crawlers on the Loose*, page 30). The surviving Xhotatse help them to load their packs with fresh supplies and a suitable amount of portable gold, jewels, and ivory. They receive a suitable farewell. The gamemaster can use the Xhotatse to mention that the valuable ivory was actually taken long ago from the Tangani, during the sacking of their Ivory Keep. Insightful player characters may then comment ironically on the cycle of wrongdoing and revenge in Zukundu.

The player characters may claim Azar's Claws of the Ape if they choose (see page 33), as well as the jade eyes of Badazeko, though the Xhotatse warn them of the eyes' sinister side-effects (see page 27). Their value if sold depends entirely on the purchaser, to be determined by the gamemaster.

If the adventure went badly for the player characters, it is possible that one or more hostile tribe (the Mekutu and/or Tangani) survive in sufficient numbers to hurriedly drive the meddling outsiders out of the city at spear point, carrying little but their weapons and the clothes they wear, though, perhaps they might pocket a few precious trinkets as they flee.

To add an extra twist, Queen Chitaka and a new advisor (if the Xhotatse survive) try to persuade the player characters to remain in Zukundu to *"revive our weakened bloodline"*. They may even try to enforce this decision on the player characters at spear-point, forcing them to stay as concubines or breeding slaves. This show of bravado collapses at the first sign of player character resistance. They back down and allow the player characters to leave peaceably.

Bypassing the great reptiles outside Zukundu can be made simpler either by the grateful Xhotatse survivors showing the player character a secret tunnel out of the city or else by a resourceful player character salvaging some bone pipes from a fallen Mekutu and employing their soothing notes to calm any great reptile they need to bypass on their way back to civilization.

EXPERIENCE

Experience point rewards should be granted as suggested by the **Conan** corebook, with additional bonuses rewarded for noteworthy roleplaying or ingenuity.

CHAPTER 2
THE PACT OF XIABALBA

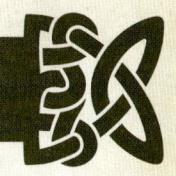

At first he thought it was a phantom, one of the mirages which had mocked and maddened him in that accursed desert. Shading his sun-dazzled eyes, he made out spires and minarets, and gleaming walls. He watched it grimly, waiting for it to fade and vanish. Natala had ceased to sob; she struggled to her knees and followed his gaze.

"Is it a city, Conan?" she whispered, too fearful to hope.
"Or is it but a shadow?"

— *"Xuthal of the Dusk"*

A city ripped from time, the unimaginably costly sacrifice of a Giant-King sorceress bent on immortality. For millennia, she has wandered the earth, ultimately regretting her decision and seeking redemption. But how does one reverse acts which occurred before the Cataclysm itself?

A group of seasoned adventures, ship-bound to their next destination when a squall appears and smites their boat, wrecking them upon a lonely island.

There, two times meet and what was done might be undone, as the sorceress and the heroes find themselves in a city forgotten by time, during the great siege which, in ages past, resulted in its fall. Can the heroes escape before the city is destroyed? More importantly, can they escape before the city is drawn inexorably into a nightmare realm, doomed to exist forever out of time and space?

INTRODUCTION

The Dreaming City demonstrates what the raw power of sorcery, coupled with personal ambition, can do to time itself. The player characters find themselves aboard a ship called *The Sea Witch* when a localized maelstrom wrecks their craft on a slender finger of beach upon an island rumored to be haunted.

What appears to be a tale of castaways and survival quickly becomes more complex, as the player characters realize the island holds the ruins of the last outpost of the mighty Giant-Kings civilization. Said civilization vanished before the Cataclysm, and now remains only in dusty tomes and the whispers passed between scholars. The player characters, however, discover that on this island, the civilization of the Giant-Kings isn't quite as dead as history supposes. In fact, this isle, at this particular time, sees the ghost of a city emerge from its dream-like imprisonment, drawing those unfortunate enough to be in its vicinity into the remote past — to the very day the city fell to an opposing army. The player characters happen to be such unfortunates and must escape both the marauding army and time itself!

HOW IT BEGINS

For the player characters, the tale begins aboard ship just as a storm appears without warning. Experienced sailors realize this is no common occurrence, but they can do little save survive. The ship soon sinks, and the player characters find that they and the first mate alone make it to safety. But safety is relative in the Hyborian Age. The island upon which they find themselves is cursed — or so the first mate says.

The preamble done, the sodden, cold adventurers must now tend to the immediacies of survival while looking for a way off this desolate isle.

Chapter One: A Private Little Maelstrom

Fresh water is the first need of anyone trying to survive, and the first mate tells the player characters that an ancient well exists at the center of ruins somewhere in the foreboding jungle ahead. Such impetus or another drives the group further inland. The jungle itself poses no mean threat, as wild creatures stalk the group. More than that, though, are creatures which "man was not meant to know". On the way to the ancient well, other ruins are discovered — foreshadowing the city ahead. The city itself is Xeiros, the last holdout of the so-called Giant-Kings whose rule ended when barbarians pulled down its walls and killed its citizens.

It is said that the city did not go quietly, but instead was destroyed by its sorcerer queen — a final act of resistance against creeping barbarism. The struggle between the savage and the civilized is a cycle of tumult punctuated by cataclysmic climaxes. Such philosophy is not the daily bread of adventurers, but a strange — yet beautiful — hermit relates such musings in her mad way as she approaches the player characters near the well. She also shows an uncanny familiarity with the player characters. As she speaks with them, the sky darkens much as it did during the squall, and an eldritch force plunges the city, and all within, into the distant past.

Chapter Two: Xeiros, the Dreaming City

From the relative calm of the ruined city, the player characters suddenly find themselves in the chaos of a living city under siege. Where there lay tumbled arches now rise the full splendor of the Giant-Kings' civilization. The city of Xeiros is itself a storm of citizenry and soldiers dealing with the barbarous besiegers who even now clamber over the walls. Screams, war drums, and the sounds of battle surround the confused group. Fighting, or running to relative safety, led by the hermit, the player characters have a chance to catch their breath as she relates her tale. In brief — the woman claims to be Xiabalba of Xeiros, Last Queen of the Giant-Kings!

Her claims become wilder as she goes on. Xiabalba asserts that she sacrificed her city to a dream realm of the Outer Dark called Kuth of the Star-Girdle. In return for this unimaginable human sacrifice, Xiabalba was granted immortality. That gift, over the ages, turned into a curse as she had all the more time to regret what she'd done. Over painful centuries, Xiabalba drew upon all the knowledge she could find, made laborious calculations, and determined that once, in this so-called Hyborian Age, the city would briefly return from the Star-Girdle, thus granting her the chance to undo what she'd done millennia ago. (For her full story, see *The Story of Xiabalba and Xeiros*, page 37).

The player characters, whether they like it or not, are now enmeshed in a doomed city's fate. Xiabalba, whether mad or not, looks like their only avenue out. The final part

THE STORY OF XIABALBA AND XEIROS

The civilization of the Giant-Kings fell many thousands of years ago. The City of Xeiros is among the last outposts of that civilization as it falls to internal decay and outward threats. One of the great themes in Howard's Conan tales is the clash between civilization and barbarism and the endless cycle in which one tops the other. The Giant-Kings are at the end of the civilized arc of that cycle and collapsing.

Xiabalba, the Sorcerer Queen of Xeiros, is not going quietly into history, however. She has no intention of letting her city fall. However, she does not have the soldiers to defeat the barbarians who are literally at the gates. She therefore searches for a solution outside the realm of the mortal world. What she comes up with is as ingenious as it is mad — preserve the city from time itself by pushing it into the realm of dream. There, in Kuth of the Star-Girdle (described further in *The Book of Skelos*, the city would remain preserved until such time as Xiabalba could find a way to return it to the real world).

Ah, but the gods of the Star-Girdle do not easily allow such intrusions into their domain. Yes, they would allow a mortal city to hide there from its enemies, but the price would be the soul of every citizen in that city. In return, they would grant Xiabalba immortality thus preserving, at least in a single person, the Giant-Kings' civilization forever. Xiabalba took the deal. Why should she die with the rest of her people if she could not save them? This, at least, was what she told herself. In the thousands of years since, that decision has lain upon her with the crushing weight of guilt.

However, she did take the deal. As the barbarians stormed Xeiros, she opened a portal to Kuth and the city, along with everyone save herself, was pulled into the dream realm. There, the citizens' minds were eternal feasts for the nightmare creatures which dwell in the Star-Girdle. However, they remained good to their compact, and Xiabalba herself was granted immortality.

As history records it, the city disappeared in an eldritch storm consuming both the Giant-Kings and their enemies. There, history ends. Xiabalba's story just begins. Undying, she spent many hundreds of years trying to find remnants of the Giant-Kings, only to find that, each time she found a redoubt, it fell to similar foes. History would have its way with all cultures — none are eternal.

As the years went by, though, the guilt of Xeiros gathered, accreting around her like shipwreck collects coral. The old Xiabalba gradually became a hard, hollow shell under layers of regret. She wandered from one nation to another. At first, she sought a way to break the pact she made and return her city to this day and age. This, however, was impossible and so she turned herself to undoing the decision itself. If she never made the deal, then the city would fall, yes, but it would not be tormented forever by the demons of Kuth.

Hundreds of years were spent gathering the necessary information, arcane lore, and astronomical calculations necessary to her task. As time has its cycles, Xiabalba realized that the stars not only align but realign as once they were. Upon a day where such alignments were identical to those on which she performed the ritual, the city would appear briefly in this world. She could, with the proper sorcery, enter the past and, perhaps, unmake that terrible decision.

of her story is, perhaps, the strangest — to get back to their own time with their hides intact, the player characters must kill Xiabalba. But they must kill her not as she stands before them, but as she was millennia ago, in the great tower of her palace. There, then-becomes-now as she enacts the ritual which condemns the city to Kuth and herself to regretful immortality.

The player characters must fight their way to the tower, find a way to the top, and kill their would-be savior/guide. Simple, right?

Chapter Three: The Hourglass

The player characters must now find a way into the tower even as the barbarians pour over the city walls. Xiabalba offers them options, but the decision about how to infiltrate the tower is theirs. Whether they fight their way up or sneak their way in, they must reach the tower's summit where the ritual now takes place.

As the player characters arrive, the past iteration of Xiabalba is near the end of her ritual — a portal rends the fabric of space and time inside the chamber itself. From said portal come ghastly things literally drawn from nightmare, and the player characters must cut through them to get to Xiabalba. Should they succeed in dispatching her, her modern counterpart fades away, much as the city itself begins to do. Time is now, literally, against them, as the player characters race to escape the city before it is reclaimed by the past.

They barely make it out of the city as it falls to barbarism and time's arrow, as it would have had Xiabalba not interfered. Just as they begin to catch their breath, though, they find the portal is not quite closed, and a dread being from Kuth tries to push its way into the waking world.

Their involvement in the past has altered the flow of history, and a fishing village populated by the descendants of the barbarians and Giant-Kings, lies quietly along the shore. As the player characters prepare to debark from that small village, they see a storm begin to gather out at sea, but this time, it seems almost benign.

CHAPTER ONE: A PRIVATE LITTLE MAELSTROM

All of the preceding, the city and the sorcerer queen, the grand cycles of history, matter little, at present, to a group of adventurers aboard a small boat called The Sea Witch. They have their own concerns, but these are blown to and fro by the same wind that fills their sails on a calm, clear day in the open sea. Whether this be The Western Sea or the Vilayet Sea is up to the gamemaster. The isle upon which the ruins of Xeiros are found can be located in either great body of water. The adventure is designed so that the gamemaster might easily insert it into a campaign. In fact, the set-up presupposes the player characters are on their way to some other destination altogether, when the hand of fate — in the form of Xiabalba — blows them off course and into an entirely unexpected adventure.

The gamemaster can play out time onboard the ship if desired but it is more dramatic to open with the clear day turning suddenly dark.

THE STORM BREWS

Calm skies can turn on an Aquilonian luna, as any experienced sea-dog knows. Yet this storm comes out of nothing, as if some forgotten god points his finger at The Sea Witch and focuses all its ire upon her wooden hull.

The very sea rises as a wall around the ship, while the sky grows as black as Set's heart. Rain comes from above. Waves wrack the ship, and the crew have all they can do to even react. A man is blown from the rigging, his screams lost to the wind as he is sucked up into the vortex of wind and rain. The mainmast cracks with a sound like thunder. A wave twice as tall as that broken mast washes men overboard like grime from a plate scrubbed by a scullery maid. The gamemaster should set the dire nature of the scene as seems appropriate.

As the ship is assailed and eventually sinks, player characters should make tests to survive. However, be lenient here; it is little fun to die at the start of the adventure. Penalize, rather than kill, but don't tell the players this beforehand. When a wave hits, it takes a Challenging (D2) Brawn test to prevent being washed overboard. When the mast falls, player characters must succeed on a Daunting (D3) Athletics or suffer 2 💀 damage. Any player characters caught by the falling mast must then make a Challenging (D2) Brawn test to extricate themselves from beneath the mast and clamber over the ship's sides. Failure, again, means a penalty when a player character is washed ashore, not death. There is plenty of opportunity to die ahead.

No matter what they do, the ship is doomed — of course, a ship of corpses is of little use to Xiabalba. Because she created the storm to draw assistance, the gamemaster may grant any player character about to suffer grievous injury or die one free Fortune Point with which to fend off such a fate. In such cases, the gamemaster should inform the player that such a stroke of luck *feels* unnatural, as if some force wishes them spared. This is also a great way to foreshadow the events to come.

ON THE BEACH

Crawling like their ancestors from the sea to land, the player characters collapse in the surf and sand along with the first mate, Khaskh, who survives the wreck through sheer chance. Should the player characters have elected to try and save other members of the crew, the gamemaster can determine their fates as they see fit — do the player characters struggle desperately to rescue a non-player character they had become friendly with aboard ship, but fail? Do the player characters manage to bring several of their erstwhile colleagues to shore? The choice is the gamemaster's.

This sliver of beach abuts a small cliff beyond which the verdant green of jungle rests against a once-again-perfect blue sky. The storm dissipated almost as quickly as it began. Out to sea, some few pieces of the ship remain, and the player characters may decide to see what supplies wash ashore. This is largely up to the gamemaster, but should not include food and water. The player characters must press inland to find these. Other sundry items are at the gamemaster's discretion but rope, weapons, and the like are probably advisable. However, the gamemaster may wish to make this an even tougher trial of survival by stripping the player characters entirely of their usual arms and armament.

It is unlikely the player characters have any idea where they are, but a Dire (D4) Lore test affords them the approximate information contained in *What Khaskh Knows* (sidebar). Otherwise, they'll have to rely on the first mate's knowledge of the area, and superstitions about this island, to inform them. As they crawl further up from the beach, Khaskh already begins to pray, visibly disturbed.

KHASKH, SAILOR AND RACONTEUR (TOUGHENED)

A dark-skinned Vendhyan, Khaskh is middle-aged, thin, with sharp blue eyes and a blue-black goatee. He tends toward superstition and regularly invokes his god, Asura. He spent the first part of his life as an ascetic monk, in fact, but found he lacked the discipline to pursue such a life. The pleasures of the world were too many to resist, and Khaskh became something of an outcast from his family and former friends. He headed west, hoping that Asura would guide him. From Vendhya, he set sail aboard a Turanian galley.

He has spent the last twenty some odd years of his life at sea, rising from lowly sea-dog to first mate on a series of ships. His own restless nature seems to perpetually prevent him from captaining his own ship, but the truth is that he is afraid. Khaskh has never felt the direction or clarity he thinks a captain should possess.

Many sailors are superstitious: it goes with the life of the sea, but Khaskh is an extreme example. Asura is his preferred deity, but he wears a tangle of holy symbols around his neck from other gods — operating on the grounds that one of them is bound to be real and in need of new followers. When it is late, and rain begins to pock mark the deck of the ship, he'll tell the crew of whatever ship he happens to be on about the time he saw a sea serpent. His description is horrific, and the event — real or imagined — clearly haunts the man.

ATTRIBUTES

Awareness	Intelligence	Personality	Willpower
8	8	9	10
Agility	Brawn		Coordination
9	9		8

FIELDS OF EXPERTISE

Combat	—	Movement	1
Fortitude	1	Senses	—
Knowledge	1	Social	—

STRESS AND SOAK

- **Stress:** Vigor 9, Resolve 10
- **Soak:** Armor 1, Courage 4

ATTACKS

- **Cutlass (M):** Reach 2, 5 🜂, Unbalanced, Vicious
- **Handy Rock (R):** Thrown, 2 🜂, Improvised, Stun
- **Mouth of a Sailor (T):** Range C, 3 🜂 mental

INTO THE JUNGLE

As their situation becomes apparent — trapped on an island with no food or potable water — the player characters will no doubt begin a search for, at the least, the items necessary to survive. Along the narrow beach, there is little to be found. The only item of interest is a stone jutting from the surf. At low tide, it sits on the edge of the beach in the sand. It is totemic in nature, and roughly hewn on first glance. Closer inspection — requiring a Daunting (D3) Observation check — reveals that the statue appears to be the defaced remnants of a previous, much more sophisticated work.

The current statue is a squat, misshapen form, somewhere between a spider and a toad. A Dire (D4) Lore check identifies the god as Tsathoggua, a demonic entity of the Outer Dark. The erosion and wear on the statue indicate it is very, very old. In point of fact, this statue began life as a monument to a much less nefarious, but now forgotten, deity. This was a deity of the Giant-Kings, but their barbaric conquerors re-carved the statue when they established a beach head here — a Challenging (D2) Craft or an Awareness at Dire (D4) — to realize it's been re-carved. Of course, their further excursions resulted in the events described previously. They did not conquer Xeiros itself.

The cliffs are not hard to scale — requiring only an Average (D1) Athletics test — and a fall only inflicts 1 🜂 damage. The first character over the rise hears, vaguely, war drums. Have that player make a Challenging (D2) Observation test to determine that the drums seem to be

Roll	Result
	JUNGLE ENCOUNTERS
1–4	**Giant-King Patrol:** Bronze armor, green with age, clings to skeletons whose flesh has long since rotted away. The skeletons are covered in foliage. They are those of Giant-King patrols. The players can recognize them from actual encounters with living Giant-Kings, flung backwards through time, before or after this discovery.
5–8	**Charnel Pit:** The player characters come upon a stone-lined pit filled with bones, many of them human. It is long since overgrown and only spotted with a Daunting (D3) Observation check. Player characters that fail this check tumble into the pit, taking 2 damage, unless they succeed in a Daunting (D3) Athletic test.
9–12	**Venomous Snake:** See page 330 of the *Conan* corebook. It attacks the nearest character.
13–16	**Grey Ape:** These are the last native inhabitants of the island and were once kept as servants by the Giant-Kings. There is one ape per player character. (See page 322 of the *Conan* corebook).
17–20	**Corpse:** The headless body of someone in a barbaric outfit of an unknown culture. This island is supposed to be uninhabited, isn't it?

> ## WHAT KHASKH KNOWS
>
> In his years on the seas of the world, Khaskh acquired a wealth of folklore, superstitious nonsense and real truth. He can speak about a number of subjects on nearly any locale that lies near a major body of water. Some of his seemingly random knowledge is of interest to the player characters, but his knowledge of this island is certainly pertinent.
>
> Khaskh has not been here himself, but has heard stories from several sailors who have. He knows the island is uninhabited (more or less), but cursed. He certainly wants to find a way off. Some of the stories he has heard involve strange creatures. Others speak of vague but persistent feelings of fear. All the sailors who returned to tell stories said they had nightmares while on the island. Some sailors did not return.
>
> There are ruins of the city of Xeiros here. Khaskh knows it to be a city of the Giant-Kings, though he thinks these were literally giants. Near the center of the ruins is a fresh water well, which he believes is their best chance for water. He is very afraid of going, but he knows he must to survive.
>
> Khaskh "knows" that the Giant-Kings destroyed themselves in a savage civil war over the love of a woman and the destiny of a dynasty. This is not true; in fact, it is heavily romanticized nonsense. After all, oral legends passed down for generations are not the most reliable source of knowledge about civilizations millennia-dead. That said, the gamemaster may prefer to omit this detail, as it could confuse players.

coming from further inland. The next player character over the cliff does not hear these drums. Khaskh claims this does not bode well for any of the group.

Jungle Travel

Pushing through the hot jungle can largely be abstracted. For every hour or two (the jungle is slow going) player characters should make a Challenging (D2) Discipline or Resistance test or suffer 1 Fatigue and Despair. Certain encounters are inevitable, unless the gamemaster wishes to dispense with them. The table above offers some random encounters the gamemaster can use to break up any monotony. The gamemaster should either pick an encounter, or roll 1d20.

PLANNED EVENTS

A couple of events ought to occur before the player characters reach the ruins proper. The first is an encounter with a Giant-King patrol displaced in time. The second is the discovery of a petrified ship in the middle of the jungle. Both foreshadow the fuller story of Xeiros and Xiabalba.

Giant-King Patrol

The sound of war drums presages this encounter. Have each player character make a Daunting (D3) Observation test. Those who succeed hear the drums in the distance. These are drums of the barbaric invaders. Each drum is covered in the leathered human skin of an enemy. They beat for battle and for the dark gods whom these soldiers worship.

This patrol consists of one Giant-King soldier for each player character. They are not looking for the player characters, but for their enemy. That said, the player characters are unknown to them and assumed to be barbarians and, given that the Giant-King troops believe themselves to be (and *are*) in the midst of a bloody siege, they will not pause to ask after the player characters' intentions but instead attack immediately.

THE PACT OF XIABALBA

This patrol is temporally displaced. The magical energy which Xiabalba is drawing to herself in order to return to the past is distorting reality around her and across the island. To represent this, if a player character generates a Complication, the Giant-King being attacked suddenly becomes insubstantial. The weapon passes through the man momentarily and becomes fused in his shield. The player character loses his weapon. Ignore this if the player character is using only his fists as a weapon.

GIANT-KING SOLDIER (TOUGHENED)

These are soldiers of Xeiros and bear the crest of Xiabalba on their breastplates and shields. Each swears allegiance to her unto death. The crest is that of a severed head, eyes wide, tongue hanging from an agape mouth. It is fairly hideous to look upon.

The soldiers keep the heads of the dead they send to the House of Shades. Each soldier has one or more rotted, desiccated severed heads ties to their belts. These reflect the growing culture of human sacrifice the fading Giant-King culture fell into (see page 37 for more details). The practice of human sacrifice stretched, in the final days of Xeiros, to the ritual consumption of those men and women butchered in offering to the gods. It is for this reason that Xiabalba could not call upon her old, fanatically loyal troops to prevent the atrocity she committed; her citizens were too maddened and corrupted by the insane rituals they conducted to do aught but eat, hunt, and kill.

ATTRIBUTES

Awareness	Intelligence	Personality	Willpower
8	8	9	9
Agility	Brawn		Coordination
9	10		9

FIELDS OF EXPERTISE

Combat	1	Movement	—
Fortitude	1	Senses	—
Knowledge	—	Social	—

STRESS AND SOAK

- **Stress:** Vigor 10, Resolve 9
- **Soak:** Armor 2 (Bronze Cuirass and Greaves), Courage 2

ATTACKS

- **Spear (M):** Reach 3, 6 ⚅, Unbalanced, Piercing 1
- **Shortsword (M):** Reach 1, 6 ⚅, 1H, Parrying
- **Shield (M):** Reach 2, 4 ⚅ 1H, Knockdown, Shield 2
- **Warcry (T):** Range C, 3 ⚅ mental, Area, Stun

DOOM SPENDS

- **Gleeful Murder:** If a Giant-King soldier injures a character, he can spend 4 Doom to deal 1 additional Wound as if his attack had the Intense quality

SHIP

From a distance, an Average (D1) Observation test reveals a form rising from the jungle loam that is entirely unnatural. The closer one gets, the clearer the object becomes — Daunting (D3) Observation to discern that it is, in fact, an overgrown ship. The bow juts up from the earth at an angle, as if it came to rest this way on the ocean floor.

With a Dire (D4) Knowledge test, the player characters may think that perhaps this is the case. The ship might have been thrust up from the sea floor during the Cataclysm, though it is more likely that it was dragged from the sea when the city was pulled into Kuth. It is a Giant-King war galley. The mast is missing, but bronze shields, of the same type carried by those soldiers the player characters recently fought, flank the sides. These are curiously uncorroded, just as the wood is mysteriously not rotted away. Some aspect of the temporal ritual preserved both.

They are, however, entirely overgrown with lichen and moss.

Once the player characters climb aboard the boat, they discover that it never sank. The skeletons of the crew remain, some fused entirely to the decks, arms and feet seemingly sunk into the timber the ship was built from, as if the crew and the ship began to grow into one another; the remains of organic tissue compose portions of the bulkheads. The broken oars jutting from the side of the ship indicate a slave galley below. However, the skeletons which the player characters can find there are those of Grey Apes, not men. How such creatures were once trained and made subservient is not apparent. Witnessing such strange and impossible things requires a Challenging (D2) Discipline test, taking 3 ⚅ mental damage on a failure.

In addition to preserved bronze shields and steel weapons, there is a quite a treasure below. The galley was attempting to make a run through the blockade formed by the barbarian's ships, so that it might hire mercenaries to assist Xeiros. This was not to be, but the coin intended to hire these mercenaries' remains below. A total of 10 Gold is in the hold, though carrying such an amount is impractical as it comes in the form of gold bars stamped with the queen's seal. An individual character may only carry one gold in such heavy loot without being encumbered.

Of particular interest is a ship's log, which has also been preserved. It recounts the war between the barbarians (who are only ever called thus) and the Giant-Kings (who are simply referred to as Xeirosans). Reading the log is a Dire (D4) Language test, as this language has been dead nearly as long as its author.

The log exists to help fill in a few details before the player characters meet Xiabalba. What it contains is up to the gamemaster, but it definitely does not include her full story. It may indicate a civilization in decline. Some salient points from the log include:

- The Giant-Kings once ruled a mighty empire but do so no longer.
- The log's author remembers his grandfather's stories of the height of empire. Human sacrifice was rare then.
- Xeiros is ruled by Xiabalba, the Sorcerer Queen. She deals with demons hailing from a realm called Kuth of the Star-Girdle, requiring a Daunting (D3) Lore test to recall information on this realm.
- Barbarians have beset the empire on all sides — apparently because of the increasing tyranny and rapaciousness of Xeiros and its ruler, although the author of the log implies it is as much because of the barbarians' lust for gold. The remaining outposts of a once great Empire, of which Xeiros is one, cannot hold out much longer.

These two encounters comprise the planned events which precede the player character's arrival in the ruins of Xeiros. The gamemaster should feel free to expand on these to extend the adventure, but delaying the crux of the plot lessens the tension and drama. With luck and good pacing, the gamemaster could finish this scenario in one or two sessions.

CHAPTER TWO: XEIROS, THE DREAMING CITY

Having ventured through the jungle and encountered ill-omens of things to come, the player characters arrive at the ruins of The Dreaming City of Xeiros. There, they find freshwater but also the impossible — they soon travel back in time! Guided by the hermit Xiabalba, former queen of the city, the player characters must find a way back to the Hyborian Age before they die with the rest of the city in the Thurian Age.

THE RUINS OF XEIROS

Broken teeth rise from the earth's maw in the form of shattered columns, clearly built by superior craftsman for they are worked with an artistry of the highest order. Tumbled arches and stone roads overgrown with grass speak of a great civilization and the means by which its people once traveled. Now, only ghosts remain. In the very center of the ruins, in a clearing, littered with the vestiges of a dead culture, lies a large well.

The well itself would once have been splendid and, in times past was in the center of an even greater fountain. The remains of the fountain suggest the statue of a woman surrounded by strange creatures, perhaps born of the Outer Dark. There is no birdsong, no wind, only an absolute stillness. A Challenging (D2) Observation test instills the sense that someone watches the player characters. Indeed, Xiabalba does observe them from a grove of trees grown up on the northwest corner of what would have been a grand square. A Daunting (D3) Observation test causes the

THE PACT OF XIABALBA

player character to hear voices, snatches of conversation in a language they don't understand. This, then, is followed by the din of distant battle — steel on steel recognizable to any warrior. Also, the drums are louder here, like a thumping, angry heart clenching itself into a desperate fist.

Spotting Xiabalba before she wishes to reveal herself is a Dire (D4) Observation test made once, and only once, as a group. She is well camouflaged.

The first player character to approach the well, should any now do so, hears the distinct sound of a coin falling onto stone. For a moment, they glimpse a child bend down to pick up the coin but, before the child can retrieve the coin, an adult scoops them up desperately and runs. Their forms seem to dissolve into mist as they flee. The coin remains on the ground. It's real and marked with the queen's profile. However, the image on the coin isn't easily recognizable as Xiabalba herself.

The sky darkens above, at which point Xiabalba reveals herself. The ritual was planned to begin soon after the player characters arrived, in order to protect against threats to her life, should the group decide to attack her. She has not come through thousands of years without being prepared.

When she steps forth from the grove, Xiabalba looks as though she too is a shade of some former existence; the shadows seem to disgorge her, suddenly, unexpectedly. The characters can see plainly that she is beautiful, though she looks quite the hermit. Her hair is intertwined with leaves; her garb is lichen-colored and likewise mixed with flora for camouflage. Over time, and her many trips back into the past, her mind encountered iteration after iteration of itself, to say nothing of the toll the travel itself took upon her, physically and mentally. Xiabalba is not quite sane. Sorcery warps the mind, however ancient and wise one may be.

When approached, Xiabalba almost immediately launchs into a garbled, hard to follow stream of disjointed words, metaphors, incantations, and nonsense. It has been many years since she has spoken any words aloud, and even longer since she needed to communicate her thoughts to another living being — at least, a being who inhabits the mortal plane. If any of the player characters can make a Challenging (D2) Lore test, they are able to gather that she is attempting to explain something about the nature of this island, and of its former ruler, Xiabalba herself. If the player characters try and calm Xiabalba, or begin to speak to her in measured tones, she quickly becomes comprehensible. The sorcerer possesses a formidable intellect, and, once prompted, it does not take her long to attune herself to conversation involving people other than herself.

The player characters receive answers to almost anything they ask, though the answers themselves may be gnomic. When roleplaying Xiabalba, the gamemaster might use strange, arcane imagery in her responses, and glance suddenly, as though Xiabalba hears dissenting voices calling from a fathomless distance. Xiabalba's answers to a number of likely questions are below. However, even these responses are wrapped in esoteric references and language:

- **If asked who she is:** *"I? You do not recognise me? Me? I am Xiabalba... Do they not know me? Have my images fallen? My scythes gone blunt? Great Queen. Greater sorcerer. I am such before whom the spirits would once bow...no more, perhaps, but for all that glory to be gone from me... from the world..."*

- **If asked about the island itself, or the kingdom that once stood here:** *"Ancient, beautiful. City of the ages. City of all the ages. Torn down, stone by stone and life by life, hunting it."*

- **If asked about any of the strange sights in the jungle:** *"The pollen of the centuries, the seeds released and floating and settling. Yes. More to come. More to spring from the earth and the air. I have seen them before. I want to never see them again. What sweetness that would be..."*

- **If asked about the nature of the storm beginning to spring up around them:** *"This is the great hope. The great chance. The throw of the dice that I must make. Will you be my Kings and Queens of Swords? Great wealth, the glinting of eyes, the testament of gods...yes. Yes."*

- **If asked whether she caused the storm that sank the ship:** *"Wind waking. Rain rampant. The dance of the elements. It was necessary. Unfortunate, but necessary. But you may right a great wrong. You may make the new from the dust, the phoenix — Mitra's mark. Yes, you know it..."*

- **Should the player characters seem liable to attack her, either upon hearing the above or for some other reason:** *"Ha! No children, pretty things, babes in arms. You have not time for that...this wind and rain and darkness will not let you cut or gut me. Time...the sand and the centuries vanish. It is our chance! Help me take it and I will offer you the rewards of the gods themselves...!"*

XIABALBA THE ELDER (NEMESIS)

Her beauty has hardly faded in the years spent on this lonely island, but her eyes betray the madness that has pooled within her mind over that time. She is voluptuous and desirable, but her hair is a jungle itself, tangled with leaves and she has the predatory, watchful movements of a jungle cat. Her clothes, likewise, are natural riot of woven fabric and natural elements, which, far from making her seem ridiculous, simply emphasize the air of danger which surrounds her. See page 49 for further information on this version of the Sorcerer Queen of Xeiros.

ATTRIBUTES

Awareness	Intelligence	Personality	Willpower
11 (12)	13	10	13
Agility	Brawn		Coordination
7	7 (12)		7

FIELDS OF EXPERTISE

Combat	—	Movement	—
Fortitude	5	Senses	3
Knowledge	5	Social	1

STRESS AND SOAK

- **Stress:** Vigor 17, Resolve 18
- **Soak:** Armor 2, Courage 8

ATTACKS

- **Daggers (M):** Reach 1, 6⚡, 1H, Hidden 1, Thrown, Parrying
- **100 Lifetimes of Practiced Threats (T):** Range C, 4⚡ mental, Stun

SPECIAL ABILITIES

- **Enchanted Ring:** Xiabalba's ring allows her to cast *Dismember* at will (4⚡, Vicious 2), but she must make a Knowledge test to hit her target.
- **Enchanted Necklace:** Xiabalba's necklace allows her to cast *Shape of a Beast*, and allows her to maintain her extreme strength and awareness.

DOOM SPENDS

- **Sorcery:** Xiabalba is a sorcerer and can cast most spells, but it will take a lot of convincing to get her to do so. An Epic (D5) Persuasion test will get her to cast one spell, but Xiabalba will not advertise this capability. If desired, she can pay X Doom to cast any spell with a difficulty and Momentum spend total of X.

THE TEMPORAL STORM

Xiabalba continues to speak with the player characters as if she knows them, addressing them as if the coming events have already occurred. It's important that the storm come now, as the player characters are not entirely unlikely to attempt to restrain her or simply attack her.

The storm which Xiabalba summons to cast herself, and the player characters back in time, manifests much as the one which sunk the boat. The wind appears as if

---

A BRIEF HISTORY OF TIME TRAVEL

The Pact of Xiabalba does not attempt to represent the complexities of time travel. CONAN is a pulp game, and Robert E. Howard's own excursions into time travel likewise ignored the messier bits. The time action in the scenario is pretty straightforward, and it's easy to cut some of the more mind-boggling elements.

The crux of the adventure is about the player characters' trip back in time to Xeiros when it still lived on the mortal plane. That alone is enough if the gamemaster so chooses. However, Howard liked to set his Conan yarns in familiar genres and in the time since Howard wrote his stories, the time travel genre has become a staple. Thus, the gamemaster should feel at liberty to introduce as many of the paradoxes and curlicues of such stories as desired. Temporal loops, butterfly effects, and the like give a nod to the Howardian spirit of genre crossing.

The point, as always, is to have fun. Cut anything that confuses things or causes too much head scratching among the players.

---

from nowhere, coming from every direction at once until it forms a whirlwind around the group. The various sounds from the past ride upon the winds like banshee and require a Daunting (D3) Fear check. Failure means the character is Stunned until the storm abates.

The broken columns regenerate like trees regaining lost leaves in the spring, as they become their former selves. The arches rise, the grass shrinks from the stone roads which brick themselves over as if being laid in place, on fast forward. The grove of trees shrinks, rewound into the earth as the statue in the fountain is again made whole. A Dire (D4) Observation test lets the characters notice the striking resemblance of the marble statue to Xiabalba — and there's quite a bit else going on. Walls spring forth and become crenelated as the city resurrects itself in front of the player characters' eyes. Fleeing is a valid option, as is attacking Xiabalba. Both require a Dire (D4) Discipline check to complete. The player characters are enmeshed in the time shift themselves, being dragged back into the distant past; tearing themselves away from the vision of the very fabric of space and time reconstituting itself around them is likely to prove exceptionally difficult.

Figures pop into existence. First one, then tens, then hundreds. The war drums sounds, the player characters find themselves in the midst of a battle for the city itself. On one side are the soldiers of Xeiros, on the other barbarians clad in loincloths and with skin painted in the most lurid of colors. Each player character must make a Daunting (D3) Willpower test. Any failure renders that player character

THE PACT OF XIABALBA

unable to act until the following round. The dizzying trip requires some moments' adjustment.

CRY HAVOC!

Pacing is key here. The player characters have little time to absorb the time shift before they are drawn into the fray raging all around them. Before they are actually attacked, a group Daunting (D3) Observation test is made with the following results:

- **0 Momentum:** The player characters ascertain only that two sides fight, as citizens are cut down around them.
- **1 Momentum:** The player characters see barbarians coming over the city walls.
- **2 Momentum:** The player characters notice the soldiers of Xeiros attempting to form up into a square or phalanx formation, while the barbarians fight with less disciplined frenzy.
- **3+ Momentum:** The player characters notice a central palace compound dominated by a tower. A secondary wall is there, but the barbarians have made little headway against that wall. Further, the city gate to which the player characters are closest is clearly buckling. It will soon explode inward.

Success results stack. So, if the player characters get 3 Momentum they learn all of the information noted in lesser success results.

The gamemaster decides which side first attacks the player characters. In a battle as chaotic as this siege, either side (or both) might see the group as enemies. This can apply going forward, depending on how the characters play things. None of them speak the languages of the age, so communication with either side is unlikely, especially given the frenetic circumstances.

Xiabalba shouts at the player characters during the melee, explaining that she will tell them everything if they follow her to safety. Safety is at a premium during a siege, and the players may face a run-and-stop battle through the streets. It takes at least 3 ⚔ rounds of combat to break off from any attacking group, at which point the attackers are consumed by other forces attempting to kill them.

As civilians run this way and that, pursued by rapacious outlanders, the player characters can see the streets are awash in blood, several fires have broken out, and the city gates nearest them have given. A tide of battle-crazed humanity floods in. There is little doubt that the city of Xeiros will soon fall.

For parties of barbarians, use the Savages described page 320 of the **Conan** corebook.

AN EXPLANATION OF SORTS

This is the last pause, the last chance the player characters have to catch their breath before the end of the adventure. This can take place anywhere that is relatively sheltered from the surrounding chaos.

Xiabalba now explains in full the situation. The player characters have traveled back in time to the fall of Xeiros. She is their only way back home. In order to return, she explains, the player characters must kill her former self who even now conducts a ritual which will catapult the city, and all within, into the dream realm of Kuth. She answers questions, but is clearly impatient. As much of the backstory comes out as the players push for, the gamemaster desires, or Xiabalba feels she must reveal to gain the player character's cooperation. At this point, she has no reason to conceal the truth, but is not predisposed to explaining herself to mortals either. Should the players contemplate killing her, she will point out that this means nothing: Xiabalba in the past will still have completed the ritual and the characters will simply be left with no means of returning home.

The player characters are free to reject her deal and try to make it out of the city on their own. That way likely lies death, but it should not be impossible that they escape the city. However, even if they do, the city is about to be sucked into a nether realm, and the player characters would, at best, be stranded in an unfamiliar age. Some notes for such an ending are given at the adventure's conclusion.

Xiabalba explains that her other self — her past self — currently works the ritual in the tower. The player characters must either fight their way in or take the sewers. Both paths present their own peril.

THE TWO PATHS

The player characters' clearest options, as presented by Xiabalba, are to either take the sewers into the tower's base or scale the wall in the chaos and attempt to fight as few foes as possible along the way. The latter option is clearly dangerous, but at least they know the foes they face will be human. Not so with the sewers.

Even when she was young, the queen was no fool. She knew both thief and barbarous invader might attempt to gain access to the palace. While the walls are stocked with soldiers, the sewers are not. Instead, her growing research into Kuth of the Star-Girdle prompted her to replace the more mundane sewer guardians with demons from the Outer Dark. If the player characters wish to access the tower this way, they will encounter netherworld creatures. The choice is up to them.

FROM HERE ON OUT

The adventure up to this point has had its thrills, but the pace was largely set by the players. From here on out, that is not the case. Every moment is a quickly-draining hourglass. Xiabalba, the siege, and their own survival send the player characters forward ever-faster.

Once inside the tower, the player characters must hasten to the ritual chamber and kill Xiabalba. After that, time itself spurs them on. The gamemaster should not give the player characters a moment to rest, or allow time to make carefully debated decisions. If the players begin to prevaricate or second guess themselves, the gamemaster might try counting down from 3…2…1… go! Any player that does not name their action cannot perform a task that turn. This is a roller coaster leading to a multitude of endings; it is not a time to ponder, reflect, or question. If a different approach to hurrying things along is desired, the gamemaster should feel free to ignore this advice.

The Third Option

Player characters are often more clever and ingenious than any scenario can account for. Any reasonable alternative plan they come up with (or even unreasonable plans) should have a chance of success. Some of these options might include:

- Disguising themselves as barbarians. They could attempt to paint themselves and scream frenetically with the growing horde assaulting the palace walls. In the chaos, they might get away with it.

- Likewise, they could dress as soldiers of Xeiros — easier than painting themselves — and get the soldiers to let them in. Of course, the soldiers are not likely to let even their own in. Their lives are on the line.

- Travel through Kuth itself to the tower. This may or may not be possible but, thinking four-dimensionally, the players could theoretically travel in Kuth from outside the walls and return to this world inside the tower. Xiabalba would need to afford them access to Kuth, something she is loathe to do — she knows what lurks there, and it's made a deal with her other self. The demons of Kuth are not unaware of her attempts to break the pact over the years.

SCALING THE WALLS

Pandemonium does not adequately describe conditions in the city or around the palace walls. Barbarians are heaped in piles at the gate as are Giant-King soldiers. Ladders are braced against every wall and the frenzied warriors swarm up them like agile simians. The player characters can find an empty or near-empty ladder. Alternatively, no one is guarding the wreckage of the market stalls, and they could easily obtain rope and some sort of hook.

Neither option is easy, of course. The rampaging barbarians are looting everything they can find from the ruined houses and the market place is a veritable treasure trove for them. Others, intent upon stealing, are unlikely to be welcomed. Meanwhile, the Giant-King soldiery engaged in their last, desperate stand are not going to take the time to distinguish between barbarian invaders and the player characters.

The Main Gate Falls

Like the main gate which buckled earlier, the palace gate now begins to cave. Once it does, the frothing wave of barbarian fury pushes through like water pouring through a burst dam. The player characters could conceivably ride on this wave. In the shouting, bloody, gore-filled madness

THE PACT OF XIABALBA

of that moment when a gate falls, a few more screaming fools are not overly noticeable.

Each player characters makes a Challenging (D3) Stealth roll; for every failure, two barbarian warriors attack the player characters, up to a total of eight.

Ladders

Scaling the walls means fighting at the top if they go by ladder. Two mobs of three soldiers intercept anyone coming up the ladder followed by two more a round after. Two rounds after that, two more arrive. After that, the soldier's forces are depleted for that area of the wall.

Rope

Throwing a hook and rope is the last obvious option. It takes two rounds for each person to scale the rope, however. Each climber must make a Challenging (D2) Stealth test to avoid being intercepted as if they had used a ladder. If they do, two soldiers intercept the player characters, with more arriving at intervals described above.

Once Inside

Once inside the walls, the player characters encounter one Giant-Kings soldier for each player character, before they reach a secret entrance about which only Xiabalba knows. This group matches the player characters one for one.

TAKING THE SEWERS

The sewers are certainly the less obvious way to get past the walls to the tower. It is also the more uncertain route and beset by demons. The sewers are sizable, similar to the layout of a small city's aquifer, allowing room for interesting combat.

Rather than map the sewers, it suffices that Xiabalba spent her ample time on the island tracing the quickest route.

NIGHT SPRIGGAN (MINION)

A spriggan is a small imp-like creature known to some northern cultures of the Hyborian Age, but one should not mistake these for kind, ethereal beings of mischief. The night spriggan feeds on terror, particularly that of mortals. They stand about four feet tall but are hunched. Their grey skin is bark-like, covered with sprouting buds here and there. The more damage a spriggan inflicts, the fuller these buds bloom into leaves.

Sorcerers sometimes call night spriggans to harry their enemies while they sleep. Any enemy killed during sleep in this way does not die in the real world, but becomes a slave to the sorcerer who set the creatures upon the victim. In Kuth of the Star-Girdle, the spriggans serve greater demons, hanging about them as dogs do their masters. They are intelligent creatures but bound largely by instinct.

ATTRIBUTES			
Awareness	Intelligence	Personality	Willpower
9	4	10	10
Agility	Brawn		Coordination
9	8		9

FIELDS OF EXPERTISE			
Combat	1	Movement	1
Fortitude	—	Senses	—
Knowledge	—	Social	1

STRESS AND SOAK

- **Stress:** Vigor 4, Resolve 5
- **Soak:** Armor 1, Courage 3

ATTACKS

- **Bite (M):** Reach 1, 3 💀

SPECIAL ABILITIES

- Feed on Fear 2
- Horror

The Bars

Steel bars prevent people accessing the tower through the sewer — or at least, that was the intention. There is no mechanism to lift the bars. However, with enough raw strength, the player characters should be capable of bending the bars to allow the passage of one person per round. Bending the bars takes four rounds, but that time can be bought down with Momentum.

Bending the bars requires an assisted Dire (D4) Brawn test. Only two people can get into position to make this attempt. Failure means the four rounds are wasted, but the group may try again. For every round spent (where a round equals five minutes, here), there is a chance the demons arrive. The gamemaster should roll a d20. On a result of 16–20, 1d6 demons arrive. This effectively boxes the player characters into a kill zone, which the demons will exploit.

CHAPTER THREE: THE HOURGLASS

This is the end. The hourglass is overturned, and the last grains of sand fight to push through to the bottom. The players must be among those grains or be trapped forever. First, they must climb the stairs to the top of the tower — fighting as they go. Then, they confront the younger Xiabalba and the demons who have come through the portal to anchor it and complete the terms of the compact.

A SKERRY OF NIGHTMARES

As the island moves closer to full alignment with Kuth of the Star-Girdle, the latter realm begins to intrude, terrifyingly, into the player characters' reality. It is this which led to the ship being marooned in the middle of a choked, oppressive forest; it is this which dragged the Giant-King troops from their place in the distant past to the present where they encountered the player characters.

As previously noted, Xiabalba draws much of her potency from Kuth of the Star-Girdle (a land far more proximate to the mercurial world of dreams than our own, and, as a result, far less stable). This power leaves traces of itself, scraps of the dream worlds which linger, stubbornly behind. In Xeiros, as Xiabalba assembled her reservoir of power for the pact she would strike that night, the remnants took root in the sewers of the city, turning the dank stone tunnels into a subterranean world of nightmare made manifest. The sewers teem with night spriggans — restless, bestial imps which consume the fear of their victims.

If the player characters choose to enter the tower through the sewers, emphasise the oneiric nature of their journey — their sense of direction does not seem to help them, passages seem — arbitrarily — to end in pitch darkness, while apertures which have no apparent purpose suddenly expand into tunnels of enormous size. The air is thick with fug, with the chittering of creatures half-seen, and with the chink of weapons of soldiers always just out of sight.

The atmosphere is deeply unsettling and will require Daunting (D3) Discipline checks from all of the player characters. The gamemaster should emphasize the growing tension, the sense of being watched or hunted and then, at a sufficiently dramatic moment, have the very darkness agglomerate into the beings, detailed below…

FIGHTING ON THE STAIRS

Though the stairs are wide, they do not easily allow one the needed room to effectively fight if too many people are on a given step. For every person over two on a given stair, increase all attack and defense rolls by one step.

Additionally, being knocked down the stairs is a real possibility. If player characters are injured they must pay 2 Doom per injury or fall. Failure finds them tumbling down the stairs for 3 ⚔ damage. Further, it takes a round to right themselves and another round to rejoin the fray…. assuming the fall didn't kill them. Player characters may spend Momentum to buy "kills" in this way. Two points of Momentum spent on a successful attack gets one kill for any opponent sent falling down the massive stairway.

Slaying Xiabalba the Younger starts the final countdown wherein the player characters must race through a city whose streets and edifices are disappearing back into history and dust.

THE TOWER

Assume that, whatever route the player characters took to get here, they wind up more or less at the same point at the base of the inside of the tower. Bodies lay heaped about the stairs where small waterfalls of blood cascade downward. Pools of it form on the tiled ground, rivers and lakes glistening on every flat surface, a topography of gore. The area is devoid of combat as the player characters enter. Outside the shattered double doors, the two sides clash, but those who have already entered the tower now war over the stairwell. The stairs are wide enough for four men to stand abreast with little room to maneuver.

The players can make a Simple (D0) Warfare test to navigate the tower and the mobs that guard it. Each point of Momentum avoids one mob of three soldiers apiece. There are as many mobs as players. The stats used previously for either side are also used here.

Doom Spend Note: Doom is used to add reinforcements as normal.

THE RITUAL CHAMBER

And so the player characters arrive at the climax of their adventure. Having been tossed on the tempestuous oceans of sea, space, and time, they now confront their final challenge — killing their erstwhile guide, the Sorcerer Queen of Xeiros. Or at least, her younger self.

The chamber spans the whole of the tower's apex — some two hundred feet in circumference. The domed roof is vaulted and, where once there was a star chart, there is now the gaping black maw which leads to Kuth. That world's eldritch light filters in from above, bathing the room in a putrid, ochre glow.

This illuminates a complex pattern on the floor, a mosaic of broken tile depicting a scene from the Star-Girdle itself. Stretched between floor and ceiling, warped optically by the differential between the two worlds, are two Unspeakable Abominations (see page 345 of the **Conan** corebook). They serve as anchor points between the two realities and guards to vouchsafe the completion of the compact. This means they are, by default, guards for Xiabalba herself.

As the two Xiabalbas eye each other across the room, palpable electricity fills the air. From either woman, a blurred trail, perhaps their single soul, stretches between them. The elder Xiabalba points, eyes iridescent with a fury borne of a millennia's worth of striving to undo this moment, this knot in time which stains her soul.

THE PACT OF XIABALBA

Xiabalba (the elder) has now done everything she can to bring her life back to this moment. She cannot, however, kill herself. She cannot further assist the player characters. The undoing of this point in time is no longer hers to meddle with. It is entirely up to the player characters to break the compact now unfolding. This means the Unspeakable Abominations and the younger Xiabalba fight the player characters alone and vice versa.

While the two parties (Xiabalba and the Abominations) are not allies except by circumstance, the moment of confluence causes them to operate seamlessly. Their full power, and their strategy, combine to fight off the player characters. The ritual is already underway. The younger Xiabalba need do nothing further save ensure it is not broken by her death. However, she cannot venture into the portal, lest her immortality be subject to the whims of the Lords of Kuth.

XIABALBA THE YOUNGER (NEMESIS)

She looks somewhat younger than her Hyborian Age counterpart but only just. The "age" difference has more to do with the way the elder Xiabalba spent the recent decades of her life — trapped on the islands, bouncing back and forth in time.

She has more fire in her belly, as it were, than her older self and has not yet learned to regret the compact now unfolding. The very idea that she will is anathema to her. From this Xiabalba's perspective, the other version of herself must be a mad fool. This Xiabalba is on her way to immortality, and she has little doubt she will find a way to retrieve her city or else discover something she finds equally satisfactory.

ATTRIBUTES

Awareness	Intelligence	Personality	Willpower
9 (12)	10	11	10

Agility	Brawn	Coordination
8	7 (12)	9

FIELDS OF EXPERTISE

Combat	—	Movement	—
Fortitude	1	Senses	1
Knowledge	2	Social	1

STRESS AND SOAK

- **Stress:** Vigor 13, Resolve 11
- **Soak:** Armor 4 (Protected by Fate), Courage 4 (Near-immortality)

ATTACKS

- **Dagger (M):** Reach 1, 6 ⚅, 1H, Hidden 1, Thrown, Parrying
- **A Hundred Lifetimes of Practiced Threats (T):** Range C, 4 ⚅ mental, Stun

SPECIAL ABILITIES

- **Enchanted Ring:** This allows her to cast the sorcery spell *Dismember* at will. The spell is cast causing 4 ⚅ damage, Vicious 2, but she must make a Knowledge test to hit her target.
- **Enchanted Necklace:** This necklace grants her the sorcery spell *Shape of a Beast*, with which she maintains her extreme strength and awareness.

DOOM SPENDS

- **Spells:** Fate is determined to make this event happen. Doom can be spent on any spell except those spells provided by her enchanted items. Xiabalba has access to all sorcery spells.

THE END OF TIME

Like the fluttering of a spasmodic eye, the portal opens and closes as the compact, now broken, fails. Moments after the younger Xiabalba is slain, the elder begins to disappear. In her final moments she seems in respose, all guilt removed from her face. Before she comes apart at the very soul, she tells the player characters to run. "The city," she says, "will now disappear like I do. If you are caught within, you will suffer the fate I averted for it so long ago. Run, you poor things. There is only the hunger of time left in this place."

She may have told the player characters this earlier, if the gamemaster wishes. However, in her singular obsession, their lives probably did not overly factor in her equations. Besides, this is a far more dramatic point at which to reveal that the danger is not over.

The final hourglass is now upended, and the player characters are in a race against time itself, an oft clichéd phrase. In this case, though, it is apt, for the city even now begins to deconstruct around them. They must first escape the tower, then the city itself.

Descending the tower, they find it deconstructing itself around them. It isn't falling down, or crumbling, but simply ceasing to exist. As they race down flights of vanishing stairs, the player characters must each make a Challenging (D2) Athletics test or fall to the floor below. Each fall is 2 🟊 damage with the Piercing 6 quality, and increases the Difficulty of the next test by one step. Players may (and probably should) spend Momentum or Fortune points here.

A CITY'S END

All around, the city slips away, dropping away into history and into the fate meant for it. Barbarian and Xeirosan citizen fall to dust, columns erode like candles melting on time lapse. There is little pattern to the deconstruction of Xeiros — one section breaks, crumbles, and turns to the powder of ages while another remains wholly intact for the moment.

Player characters must make a Dire (D4) Athletics check or be trapped in the city as it, and they, turn to dust (the gamemaster is free to lessen such a consequence). As in their ascent of the tower, player characters need to spend Momentum or Fortune points to survive failure. At this point in the adventure, they may have depleted both.

Those who do escape see the city return very much to the same ruins they entered. However, there are differences — black stains mark where fire consumed the city, the statue of Xiabalba was pulled down and smashed, the remaining sections of wall show battering ram damage, and the like — small but undeniable to any who have endured what the player characters have.

Here, the player characters may think they can catch their breath, but they cannot. One final scare awaits them.

THE PACT OF XIABALBA

The fluttering eye of the portal appears above their heads at a height in the sky approximately as tall as the domed ceiling of the tower. Tendrils block the closing eyelid of Kuth and force it open. The tendrils pry apart time and space — the writhing, screaming face of Xiabalba appears, monstrously bloated and wreathed with tentacles, which seek to seize the player characters and drag them through the vast rent in the fabric of the universe.

"*I was wrong!*" a dreadful voice screeches, an echoing suffusion of torment and agony. "*Free me! Free me! Let the city burn! Let it all burn!*" This results in an Epic (D5) Discipline test. Those who fail take 4 ⚡ as Xiabalba's pain inflicts intense mental wounds on them.

Writhing tentacles, one per living player character, rip their way out of the void which has opened around this warped, boiling visage of the woman the player characters saw only a few moments ago. The tentacles attack each player. Avoiding them requires a Daunting (D3) Parry or Acrobatics test. Failing this test results in being caught and held by a tentacle and slowly dragged toward the slavering maw of the squealing, howling *thing* that was once Xiabalba. For those caught by the tentacles, a Dire (D4) Brawn test is needed to escape, or a successful Attack roll. Otherwise, they are crushed for 3 ⚡ damage. Any player characters trapped by a tentacle have three rounds to escape the tentacles' grip or be dragged into the eternal void. Falling into this darkness causes instant death. Any player characters who are not caught by one of Xiabalba's tentacles may assist in helping their companions break free.

After three rounds, whether the player characters have managed to escape the dread grip of the now forever damned Xiabalba or she has claimed a victim or two, the rent closes, quite abruptly. The adventure is over. Those who are left may count the cost of their actions.

XIABALBA THE GODDESS (NEMESIS)

This warped, hideous thing is Xiabalba's last, eternal form. Her reneging on the pact she struck with the Outer Dark may have saved her city from its dreadful fate in the all-consuming chaos, but she has taken its place. Her monstrous size and form swarm from the darkness one last time — to consume all that she has had taken from her in her pursuit of redemption.

ATTRIBUTES

Awareness	Intelligence	Personality	Willpower
12	8	14	14
Agility		Brawn	Coordination
8		14	8

FIELDS OF EXPERTISE

Combat	—	Movement	—
Fortitude	1	Senses	1
Knowledge	2	Social	1

STRESS AND SOAK

- **Stress:** Vigor 15, Resolve 15
- **Soak:** Armor —, Courage 4 (Horror)

ATTACKS

- **Tentacles (M):** Reach 3, 6 ⚡, Grappling, Knockdown, Stun
- **Dismember at Will (T):** The spell causes 4 ⚡, Vicious 1, but she must make a Knowledge test to hit her target.

SPECIAL ABILITIES

- **Dragged to Your Doom:** A player character grappled successfully for three rounds is devoured whole and alive. Xiabalba gains 1 Doom every round a player character is grappled.

> **DOOM SPENDS**
>
> - **Spells:** Doom can be spent on any spell. Xiabalba has access to all sorcery spells.
> - **Writhing Smashing Tentacles:** Xiabalba can spend X Doom to inflict X 🗡 damage on all within Close range.

> ### ALTERNATE ENDINGS
>
> Two alternate endings immediately present themselves. What if the player characters are trapped in the Thurian Age? What if they are trapped in Kuth? Below are some ideas to get the enterprising gamemaster started. Either option is likely to lead to a whole other adventure.
>
> #### Trapped in the Thurian Age!
>
> The player characters never make it back to the Hyborian Age during the course of this adventure. What now? Well, since Xiabalba found a way back in time, it stands to reason there is a way forward, but how? She's gone, tacked to history's original script. There are, however, many other sorcerers in this age. One of them might know a way back. Isn't Thulsa Doom active right about now?
>
> #### Trapped in Dreams!
>
> It is by no means certain that the player characters can prevent the ritual from completing. If they fail, the city and all within are sucked into Kuth of the Star-Girdle. That means the player characters are dragged in too. However, they need not suffer the same fate as the citizens — to be forever tormented by demons. The pact may only apply to citizens of the city, not people there when the city moves into dream. In this case, both the player characters and the outlanders would be pulled into Kuth, but their souls would not become immediately forfeit. Perhaps the player characters rally the barbarians and make a push to take the city back from demons? If they succeed, what then? They must still return to their own world. An adventure in the Star-Girdle could turn into a mini-campaign, as the player characters attempt to find a route through the nightmare realms to the waking world.

EPILOGUE

The player characters have survived the day, or at least, some of them have. If Khaskh lives and sees the player characters emerge from the darkness they vanished into, he gets on his knees in deference to Asura and in thanks for their deliverance. The characters can breathe. They can drink from the well… but they are still trapped on an island.

But that night, they see lights through the jungle, coming from the opposite shore on which they arrived. They are cooking fires from a tiny fishing village. The peoples here are the descendants of the bloodlines of the barbarians and the Giant-Kings. Their lore tells of the city's last day — in which it fell to mortal men of rude savagery rather than unnatural sorcery. The player characters' role in this mythic past has been effaced by time and by myth, but there are references to a sorceress within the city who vanished, leaving her people to be slaughtered. The cycle of history has not been kind to Xiabalba.

They speak a hybrid language recognizable as partly comprised of the former tongues of both groups. With effort, the player characters can understand them. The fisherman are happy to take the player characters out with them to the mainland where they sell their excess catches.

That morning, against a once-again perfect sky, the player characters set sail. Perhaps, as they depart, they see the ominous gathering of storm clouds — this time however, the clouds are entirely natural.

EXPERIENCE

The gamemaster should award any of the player characters who successfully save the city of Xeiros from the pact which the young Xiabalba struck with the Outer Dark 300 experience points. The gamemaster should also feel free to award 50 or more additional experience points to any player characters that did any of the following:

- Try to save or assist the crew of their ship when it begins to capsize during the storm.
- Slay Xiabalba the Younger and prevent her striking her bargain.
- Rescue a comrade from the grip of Xiabalba the Goddess' tentacles.

The gamemaster should avoid awarding more than 100 additional experience points to any single player character. This ensures that player characters progress and develop at roughly the same rate, rather than any one player character suddenly surging ahead and leaving their companions struggling to catch up!

CHAPTER 3
THE CAVES OF THE DERO

> *It made a ghostly half-light, in which he was able to see a bestial image squatting on a shrine, and the black mouths of six or seven tunnels leading off from the chamber. Down the widest of these — the one directly behind the squat image which looked toward the outer opening — he caught the gleam of torches wavering, whereas the phosphorescent glow was fixed, and heard the chanting increase in volume.*
>
> — "Servants of Bit-Yakin"

INTRODUCTION

Many speak of long dead Acheron and the unfathomable marvels of its diabolic sorceries. At its peak, the terrible power of Acheron shook even far-off Khitai. Those who did not outright bow to its might nevertheless deferred to its sorcerous leaders. All manner of tribute and treasures were heaped upon the empire of Acheron, plucked from the ground to sate the desires of its jaded rulers and avaricious nobility.

The Caves of the Dero finds the player characters in possession of a unique map, supposedly showing the location of a legendary mine from the time of Acheron. Whether they have taken the map as plunder, or been hired by some sage to prove the map's veracity, the adventure assumes that they hold the map and have already set forth to uncover its mysteries. The map is unusual, on masonry rather than paper, laid out in a cracked mosaic. Several crucial details are missing from the map, lost as the ages passed. To read it in full, the player characters must return the map to the villa Hybris, where additional details will help them locate the mine.

Chapter One: Hybris takes the characters to Hybris, the site of an Acheronian villa marked on the map. As the map is thousands of years old, gone are the modern, navigable features. Such landmarks vanished with the passage of time. The gamemaster can locate Hybris in nearly any kingdom which was once part of mighty Acheron, but this scenario works best if set within the bounds of the so-called Hyborian kingdoms. The player characters explore Hybris, where they eventually find their way to the long lost mine.

Chapter Two: The Mines of Acheron follows the player characters as they enter the horribly unstable mine and discover the time-lost Dero tribe. A cave-in traps the player characters, forcing them to find an alternative exit, while the Dero attempt to mete out savage vengeance on the trespassers.

Chapter Three: What Lies Beneath finds the player characters in the lair of the Dero, where a ruined statue dominates an impossibly large cavern. Here, in the dark of ages, they witness the strange rites of creatures forgotten by mortal minds.

CHAPTER ONE: HYBRIS

SCENE ONE: THE RUINS ABOVE

The player characters arrive at Hybris during the day, with several good hours before nightfall. Hybris is a ruin, shrouded by a tangled claw of fruit trees. The smell of rot

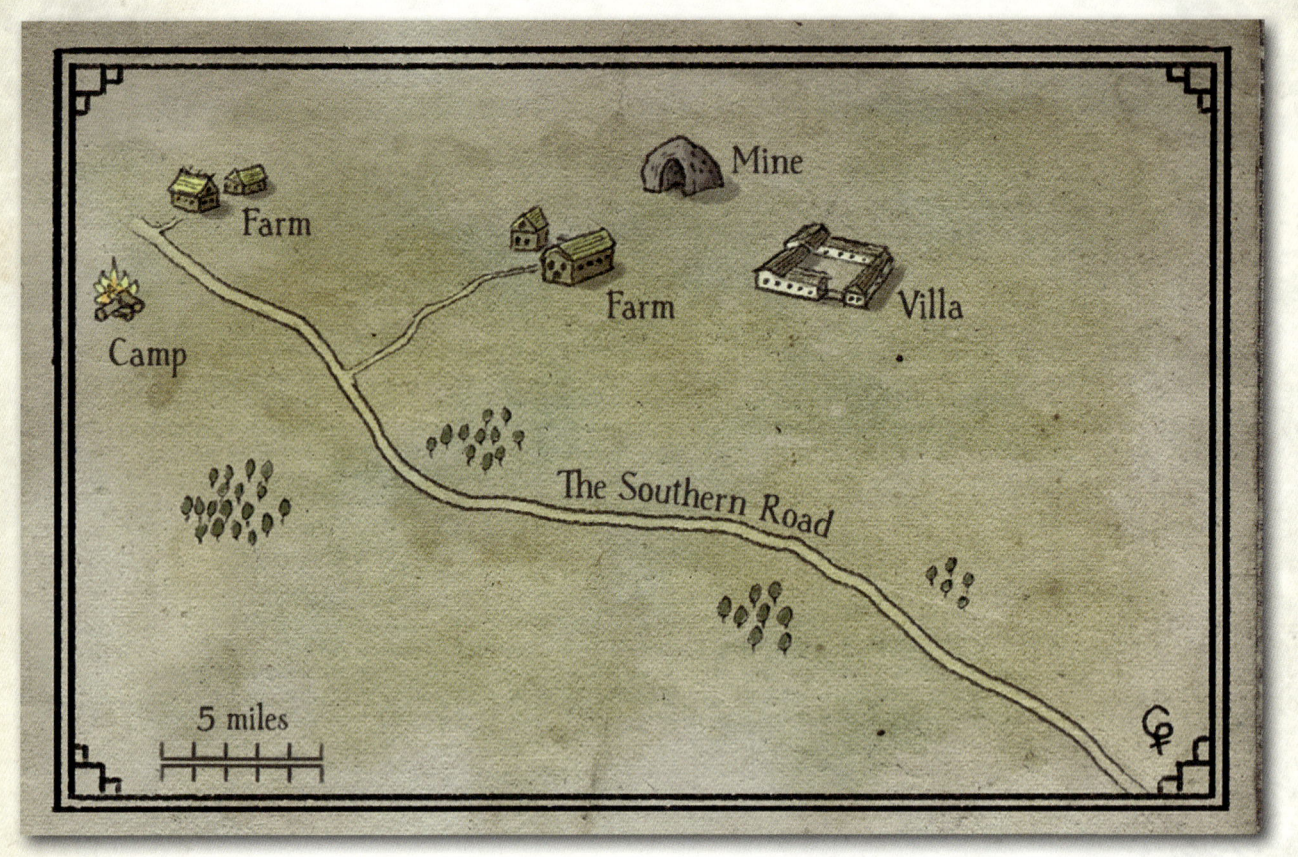

[Map: Shows locations including Camp, Farm, Farm, Mine, Villa, and The Southern Road, with a 5 miles scale bar]

pervades the air, and animals shun the ruin. Fog lingers in the air, and the player characters occasionally cough from the cold.

Approaching on horseback requires a Daunting (D3) Animal Handling test. Leading the animals is the slower way to advance, but it reduces the Difficulty to a Challenging (D2) Animal Handling test, as the beasts cannot shy away from the villa as do other animals. Characters have little difficulty understanding their mounts' apprehension — an Average (D1) Insight test is enough to note there is something off about the place.

What once was a mighty structure fit for a lord and his retainers is now but bare stone walls and rubble. Only one quarter of the building remains standing, with the rest consigned to history. The atmosphere here is a curious mix of grandeur, dilapidation, and wild forest. Where once perfumed maidens would have attended a garden pool, there is now a stagnant pond and the smell of decay. Where mighty walls once protected the court, there are only gnarled trees laden with untouched fruit.

Hybris fell to ruin very long ago. Having the feel of a haunted house, it should be appropriately creepy and oppressive. The villa was the home of a sorcerer, and remnants of his experiments are occasionally unearthed by the overly curious.

The gamemaster should keep careful track of the amount of time spent in and around the villa. The villa is a curious place, and time passes strangely here. If the player characters become separated, the gamemaster should emphasize a feeling of unease. The gamemaster should be vague about the amount of time a player character spends in any place, explaining that it feels like mere minutes, telling other player characters how long the first one has been away, implying that it feels like several hours. Should the player characters think to use one, timepieces such as hourglasses cannot be trusted.

Most of the rooms in the villa are in various states of disrepair, and any character with a Craft Expertise of 2 or higher should be told that no current means of construction would have weathered the ages so well. Though the forest has taken over the ruined fragments of stone, pots litter the ground around the massive apple trees that have taken over.

Room One: The Triclinium

The triclinium was a formal dining area, now overgrown with weeds. The floor has gone from hard wood to a soft bed of lichen and moss. The ceiling and walls are filthy with age, but a success on an Average (D1) Observation test reveals that the original paint is intact under the filth. If the observation test generates 1 or more Momentum, the player character will realize that one wall in particular has had mud added to the general filth in an effort to obscure something. Removing the ceiling filth will reveal a beautiful pattern of the night sky. Player characters with Lore

THE CAVES OF THE DERO

Expertise of 3 or Sorcery Expertise of 2 will realize that it does not feature known constellations. Removing the filth uncovers the original mosaic, allowing characters to complete their map and reveal the location of the mine.

The mosaic is a rendition of the local countryside around Hybris in spectacular detail. When the mosaic was originally placed this would have been a remarkably beautiful work of bright colored stone cut so close that they would have seemed as one. Now, age has taken its toll, and the joins are filled with dirt and the glittering trails left by slugs.

The mosaic has a cunningly concealed map of the villa in the design. Before anyone can read the map, it must be repaired. This is a simple, but time consuming, matter. The player characters don't need perfection, just the ability to read the map, after all. A Simple (D0) Craft test will accomplish this in an hour or so, long enough for other characters to explore. Momentum can be spent to decrease the time. The gamemaster can allow the player characters to spend 1–3 Momentum to reduce the time by 10 minutes. The actual amount of time isn't as important as the fact that time passes and the other player characters have the opportunity to explore. As characters return, tell them they were away for only a few minutes. The different perceptions of time passing is but one hint that Hybris harbors many secrets.

Once the player characters repair the mosaic, an Average (D1) Languages, Lore, or Sorcery test, or a Challenging (D2) Insight or Observation test will reveal the true nature of the map after a few moments of examination. The map is revealed by viewing the map from an extreme angle, achieved by pressing one's face tightly against the wall; the compression of perspective alters the composition of the image, revealing it not to be a landscape image but a map, including the villa as a minor detail. The villa is on top of the mine. Somewhere within its fallen walls is the pathway to unimaginable riches.

Room Two: The Bakery

Fire damage in the bakery hints at what may have led to the abandonment of the villa. Even being in this room is dangerous, as small pieces of the roof fall constantly. Whenever a Complication occurs inside the villa, a large chunk of masonry, tiles, and dead leaves can come crashing down. The shock of this causes all characters to make an Average (D1) Discipline test or suffer 3 ⚜ mental damage to Resolve. If player characters are in this room, they are in considerable danger. The collapsing roof starts as a creaking noise from above and a small shower of dust. This requires no test to hear but, unless the characters leave the room immediately, they must make a Challenging (D2) Acrobatics test or be hit by the roofing as it collapses.

The roofing deals 4 ⚜ damage with the Knockdown Quality. Those knocked down are automatically pinned by masonry and need rescue. Lifting the masonry is a Daunting (D3) Athletics test or an Average (D1) Craft test. Those pinned and trying to free themselves increase these Difficulties by one step.

Room Three: The Baths

With water bubbling up from some unknown spring, the baths are slick and dangerous to explore. Numerous holes in the walls and floor prevent the room from flooding too badly and, while the pattern has long since worn away, the original tiles are still intact. Player characters who brave the slick floors and succeed in an Average (D1) Acrobatics test are in a position to see numerous tracks leading from this room to the kitchen. An Average (D1) Survival test will determine that the tracks are about a week old.

Room Four: Kitchen

The kitchen lays in disrepair like the triclinium. Tracks abound, leading into the forest before returning to the yard. These tracks lead all the way to the mine. It requires an Average (D1) Survival test to follow the tracks.

Room Five: Stock Pens

This room is long overgrown with weeds. A quick search uncovers piled bones on the ground. Most are very old. An Average (D1) Healing test separates human remains from those of donkeys and cattle. They have been badly mutilated and, potentially, gnawed at, by humanoid mouths.

Room Six: Yard

What remains of the yard is overgrown and lousy with rotten apples and the occasional shattered remnants of cider presses. Most of this side of the villa is now a murky, stinking pond. From time to time, a burble of bubbles comes to the surface as if a single, giant fish made the pond its home. On an Average (D1) Survival check, a player character investigating the trees around the pond will discover that something broke most of the tree branches under five feet in height. Spending 1 Momentum for Obtain Information will reveal that this occurs often enough that new growth hasn't replaced the broken branches.

Player characters entering the pond disturb the horror that lurks there (see *Part Three: Waking the Locals*, page 60), but might discover a Dero periscope prior to doing so. The stench of the pond is unbearable, and a Challenging (D2) Discipline check is needed to conduct any sort of search. If characters do engage in a search, the Dero periscope is so well camouflaged it requires a Daunting (D3) Observation test to find it.

At first, the periscope looks like a broken potsherd lying on the bottom of the pond but, when nudged, it feels too firmly lodged. If lifted, a bronze tube with curious openings lies beneath. Angled mirrors fill the tube. Anyone lifting the tube discovers it reaches a full foot above the pond's murky depths before refusing to rise further. Suddenly, the

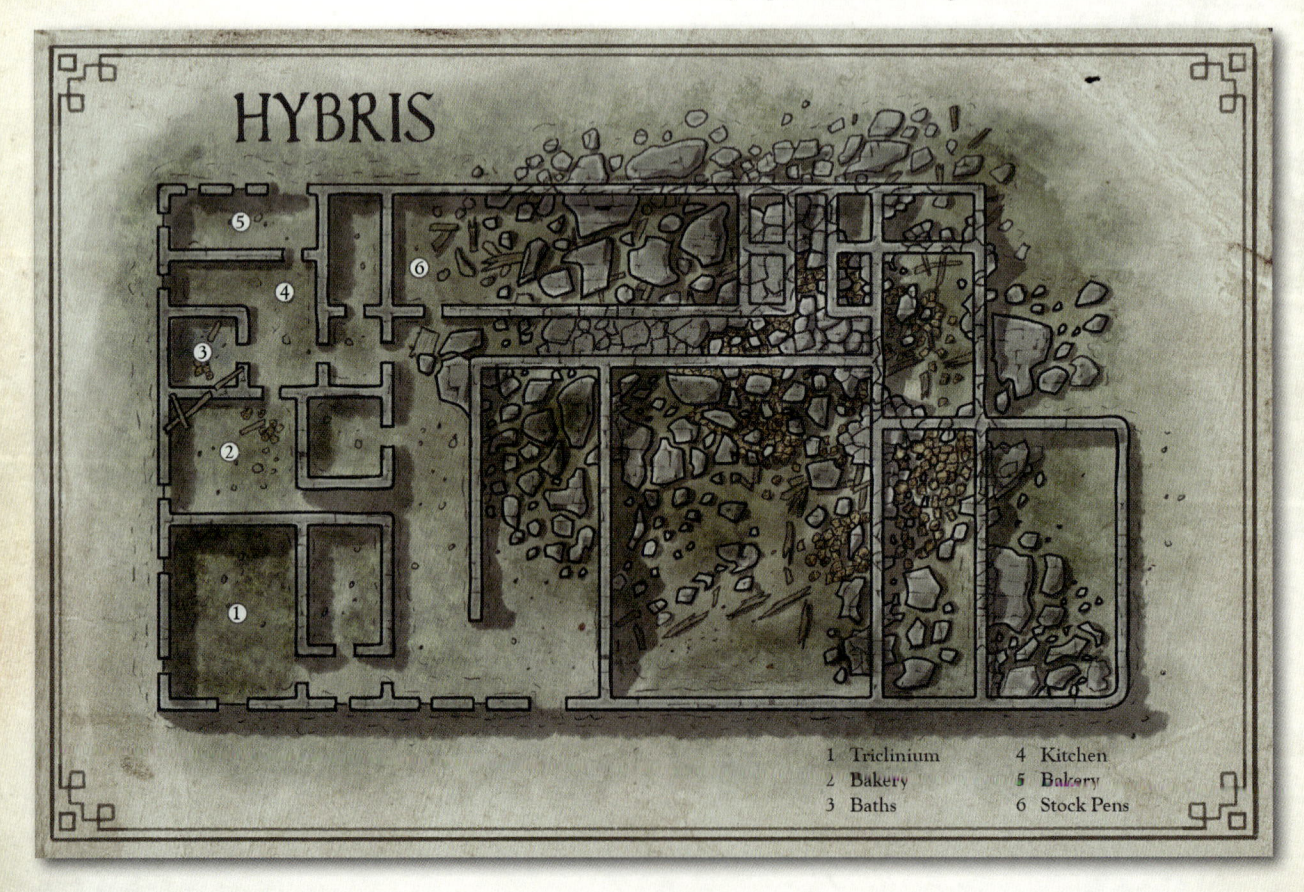

HYBRIS

1 Triclinium
2 Bakery
3 Baths
4 Kitchen
5 Bakery
6 Stock Pens

THE CAVES OF THE DERO

STRANGE EVENTS AND EFFECTS

The player characters might observe a variety of phenomena while exploring the ruins. These range from the subtly strange to the uncanny and terrifying. The gamemaster should use the example events below as a means of adding flavor to the exploration, picking them as appropriate or rolling a d20 whenever desired. These can be introduced as Complications or as effects to emphasize the overall feeling of being in a haunted place.

If a player character thinks to check, a Challenging (D2) Sorcery test will reveal that there is a place of power somewhere nearby.

Strange Events

1–2	One player character witnesses a doppelganger of a party member (or someone else known to be dead) stride confidently past, though no one else can see them. However fast the player characters chase the figure, it remains the same distance away from them. The doppelganger, if pursued, walks through a wall and vanishes.
3–4	Shadow people are seen in the corner of the eye, dancing, cavorting in acrobatic display, before falling to the ground dead. The bodies linger for a few moments before melting into the stone of the floor.
5–6	Water drips upwards so that a puddle on the floor is now soaking through the ceiling.
7–8	A rain of soft blue spheres filled with salt-water starts to fall in an incredibly localized area — often no more than a few feet in diameter. They pop, quietly, leaving behind a scent of burnt flesh.
9–10	A hot, wet wind blows through the trees, causing leaves to scatter everywhere. It disturbs everything it touches, except for the player characters.
11–12	A hissing from under the ground sounds like words if one could just listen closely enough. The more one concentrates, however, the harder it is to hear anything.
13–14	Strange voices speak unknown languages in lilting voices, from behind walls or trees. The end of these odd recitations always devolve into screams.
15–16	It feels like someone is watching, from inside the walls. In places where the original surface has crumbled away, one player character is certain that they can discern the gelatinous whiteness of an eyeball — but whenever they investigate, it is gone.
17–18	A player character feels like someone just stroked their shoulder, with the soft tenderness of a loved one. The pressure remains, comforting and warm, until they try to turn and see who it is. There is, of course, no one there.
19–20	A player character feels like someone just pushed them, savagely. Make a Challenging (D2) Athletics test or fall over onto the hard flagstones for 1 ♦ physical damage. There is no one behind the player character and no evidence of any supernatural presence. In fact, thinking about it, didn't they trip over an uneven paving stone?

Most of these events are figments of the imagination caused by being too close to a place of power, but some are the player characters recognizing that they're being watched. The Dero have numerous hiding places from which can listen to trespassers, and utilize complex hidden periscopes through which they can observe. In addition to this, the Dero overlord is a sorcerer and can view all the goings on in the triangular room due to his mental connection with Watcher in the Pond (see page 60).

periscope jerks to life and turns so that the glass faces the player characters. It appears to study them in detail before slowly turning fully around until it stares at them again.

A Dire (D4) Alchemy or Sorcery test might reveal the device's purpose, but it's more likely that the periscope remains a mystery of Acheronian sorcery and, thus, unknowable. Excavating the mud around the periscope reveals solid rock and a metal box into which the scope retracts. The periscope connects through a series of lenses to a wire similar to that which holds up the chandelier in the triangular room (see page 58). A thorough search of the villa — once the periscope is found — uncovers four more such periscopes in varying locations. The periscopes are fragile things, and any effort to break them is successful.

Further examination of the yard, including a long search and a Daunting (D3) Observation test, reveals a set of filth covered steps leading down below. These slick steps are hidden near the pond. Player characters wishing to explore this area wake the thing below, provoking a fierce battle, after which they can progress to *Chapter Two: The Mines of Acheron* (page 61).

SCENE TWO: THE RUINS BELOW

Part One: The Green Door

The room with a star is a ramp heading downwards. Player characters walking past the room should make a Daunting (D3) Observation test and, regardless of the result, be advised that, as they pass the room, the hackles on their necks stand up. To those that have deciphered the map, this would seem like the obvious entrance to the mine. The room consists of a ramp leading to pair of verdigris-covered doors.

Water has accumulated at the bottom of the ramp and blocks the doors from opening. There are no obvious handles, or keyhole and the hinges are on the other side of the doors. The doors have been dented and buckled by all manner of hammers and rams, but one thing stands out. The doors have three dents about two feet in diameter where something has cracked the finish and exposed lines of gleaming metal. None of the other blows have gotten past the verdigris so this must have been a very powerful force.

The doors are an alchemical wonder and respond to aggression by becoming more firmly stuck the more violence is applied to them. A player character who softly presses on the doors hears a click as the locking mechanism relaxes. After a count of three, the doors can be opened normally. After a count of six, the mechanism resets, and a second click can be heard. The clicks are incredibly quiet and, unless the character is actively listening for them, require a Dire (D4) Observation test to notice them. If anyone tries to walk through normally, or batter their way in, they hear two clicks as this works the mechanism past its grace point and seals it for the next few minutes.

Salvaging the doors in such a way that they can be resold requires an Average (D1) Craft test. The doors could fetch a price in any large city equal to the Momentum rolled when the doors are removed. Salvaging the doors is an incredibly noisy affair. It alerts the Dero who send a small party to investigate.

The mechanism opens with a Daunting (D3) Thievery test (which includes listening for and hearing the above clicks) or battered down. The doors are only battered down if the door suffers a break (see page 122 of the **Conan** corebook). The doors have a Soak of 8 and a Structure of 20. Every blow on the doors that deals 2+ damage will make an incredible metallic ringing noise, alerting the Dero.

Part Two: The Triangular Room

Upon breaching the doors, the player characters find themselves looking at a strange triangular room. The room is 20' × 15' × 25' and has a curved upas-glass mirrors in each corner. Two circles, etched into the floor, are adorned with occult symbols. The smaller circle is decorated with additional wards and symbols while, above the greater circle, a chandelier hangs off-center. The chandelier is constructed of amber rods, prisms, and golden wires.

The triangular room is a circle of power (see page 185 of the **Conan** corebook). Anyone with the *Sorcerer* talent or Sorcery Expertise 2+ knows this automatically. Anyone else with Expertise 1+ in Sorcery or Insight suspects this, but remains uncertain. A Daunting (D3) Sorcery test reveals that the circle has been enhanced somehow so that, in addition to the Difficulty decrease such a circle would normally provide, the circle also provides 1 Momentum for the purposes of banishing a summoned creature. If a sorcerer wishes to understand the construction, they must take very precise notes over the course of a day and a night to learn the *Talent: Acheronian Summoning* (seepage 60).

Spending a night in the ruins of the villa likely attracts the attention of the Dero and isn't conducive to rest. Player characters must make a Dire (D4) Discipline check to get proper sleep. Those who fail this test suffer 1 Fatigue and 1 Despair throughout the next day.

Should the player characters enter the circles, touch, or in any other way affect the ground inscriptions, they

THE CAVES OF THE DERO

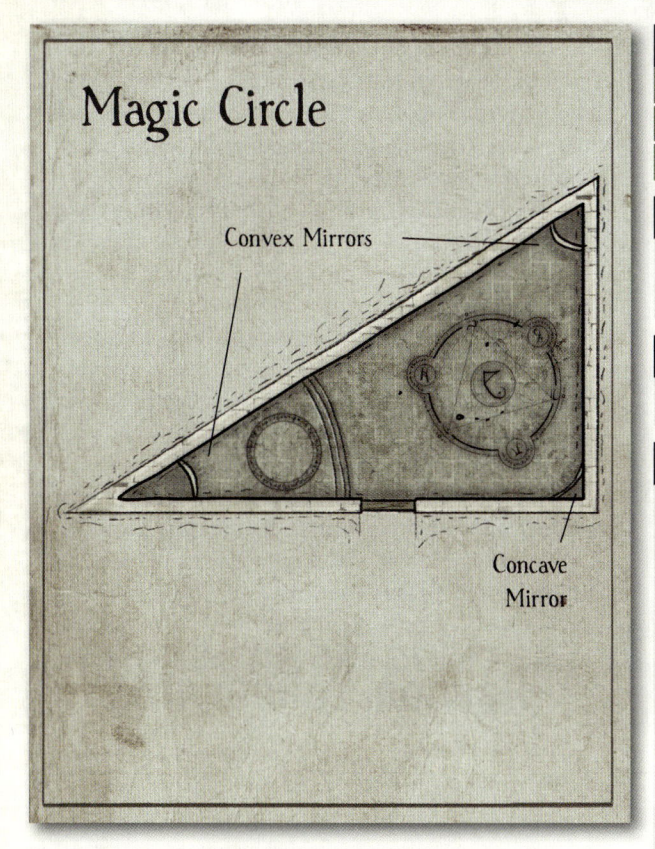

Magic Circle

Convex Mirrors

Concave Mirror

will awake the Watcher in the Pond. This creature was summoned by the former sorcerer that inhabited this villa and has since been made the slave of the Dero. If the player characters do not touch the circle, then pressing on into the corridor attached to this room will also cause the Watcher to clamber out of its lair, searching for blood and flesh.

THE WATCHER (HORROR, NEMESIS)

The Watcher is an infant god left behind during one of the summonings that took place long ago. While constrained by the circle, it is well fed, bored, and feral. While the Watcher is listed as a Nemesis, it is more of a long-term nuisance than a villain to be immediately overcome.

ATTRIBUTES

Awareness	Intelligence	Personality	Willpower
10	4	5	10

Agility	Brawn	Coordination
5	5	5

FIELDS OF EXPERTISE

Combat	—	Movement	—
Fortitude	—	Senses	2
Knowledge	—	Social	—

STRESS AND SOAK

- **Stress:** Vigor 5, Resolve 10
- **Soak:** Armor 4 (Horror), Courage 4 (Horror)

ATTACKS

- **Transdimensional Spine (M):** Reach 1, 3 🜂, Piercing 5

SPECIAL ABILITIES

- Familiar
- Fast Recovery (Vigor and Resolve) 2
- Feed Upon Fear
- Flight
- Unliving
- **Worship Me!:** The Watcher is an infant god and desires worship. At any point, a sorcerer can worship the Watcher. In return it will act as a familiar for the sorcerer. The Watcher will grow bold over time. While it might initially provide this service for an occasional offering (beginning at 1 Gold, Vigor, Resolve, or some other price), every time a Complication is rolled when casting a spell that the Watcher aids, the offering's frequency or cost increases. The first Complication increases the offering's frequency to one offering per day. Every Complication rolled after this increases the price by +1 offering until the price reaches a total of 5 offerings. If the sorcerer is foolish enough to pay this price, the Watcher will hatch into a larger, more horrible adult form. Witnessing this transformation requires the sorcerer to make a Dire (D4) Discipline test, with failure causing 6 🜂 mental damage. Once the Watcher matures, it will be capable of functioning as a Patron and will be more than willing to assist its worshippers in bargaining their souls away. That said, it is just as likely to eat anyone within reach as it is to engage in a lengthy discussion. The adult form of the Watcher can be any horror that the gamemaster sees fit, perhaps Devil of the Outer Dark, described on page 347 of the **Conan** corebook.

DOOM SPENDS

- **Leech:** While the creature can draw sustenance without drawing suspicion, it occasionally enters a feeding frenzy. When in a feeding frenzy, the Leech spends 1 Doom to increase the Difficulty of any casting by two steps.

NEW TALENT: ACHERONIAN SUMMONING

The following talent, lost to ages, was a standard part of the sorcerous training in the empire of old Acheron.

Acheronian Summoning

PREREQUISITES: *Summon a Horror* (spell), *Barter Your Soul* (talent), exposure to an Acheronian summoning site

The empire of Acheron was one of sorcery and deviltry. Prodigious summoners in that fell land learned secrets now lost to men. Those with this talent can construct a circle of power (see page 185 of the CONAN corebook) for the purposes of summoning. This circle, while unable to enhance any other spell, provides 1 Momentum for the purposes of banishing a summoned creature.

These circles are incredibly fragile, and placing them near other circles can have serious consequences, the exact nature of which determined by the gamemaster.

Part Three: Waking the Locals

The player characters likely wander the ruins before they think to try cleaning the walls. Sorcerers looking to unlock the secrets of the triangular room need to remain for a considerable amount of time.

If the player characters touch the circle in any way, the creature rears up from the stagnant pond and crawls towards the mirrors in the triangular room. Once inside, it destroys the room, leaving nothing standing and no circle unbroken, before heading outside looking for food. If the player characters have not opened this chamber, the creature hits the door in frustration before wandering the ruins.

The creature is not particularly bright and doesn't race to fight the player characters, if they seek to spring an ambush, it almost certainly works. The creature is, however, a significant threat and players might get more than they bargain for if they face it head on.

THE THING FROM THE POND (HORROR, TOUGHENED)

Looking for all the world like a giant slug, this horror is capable of changing its form to exude tentacles from its head. It uses these tentacles like mandibles, to grapple and tear its prey before finally devouring the dead meat. A clumsy beast, it is unused to being injured and reacts poorly to the sensation. The Thing From the Pond is the reason the villa was originally abandoned.

ATTRIBUTES

Awareness	Intelligence	Personality	Willpower
7	7	7	10
Agility	**Brawn**		**Coordination**
8	12 (2)		8

FIELDS OF EXPERTISE

Combat	1	Movement	1
Fortitude	1	Senses	—
Knowledge	—	Social	—

STRESS AND SOAK

- **Stress:** Vigor 14, Resolve 10
- **Soak:** Armor 5, Courage —

ATTACKS

- **Grappling Tentacles (M):** Reach 1, 7 🔥, Grappling
- **Mighty Slap (M):** Reach 2, 7 🔥, Knockdown
- **Monstrous Form (M):** Reach 2, 5 🔥 mental, Area, Piercing 1

THE CAVES OF THE DERO

SPECIAL ABILITIES

- Fear 2
- Inhuman Brawn 2
- Unliving

DOOM SPENDS

- **Poisonous:** When player characters cut the creature, its thick poisonous blood leeches out. When the creature is injured, the gamemaster can spend 1 Doom to force the attacking player characters to make a Challenging (D2) Resistance test or take 3 🐲 damage with the Persistent 2 Quality.
- **Rend!:** When player characters are caught by its grappling tentacles, the creature can spend X Doom to inflict X 🐲 Vicious 2 damage as it attempts to rip its meal into smaller pieces. If this causes someone to suffer a Wound, all witnesses must make an Average (D1) Discipline test or take 5 🐲 mental damage as they see the spray of blood.

ON THE ROOF

In the bakery, the roof is particularly fragile and could easily be used as a trap. Player characters that recognize the danger in this room and take steps to make a temporary repair, can rip this repair away as a Free Action. This instantly triggers the trap. As a reward for this cleverness, the creature is Pinned and Prone with no guard for one turn, in addition to any damage done. Those wishing to drop the roof without this sort of preparation must use a sledgehammer or similar weapon. They must either succeed with a Challenging (D2) Craft test or reduce the Structure of the room to 0. The bakery has a Structure of 5. All other roofs have a Structure of 10.

CHAPTER TWO: THE MINES OF ACHERON

SCENE ONE: INTO THE DARKNESS BELOW

Having visited the ruin of Hybris, the player characters should be in a position to find the lost mines. If the player characters have not discovered the mine, they need to make a teamwork Daunting (D3) Observation test in order to find the doors in the yard (see page 58).

The stairs plunge downwards for a long time. They are slick with the foulness of the yard above and only end after ten to fifteen minutes of descent. Once the player characters reach the bottom of this stair, they reach the initial mine.

The initial mine is key-shaped, with the final tunnel radically decreasing in size from eight feet high to a mere five feet as it shrinks. The cave has no natural light source, and player characters require torches. It quickly becomes apparent that wearing armor only makes for a very cumbersome journey. The mine from this point on is considered to be Difficult terrain (see page 97 of the Conan corebook).

If a player character chooses to wear armor of any sort in the mine, all skill tests for traversing or fighting in the mine increase in Difficulty by one step, or two steps if the character is wearing any Heavy or Very Heavy armor. Likewise, swinging a sword in narrow tunnels is much harder than doing so outside. The confines of the mine make it much harder than normal to strike a blow or parry with weapons that must be swung for effect. All Melee and Parry skill tests for such weapons increase in Difficulty by one step. These difficulties are cumulative, so a warrior in mail using a sword faces a Daunting (D3) Parry test while in the tunnels.

These penalties are a general rule for all areas in the mine.

The mine is broken into two sections: the early mine and the later mine. The later mine is covered in *Scene Four: Stranded in the Mine!* (see page 64).

The early mine is a series of five-foot-tall, straight, craggy walls bereft of any treasure. The rock was fully exploited, and small cuts in the stone show where miners searched in the past. It was an organized search conducted by master miners, so it is almost certain that nothing precious remains. The early mine can feature any of the basic cave encounters, but ends with a cave-in that traps the player characters. The cave looks very stable, but is not so stable that it can withstand sabotage. After all, the Dero know the player characters are coming and have long since rigged the mine to collapse as a precaution against trespassers!

At this point the gamemaster should trigger *Scene Two: The Ambush* (below).

SCENE TWO: THE AMBUSH

These mines stretch deep into the earth. The player characters can easily wander for an hour in the cramped tunnels before coming across the Dero. By the time they face the Dero, they will likely be tired. The real danger to this encounter is that there is nowhere suitable to rest underground.

The Dero plan for securing their home is to wait until the player characters are deep within the mines, letting the invaders tire themselves wandering. The Dero spring an ambush when the player characters approach and are

CHAPTER 3

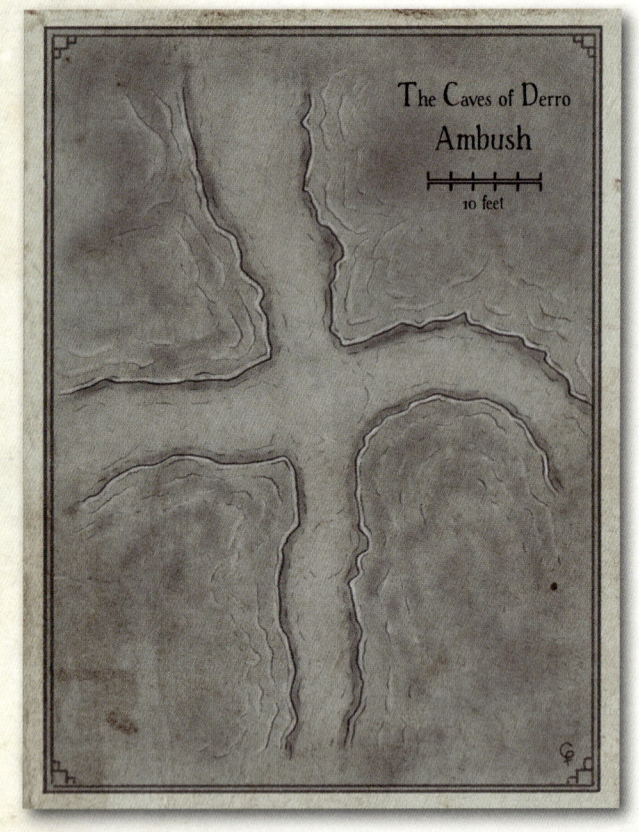

in a poor position to flee. Detecting this ambush before it happens requires a Dire (D4) Observation test. Should the ambush fail, the last Dero alive will trigger the rock fall described in *Scene Three: Rocks Fall!* (see page 63).

The ambush consists of one Dero warrior and two Dero scavengers for each player character in the mine. Only the Dero warriors contribute to the ambush's teamwork test. The fight should be fast and furious, with the player characters gaining only fleeting impressions about the foes they face. As the Dero emerge, the eerie quiet of the cave is broken by the manic screams of a horde of angry dwarf-like figures. They carry no torches, and bear mining equipment as weapons. As one, they descend upon the party with maddening cries which echo, becoming a blur of overlapping sounds.

DERO SCAVENGER (MINION)

Dero are uniform in appearance, with near-identical feral faces distinguished only by ritual scarring inflicted to make them distinct. They are all exactly four and a half feet tall, with wild hair and dirty beards. They have wide saucer-like eyes and are all entirely sexless.

The process that creates Dero is a far from perfect one. The device that creates them was not designed for human use and many of the Dero created are vicious mindless weaklings. Utterly fearless and beyond easy questions of sanity, these wretches follow their masters' bidding, not from fear but from the certain knowledge that disobedience will make them the next meal for the Dero overlord.

When the Dero device does work correctly, the Dero is a creature much smarter but no less crazed. Afforded weapons and armor, the warriors keep the scavengers in check, culling the herd as necessary and eating those they have worked to death. Warriors are occasionally sent out to gather feast items for the overlord which recently has included a farm's worth of slaves.

ATTRIBUTES

Awareness	Intelligence	Personality	Willpower
8	6	6	6

Agility	Brawn	Coordination
8	8	8

FIELDS OF EXPERTISE

Combat	1	Movement	1
Fortitude	1	Senses	3
Knowledge	1	Social	1

STRESS AND SOAK

- **Stress:** Vigor 4, Resolve 3
- **Soak:** Armor 1, Courage —

THE CAVES OF THE DERO

ATTACKS

- **Mining Tool (M):** Reach 1, 4⚔, 1H, Improvised
- **Insane Cry (T):** Range C, 2⚔ mental, Stun

SPECIAL ABILITIES

- Night Vision
- Inured to Fear
- Inured to Pain

DERO WARRIOR (TOUGHENED)

ATTRIBUTES

Awareness	Intelligence	Personality	Willpower
8	8	9	8

Agility	Brawn	Coordination
10	9	10

FIELDS OF EXPERTISE

Combat	2	Movement	2
Fortitude	1	Senses	3
Knowledge	1	Social	2

STRESS AND SOAK

- **Stress:** Vigor 9, Resolve 8
- **Soak:** Armor 2, Courage —

ATTACKS

- **Shortsword (M):** Reach 1, 5⚔, 1H
- **Maddening Cry (T):** Range C, 3⚔ mental, Stun

SPECIAL ABILITIES

- Night Vision
- Inured to Fear
- Inured to Pain

"Acheron has been a myth for more centuries than I can remember. I've often wondered if it ever existed at all."

"It was a black reality," answered Hadrathus, "an empire of black magicians, steeped in evil now long forgotten. It was finally overthrown by the Hyborian tribes of the west. The wizards of Acheron practised foul necromancy, thaumaturgy of the most evil kind, grisly magic taught them by devils."

— Conan and Hadrathus, *The Road of Kings*

TORCHES

Any player character holding a torch is considered to have adequate light for most tests but, if reliant on another's light source, may suffer a Difficulty increase for insufficient light as the gamemaster sees fit.

Torches can be also used as one-handed improvised weapons, dealing 3⚔ with the Burning Quality. Using a light source as a weapon is inadvisable, and the torch may go out as a Complication while using it in this manner. If the torch is extinguished, it loses the Burning Quality until relit. Relighting a torch froma another torch is a Free Action. Lighting a torch with flint and steel is a Minor Action.

SCENE THREE: ROCKS FALL!

With a horrible explosion, the mine starts to fall apart. Hapless Dero are caught and crushed under giant boulders raining down from above. While the player characters are safe from the largest boulders, they don't know this, and will be pelted with smaller stones. The gamemaster should require the player characters make an immediate Simple (D0) Acrobatics test, modified by the penalties described in *Scene One: Into the Darkness Below* (page 61). The damage the player characters take is dependent on the Momentum from this test (see below).

CAVE-IN DAMAGE

Momentum	Damage
0	4⚔
1–2	3⚔
3–5	2⚔
6+	1⚔

If the players themselves (not their characters) are blasé about the falling rocks, the gamemaster should spend 4 points of Doom to have a massive boulder crash right next to them, inflicting 4⚔ mental damage and requiring a similar Discipline test, with additional physical damage from the chart above. Once the player characters have made their Acrobatics tests, each should attempt a similar Athletics test to avoid boulders that chase them deeper into the mine (Momentum spends as above).

The rumbling from the crash should continue for a while after the initial shock and explosion, seemingly triggering additional collapses along the path the player characters have taken. Though they have no immediate way of knowing, a few additional deadfalls were also triggered, further blocking their way out. This is no real problem for the Dero, who have all the time and effort they require to clear the path and set new deadfalls.

Once the crash happens, any player character with an Expertise 3+ in Alchemy recognizes that the explosion was a very rare type of explosive called *hygron-pyre*, a petty enchantment in the form of a combustible liquid, requiring a Dire (D5) Alchemy test to manufacture. The scent, residue, and smoke are the clues identifying the material.

Once this scene concludes, the player characters can look back at their entrance and see that it caved in entirely. The realization that they're trapped immediately causes them to suffer 3 points of Despair. The player characters can attempt a Simple (D0) Discipline to reduce this, with each point of Momentum reducing the despair taken by 1. With unearthing the way back taking potentially days to clear, with no guarantee of success, the only immediate option is to continue deeper into the mine!

SCENE FOUR: STRANDED IN THE MINE!

The player characters are now stranded in the mine and must find a way to the surface. There is no map for the later mine, as they should progress organically through the maze of crooked tunnels looking for hope until they come across the giant statue in *Chapter Three: What Lies Beneath*. Instead of a detailed map, each round of exploration leads the gamemaster to roll or select an encounter from the *Mine Encounters* table (page 66). The gamemaster should describe the multiple branching tunnels, allowing player characters to explore and map the various perils they come across as they see fit. An example map is offered at the end of this adventure, but the gamemaster should not feel restricted by it.

This section of exploration is represented by the *Mine Tracker*, a table representing the various steps of exploration and searching while trapped in the mines. The *Mine Tracker* describes the type of surrounding terrain and types of encounters, with potential rewards should the player characters seek them.

At the end of each round of exploration, the gamemaster should have the player characters make an Average (D1) Insight test as a teamwork test. If the party generates 2 Momentum (repeatable) the gamemaster should have them progress down the *Mine Tracker* by one step. Once they pass Step Three, the gamemaster should have them progress to *Chapter Three: What Lies Beneath*.

Traversing the mine is tiring. At the end of each test, the gamemaster should require the player characters to make a Challenging (D2) Resistance test. Failing this test makes the player character suffer 1 point of Fatigue.

Player characters traversing the mine should regularly have to make Athletics and Acrobatics tests to traverse the tunnels. As noted prior, the entire mine (all of *Chapter Two: The Mines of Acheron*) counts as Difficult terrain.

ADVERSARIES

BAT SWARM (MINION)

Normally found in dank caves, these small flying vermin gather in dense swarms that, when disturbed, can overwhelm an adventurer through sheer numbers. Though not much of a threat, they can knock an unsuspecting person off their feet, or distract them at an inopportune moment.

ATTRIBUTES

Awareness	Intelligence	Personality	Willpower
10	4	5	9
Agility		Brawn	Coordination
10		5	4

FIELDS OF EXPERTISE

Combat	—	Movement	2
Fortitude	3	Senses	2
Knowledge	—	Social	—

STRESS AND SOAK

- **Stress:** Vigor 3, Resolve 5
- **Soak:** Armor 2, Courage —

ATTACKS

- **Many Tiny Bites (M):** Reach 1, 4 ⚔, Fearsome, Piercing 1

SPECIAL ABILITIES

- **Diseased (Optional):** Bats often carry diseases. Any player character successfully attacked by bats must make an Average (D1) Resistance test at the end of combat or suffer 1 Fatigue.
- **Echolocation:** Bats do not "see" as men do, but navigate by sound. They reduce the Difficulty of all Senses tests to listen by three steps, and they ignore all penalties based on darkness.
- **Flight**
- **Incorporeal:** Though bats have material bodies, they are so plentiful that any attacks against individual bats have no effect.
- **Swarm:** The bat swarm can take the Withdraw Action as a Free Action.

DOOM SPENDS

- **Swarm Attacks:** For each Doom spent, the bat swarm may make one additional attack when it makes a close combat attack as a Standard Action. Each attack must be targeted at a different enemy.

THE CAVES OF THE DERO

VERMIN, VENOMOUS SWARM (MINION)

There are many poisonous insects and spiders in the world. This description serves for swarms of all but the deadliest or greatest of specimens. These are usually encountered as parts of Mobs (or rarely, in Squads), and as such present a greater threat than that of a single swarm.

ATTRIBUTES

Awareness	Intelligence	Personality	Willpower
8	3	5	3
Agility	Brawn		Coordination
7	6		4

FIELDS OF EXPERTISE

Combat	1	Movement	1
Fortitude	—	Senses	—
Knowledge	—	Social	—

STRESS AND SOAK

- **Stress:** Vigor 3, Resolve 2
- **Soak:** Armor 3, Courage —

ATTACKS

- **Many Bites or Stings (M):** Reach 1, 2 ⚔, Improvised, Persistent 2

SPECIAL ABILITIES

- **Hallucinogenic Venom (Optional):** Remove the Improvised Quality from damage.
- **Incorporeal 3**
- **Inured to Disease**
- **Inured to Venom:** Species venom only.
- **Keen Senses (Scent)**
- **Swarm:** The swarm can take the Disengage Action as a Free Action.

DOOM SPENDS

- **Always More Where That Came From:** For each Doom spent on reinforcements, two additional venomous vermin swarms arrive as reinforcements at the end of the turn. These may join any existing Mob or Gang.
- **Swarm Attacks:** For each Doom spent, the swarm may make one additional attack when it makes a Standard Action close combat attack. Each attack must be targeted at a different enemy.
- **Venom:** When a player character takes damage from the vermin's toxin, the gamemaster may spend 1 Doom to inflict the Staggered Condition on that character. If the Venom is hallucinogenic it also inflicts 1 Despair.

CHAPTER THREE: WHAT LIES BENEATH

SCENE ONE: THE IMPOSSIBLE RUINS

With the Dero momentarily defeated, the player characters come across the true treasure of the mines, the remnants of an impossibly large statue. The Dero "city" is housed in a massive cavern of impossible size, stretching far above where the ground should be. At first the city appears to be a giant pit mine with a single white tower striking in its contrast against the anthracite of the mine. As the player characters survey the cavern, they soon recognize curves carved into the vast black rock. Only when a player character turns their head does the truth sink in. The mine is the cheek of a fantastically huge face. Scanning the horizon a player character can see where barely a hint of the massive statue protrudes. The rock walls of the cavern cover half the face, but a player character can see lone Dero prospecting over its sneering lips and gathering unknown spoils from other white structures that appear to have shattered against the statue's surface.

Occasionally, a Dero scavenger approaches the white tower cradling a bundle of wire or a handful of shining green gems. The guards take the paltry find of the scavenger, and beat them mercilessly, scattering their finds to the floor. At times, a Dero approaches with a great amber rod or some sort of strange fossil. The guards reward these more successful scavengers with the scattered findings of their other victims, as well as scraps of meat. Once the scavenger has fed, it enters the building. Only the very occasional Dero ever leaves. Every so often, a green flash comes from the buildings only window, and the guards visibly shudder.

MINE TRACKER

Step	Walls	Floor	Encounters	Riches
One	Five foot tall straight craggy walls with all the ore pulled long ago.	Flat worn floor, as if trodden down by an unimaginable army of slaves.	Basic only (see below)	None
Two	Five foot tall twisting craggy walls. Tiny holes, barely an inch in diameter, pock the walls where desperate miners once looked for stones.	Outcrops of dense stone jut where miners worked around them rather than excavate.	Basic and Strange (see below)	Occasional stone of little worth. A successful Challenging (D2) Craft test, costing 2 Momentum and generating 1 Fatigue will yield the player character 1 Gold worth in fragments of gems.
Three	Five foot tall unfinished walls. Large holes — large enough to plunge an arm into — are intermittently placed across the walls. Flickers of emerald glint in the dark.	A narrow finished path, barely a foot wide, was cut out of the rock. Impossibly ancient.	—	Handful of small gems. Make a Challenging (D2) Craft test. The resulting Momentum in Gold can be taken, incurring 1 Fatigue.
Four	Go to *Chapter Three: What Lies Beneath* (page 65)			

MINE ENCOUNTERS

Encounter	Example	Purpose
Basic	Bat Swarm	See *Adversaries* (page 64). A weak encounter equates to one Minion per player character, while a more difficult encounter represents two Minions per player character (in addition to Disease).
Basic	A Flock of Swallows	Birds fly down the corridor at break-neck speed, startling the player characters. They pass by as quickly as possible and soon leave them far behind. The player characters take 3 🕊 mental damage. A Simple (D0) Discipline test can reduce this by 1 point per point of Momentum gained on this test.
Basic	Nest of Cave Spiders	Vermin, Venomous Swarm (Minion) from *Adversaries* (page 64). A weak encounter equates to one Minion per player character, while a more difficult encounter represents a Mob of three Minions per player character (in addition to Disease).
Strange	Strange Arachnids	Vermin, Venomous Swarm (Minion) from *Adversaries* (page 64). A weak encounter equates to one Minion per player character, while a more difficult encounter represents a Mob of three Minions per player character (in addition to Hallucinogenic Venom).
Strange	Gravity Shift	All player characters must make a Challenging (D2) Resistance test or are flung against a random surface, floor, wall, or ceiling. Those affected are pinned there before being dropped. Player characters take 4 🕊 mental damage. A Simple (D0) Discipline test can reduce this by 1 point per point of Momentum gained on this test.
Strange	Rumbling from Deep Underground	Player characters take 2 🕊 mental damage. A Simple (D0) Discipline test can reduce this by 1 point per point of Momentum gained on this test. Player characters with Expertise 2+ in Alchemy or Observation discern that this is an explosion, without needing a test. Other player characters may attempt a Challenging (D2) test (for either skill) to discern this.

THE CAVES OF THE DERO

It is up to the player characters what to do here. There is wealth in the tunnels, but it is not the fortune they imagined, and any real reward will be hard-won. Still, this cavern may well offer easier and greater wealth. Should player characters decide to raid the Dero tower, proceed to *Scene Four: The Tower*. Should the player characters decide to pocket gems from the caverns as they get out of the mine, proceed to *Scene Three: Run!*

The statue should be a genuine mystery. It looks like a Stygian pharaoh, and the builders of the alabaster tower were more than happy to desecrate it. the player characters to offer conjecture as to who might have made the statue, but offer them no easy answers, even with an Obtain Information Momentum spend, or a Lore test.

Should the player characters attempt to investigate the rubble, the gamemaster should encourage them to make a Simple (D0) Observation test and a Challenging (D2) Stealth test. If player characters fail the Stealth test (which can be a teamwork test) it triggers an alarm — see *Scene Two: Cat and Mouse*. Otherwise, the player characters may continue searching, can raid the tower, or flee the mines. Momentum from the Observation test reveals treasures as below.

A competent alchemist can transform these treasures into offerings. The Alchemy test uses the Difficulty listed in the *Offering Transformation* chart (below).

SCENE TWO: CAT AND MOUSE

While the player characters are searching the rubble and avoiding Dero patrols, a cry echoes from the caverns. Dero scavengers and warriors, having discovered the corpses of their brethren, have raised the alarm and dozens more now spill from the tower. Fast-running messengers prompt the scavengers working the rubble to begin aggressively searching.

The player characters may continue their search, but every round must make a Stealth versus Senses struggle against a squad of Dero, each led by a warrior. The Difficulty begins at Simple (D0) but increases by one step every round the player characters remain on the statue.

Ultimately the player characters must decide what to do, but their options rapidly decrease into either raiding the Tower (see *Scene Four: The Tower* on page 69) or fleeing (see *Scene Three: Run!*, below). They might, given their success in the tunnels, attempt to fight the Dero. This is most likely a poor decision. The Dero overlord can send a near-infinite number of Dero at the player characters, and once they are discovered, war bands consisting of one warrior and two scavengers begin to arrive. First, one band arrives, then two more will appear every round after. If the player characters can get free of the war bands, they can attempt to use stealth again, but this chase continues as a seemingly unending number of Dero filter out of the tower in small groups, in response to the player characters' presence.

If the players query as to the number of Dero, and are in a position to watch the tower, they will see the guards dismember the corpses of any slain Dero. The guards then force Dero scavengers to take the pieces back into the tower. Moments later there is a faint green light from inside the tower and a new mob of Dero emerges from the tower.

SCENE THREE: RUN!

If the Dero have been alerted (see above) to the player characters, getting off of the statue is a challenging prospect. The Dero are not stupid and have set up a double-sized

OFFERING TRANSFORMATION

Momentum	Findings	Description	Value	Transformation Difficulty
0	Innocuous Rubble	Large chunks of anthracite. Some of it is carved with strange fluting, but otherwise it is solid rock.	None	N/A
1	Cave Drawings	A large slab of stone covered in bloody drawings and strange pictographs. See *Cave Drawings* (below).	None	N/A
2	Brass Wire	A foot or two of wire about one tenth of an inch in width.	1 Gold	Epic (D5)
3	Strange Fossil	A broken fossil that appears to be a stem of plant life or a giant starfish.	1 Gold	Dire (D4)
4	Glowing Gemstones	A one-inch gemstone embedded in some sort of ceramic tile. It glows with a pale yellow light until exposed to daylight, at which point it cracks. The tile is easily broken.	2 Gold	Daunting (D3)
5	Cracked Amber Rod	A twenty-inch long hollow wand of amber with a cracked top.	2 Gold	Challenging (D2)
6+	Amber Rod	A twenty-inch wand of amber that buzzes from time to time and glows like the gemstones.	3 Gold	Challenging (D2)

CAVE DRAWINGS

The history of the Dero is written out on a huge boulder. The level of detail that the player characters receive depends on a Daunting (D3) Linguistics, test or the use of the *Atavistic Voyage* spell.

The Dero overlord was originally a child worker in the mines. During a revolt, he fled into the mine and discovered a crack in the wall. Exploring the break, he uncovered the statue and the tower. In the tower lay the crystal coffin. There before the crystal, he accidentally made a copy of himself. It is unclear whether the copy was insane and killed the original or *vice versa*, but the survivor began duplicating himself and scouring the ruins for riches, food, and slaves.

Momentum

Every point of Momentum earned with the Linguistics test adds one detail to the above, in this order.

- Originally the crown and coffin were found. Later, a sceptre was uncovered and added.
- Strange things have been uncovered — drawings indicate some sort of strange being with a barrel-like torso and multiple branching arms, tentacles at the bottom and a star-like array of eyed tendrils at the top, with curious fan-like wings. At least one of these was eaten by the Dero.
- The Dero are cannibals that regularly go to the surface looking for meat.
- The Dero overlord is obsessed with finding more treasures to add to his crown.
- The Dero fought off the Acheronian guards over a lengthy struggle, and it has been an immensely long period of time since they were disturbed.
- The Dero overlord is immortal.
- Failing the Linguistics test leads the player characters to believe that these are the city's original inhabitants, locked beneath the earth and surviving by cannibalism and strange sorcery. The Acheronians found them, but the Dero fought them off.

A player character using the *Atavistic Voyage* spell will witness the entire tragic tale of madness and cannibalism. If the player character wishes to go back further, they discover that this whole place was once above-ground until fire fell from the sky and the buried statue was drawn through from another realm, where buildings collapsed upon it. The player character sees the tower populated by the strange barrel-shaped creature described above, using the crystal coffin to create slave animals.

A Dire (D4) Sorcery test causes a sorcerer to recognize the strange star-headed, winged barrel demons for what they are, an ancient and terrible race dating to before any known history, known only as "elder things". The player character witnesses the destruction of the towers by unknown but powerful sorcery.

First there is the statue, impossibly old and buried in iron sands; then there is a flash, and the sand turns to glass. At once, buildings start falling from the heavens. Many of them shatter against the statue but some remain standing, carving chunks of crater with their thunderous arrival. The tower appears to fend off these new arrivals, though the struggle is bitter, as more and more towers fall until a great spell creates a dome of green light and the conflict ends. Over time, the dome submerges in the ocean and is finally covered in stone.

Either voyage is maddening, with player characters suffering 4 🜛 mental damage if they witnessed the Dero brutality and 8 🜛 mental damage with the Intense quality, for seeing the arrival of the elder things. This can be reduced by a successful Average (D1) Discipline test, with each point of Momentum reducing the damage suffered by 1.

THE CAVES OF THE DERO

force at the ambush site, and potentially another force at the cave mouth. The player characters need to fight their way out of the caves, and the gamemaster should consider closing the adventure with the player characters' escape into daylight. Survival is not failure and player characters approaching the ambush with a decent strategy for escape should be rewarded with generous amounts of treasure in the aftermath, represented with gems and items scavenged along the way out.

Should the player characters choose to exit before the Dero rouse to fury, they encounter token resistance. A mob of scavengers that decided to flee the statue for some respite have yet to come across the dead from the ambush. They will react aggressively to the player characters and try to run for help. This will stir up a half-dozen Dero war bands who chase the party through the tunnels to the surface. The gamemaster should take the player characters backwards through this scene back to their entry into to the mines in *Chapter Two: The Mines of Acheron* (page 61), using Dero war bands as required to spice up the escape.

SCENE FOUR: THE TOWER

If the Dero were alerted (see *Scene Two: Cat and Mouse* on page 67) then entering the tower will require climbing in the window. The door guard has escalated from two warriors to two Squads of Dero, and even more keep dribbling out. The climb is a Challenging (D2) Athletics test. If a player character fails, they will slip down the surface. The climb is a two-story climb and player characters that roll 1 success will fall halfway. Characters that roll no successes will fall both stories. Momentum can be used to assist other climbers as normal.

From the window, the player characters see a curious sight. The tower consists of a massive room, almost like a grain store in appearance. Much of it is filled with a buzz of activity in the form of servile Dero scavengers rummaging through an astonishing clutter of broken rubble, scraps of stone, and bits of wire. In the center of the room is a curiously-shaped throne-like pedestal, but not one made for a human physique. Atop it is a particularly wizened Dero, wearing jewelry of braided wires, holding a crystal scepter, wearing a strange crown. Several scavengers attend this Dero, making more jewelry and bringing it meat. The crown and scepter appear connected to a crystal coffin about five feet in length, set into the floor upon a dais.

Dotted around the room, polished metallic mirrors reflect scenes from the villa and the surrounding countryside, although these mirrors seem out of place, almost as if they were a later addition added by unknown hands.

Every minute or so, a large paste-like substance fills the crystal coffin. The paste bubbles into the coffin from somewhere within it, extruding mouths and eyes of various sorts and screaming the same cries as the Dero until it finally settles into the shape of a Dero. With a horrible, gelatinous lurch, the Dero clambers from the coffin, dripping hands clutching spasmodically at the air. Witnessing this is a sanity-shaking moment. Player characters will take 6 mental damage unless they successfully make a Challenging (D2) Discipline test which reduces this to 3 mental damage.

During the combat, a player character might decide to destroy the crystal chamber in an effort to prevent the creation of more Dero or to simply enrage the Dero overlord. This is a Standard Action, but requires no test. The crystal coffin is extremely fragile and will shatter if struck with any amount of force. Ooze immediately begins to spill out, running onto the floor, a cascade of eyes, strange organs, and flapping tissue in the midst of becoming muscle tissue and bone, a ghastly experience to behold.

Without the coffin to contain it, this strange proto-matter quickly forms a shape not unlike that of the thing from the pond (encountered in *Chapter One: The Ruins Above*). Its first target is the Dero overlord, but the thing quickly turns on the player characters. The gamemaster should use the writeup for *The Thing From the Pond* (see page 60), spending suitable Doom to make it a formidable challenge. Additionally, should the Dero overlord be alive, he sends as many Dero as he can at the creature and the player characters, fearful of any danger.

Upon the end of the battle, proceed to *Scene Five: Epilogue* (page 70).

DERO OVERLORD (NEMESIS)

Long ago the Dero overlord was a human slave mining emeralds for Acheron. The mines were a brutal place where uprisings were common and it was common for the entire labor force to be executed in the night at the whims of their cruel masters. During one of these many uprisings, the one who would become overlord fled into the tunnels and hid. As the uprising was brought down with mighty sorcery, the earth trembled and the former slave discovered the strange tower and its otherworldly devices. The devices of the strange tower have transformed him and allowed him to thrive, albeit after a strange and grotesque fashion. He once had a name, but has long since forgotten it.

ATTRIBUTES

Awareness	Intelligence	Personality	Willpower
8	8	9	12

Agility	Brawn	Coordination
10	9	10

FIELDS OF EXPERTISE

Combat	2	Movement	2
Fortitude	1	Senses	3
Knowledge	3	Social	3

STRESS AND SOAK

- **Stress:** Vigor 10, Resolve 13
- **Soak:** Armor 2, Courage —

ATTACKS

- **Shortsword (M):** Reach 1, 5 ✦, 1H
- **Rod of the Old Ones (R):** Range C, 5 ✦, Stun
- **Maddening Cry (T):** Range C, 3 ✦ mental, Stun

SPECIAL ABILITIES

- Dread Creature 3
- Night Vision
- Inured to Fear
- **One Mind, Memory, and Soul:** The crown ensures that the wearer knows everything that any Dero (living or dead) within close range knows. However each of the Dero is a soulless replica. Should the overlord die, all his copies will revert to being semi-sentient paste, having lost the energetic force that shapes them into humanoid form.

DOOM SPENDS

- **Dero Device:** While connected to the crystal coffin, the overlord can spend 1 Doom to generate a Dero. When this Dero is born, the gamemaster should roll 1 ✦. If an Effect is rolled, the Dero is a warrior (see page 63); otherwise it is a scavenger (see page 62).

Plunder

Should the player characters manage to survive this encounter in the overlord's chamber, they will each be able to find six lengths of wire (see the *Offering Transformation* table on page 67), one broken and one functioning amber rod, and one glowing gemstone for every player character.

SCENE FIVE: EPILOGUE

At last, daylight! With the player characters having reached the surface, it seems for a moment as if they can finally breathe. Then the screams begin. Something unknowably horrible is happening deep below the surface, continuing on for several hours. At times, the ground tremors slightly, as if something is shifting and collapsing. Eventually, all becomes still.

Escaped from the caves of the Dero, the player characters may cling to whatever treasure they have clawed from deep beneath the earth. Certainly, the statue offers great mysteries for those inclined to return and investigate them, but likely untold horrors remain undiscovered. There are certainly emeralds as promised, but the effort to reclaim them might cost more than one could make in return. Plans need to be made, but for now the player character should be content enough to breathe in the air of a cool autumn night and to take a swig of wine, happy that they are out of that loathsome darkness.

EXPERIENCE

Experience point rewards should be granted as suggested by the **Conan** corebook, with additional bonuses rewarded for noteworthy roleplaying or ingenuity.

CHAPTER 4
THE GHOST OF THUNDER RIVER

> *In the Conan story I've attempted a new style and setting entirely — abandoned the exotic settings of lost cities, decaying civilizations, golden domes, marble palaces, silk-clad dancing girls, etc., and thrown my story against a background of forests and rivers, log cabins, frontier outposts, buckskin-clad settlers, and painted tribesmen.*
>
> — Robert E. Howard, letter to H.P. Lovecraft

In *The Ghost of Thunder River*, the player characters are in Velitrium, a border town in the Westermark in the Bossonian Marches, the buffer Aquilonia maintains between its border and Pictish territory. Led by a mysterious pale devil risen from ancient days, the Picts are hell-bent on destroying Aquilonian settlements, and are brazenly crossing the Thunder River. The garrison commander needs volunteers to defend the frontier town while waiting for reinforcements. The player characters, for reasons of their own, have answered his call.

The adventure begins, however, with the players taking on *alternate* roles, playing out an initial Prelude in which the adventure's primary antagonist, the "Ghost" of the title, is introduced, enshrouded in mystery. Robert E. Howard employed this technique to great effect in "The Phoenix on the Sword", "Black Colossus", "The Devil in Iron", *The Hour of the Dragon*, and others, and here it is used as a means of dramatic foreshadowing, as well as giving insight into a group often only seen as enemies, the Picts themselves.

Should the gamemaster wish to forgo the prelude, the adventure can be run by starting with the player characters in the opening scene, *Death at Their Heels*, on page 78.

PRELUDE: A TORCH SHINES ACROSS THE AEONS

The gamemaster should introduce the adventure and read or summarize the following text aloud:

> *The endless tide of invaders has come into your land time and again, committing atrocities upon your people. They have trod in your sacred spaces, their iron axes and saws cutting great swaths out of a forest that has lasted since the waters receded from this land. Once there was enough for all, but they have hunted and cleared and burnt so much, feeding some endless hunger behind them, that you and your people are pushed back each day. Now their hatred has fallen upon you. They brazenly cross the Thunder River in metal-clad bands, and wage war against you in your own villages.*
>
> *Two days ago, while you were on a hunt, a band of these soulless ones attacked your village. They could not kill everyone, but set fire to your huts in the night, killing many — including children and elders. As the*

village burnt, they defiled the bodies, taking their ears to sell as bounty, and they took all the gold and precious items they could find, treasures that had been with your people for generations beyond counting. You returned to smoking ruin, the people of your village fled deeper into the wilderness, and when you had laid the dead to rest, you went on the hunt once again.

Since then, you have harried them as they attempted to return to safety on the other side of the river. Your arrows have thinned their number, and the sole survivor — wounded by one of your arrows — has cut deep into your territory, perhaps lost or trying to draw you into the land of a rival tribe. You have followed him for half a day now, and as the moon rises and shines through the forest, he is finally within your reach. However, he has gone into the Place of the Whispering Fog…

At this, the gamemaster should hand out the alternate Pict characters, members of a Pict hunting party turned war-party. These are presented on pages 73–75. Because these are essentially non-player characters during this encounter, the players will not have any Fortune points available.

The gamemaster should encourage the players to introduce these characters to one another, preferably in character. This will let them know each other as they try on these new roles. After that introduction is provided, begin with *On the Red Spotted Trail* on page 75.

MORE PICTS

This adventure presents five sample Pict characters, but the gamemaster can make additional characters if needed, by copying one of the existing characters and changing minor details, or by using them as a guideline and creating a new character entirely.

Suitable female Pict names are Mitena, Wyome, and Zihoa; and suitable names for male Picts are Hinun, Matoskah, and Teetomeq.

These names can also be used should it become relevant later in the adventure.

THE GHOST OF THUNDER RIVER

CHOGAN, PICT WARRIOR (TOUGHENED)

Named "Black Bird", this sturdy warrior is the deadliest of the Ravens and the leader of this war-band. He hates the soft invaders, and has been fighting them for all his life. Though not much liked in his village, most would follow him into battle, confident of victory. Chogan is larger than most Picts, standing almost a half-head taller, with broad shoulders and a fierce jaw-line. His head is shaved, and he wears coal paint and crow feathers on his face and shoulders, a fearsome appearance that suits him perfectly.

ATTRIBUTES

Awareness	Intelligence	Personality	Willpower
8	8	8	9

Agility	Brawn	Coordination
10	12	11

FIELDS OF EXPERTISE

Combat	2	Movement	2
Fortitude	1	Senses	3
Knowledge	3	Social	3

STRESS AND SOAK

- **Stress:** Vigor 12, Resolve 9
- **Soak:** Armor 1 (Leather, Arms/Torso), Courage 2

ATTACKS

- **Bladed War Club (M):** Reach 2, 7🔱, Unbalanced, Stun, Knockdown.
- **Throwing Axe (M):** Reach 2, 6🔱, 1H, Thrown, Vicious 1
- **Knife (M):** Reach 1, 6🔱, 1H, Hidden 1, Improvised, Unforgiving 1
- **Savage Glare (T):** Range C, 2🔱 mental, Stun

SPECIAL ABILITIES

- **Forest-Born:** While in a home forest, Chogan may reduce the Difficulty of any action relating to stealth or movement by one step.
- **Wrathful Warrior:** If using an Unbalanced weapon in two hands, Chogan rolls +1🔱 and can make Swift Strikes for 1 Momentum instead of the usual 2.
- **Savage Glare:** When making a Threaten attack, Chogan can spend 1 Momentum to gain the Vicious quality.

AHANU, PICT SCOUT (TOUGHENED)

Ahanu's name means "Always Laughing", for good reason. Though he has seen much suffering at the hands of the Aquilonians and Bossonians, he is constantly amused, as if amused by some jest made in a voice only he can hear. This is true. He speaks to the gods, and they to him, telling him to hunt the pale devils that trespass on sacred land and hunt wantonly, selfishly withholding their offerings to the forest gods. Ahanu is tall, rangy, and smiling, and wears a bone breastplate.

ATTRIBUTES

Awareness	Intelligence	Personality	Willpower
9	9	10	9

Agility	Brawn	Coordination
11	8	10

STRESS AND SOAK

- **Stress:** Vigor 8, Resolve 9
- **Soak:** Armor 1 (Bone Breastplate, Torso), Courage 1

FIELDS OF EXPERTISE

Combat	2	Movement	2
Fortitude	1	Senses	3
Knowledge	1	Social	1

ATTACKS

- **Club (M):** Reach 2, 3🔱, 1H, Stun, Knockdown
- **Knife (M):** Reach 1, 3🔱, 1H, Hidden 1, Improvised, Unforgiving 1
- **Hunting Bow (R):** Range C, 4🔱, 2H, Volley, 2 loads
- **Savage Glare (T):** Range C, 4🔱 mental, Stun

SPECIAL ABILITIES

- **Forest-Born:** While in a home forest, Ahanu may reduce the Difficulty of any action relating to stealth or movement by one step.
- **Savage Glare:** When making a Threaten attack, Ahanu can spend 1 Momentum to gain the Vicious quality.
- **Whispers From the Spirits:** When in an ambush, Ahanu can reroll any dice that don't initially roll a success.

ROWTAG, PICT HUNTER (TOUGHENED)

For reasons that are obvious, he is named "Like Flame". Rowtag is quick to anger, fast to act, his appetite voracious, his attention fleeting. Unlike many of his kin, he has not been overly concerned with the oncoming tide of settlers from the east. He drives Aquilonians out of his homeland more for the thrill of killing them than an action born out of outrage. Rowtag wears a metal cap he took from the first Aquilonian he killed, and he is more squat than his brethren, though stronger than any in the tribe.

ATTRIBUTES

Awareness	Intelligence	Personality	Willpower
8	7	7	10
Agility	Brawn		Coordination
8	13		9

FIELDS OF EXPERTISE

Combat	2	Movement	2
Fortitude	2	Senses	2
Knowledge	—	Social	—

STRESS AND SOAK

- **Stress:** Vigor 13, Resolve 10
- **Soak:** Armor 1 (Metal Cap, Head), Courage 2

ATTACKS

- **Throwing Axe (M):** Reach 2, 6🦅, 1H, Thrown, Vicious 1
- **Knife (M):** Reach 1, 6🦅, 1H, Hidden 1, Improvised, Unforgiving 1
- **Bow (R):** Range C, 3🦅, 2H, Volley, 2 loads
- **Savage Glare (T):** Range C, 2🦅 mental, Stun

SPECIAL ABILITIES

- **Forest-Born:** While in a home forest, Rowtag may reduce the Difficulty of any action relating to stealth or movement by one step.
- **Savage Glare:** When making a Threaten attack, Rowtag can spend 1 Momentum to gain the Vicious quality.
- **Whirlwind:** If Rowtag throws a weapon and successfully hits his target he can make a Swift Strike for 1 Momentum.

TOGQUOS, PICT WARRIOR (TOUGHENED)

Named "Like the Other", Togquos is the spitting image of the old chief, and has grown up in that man's shadow. The youngest of this band, Togquos was eager to score his first kill and sit at the fire with the other warriors and elder council, but now that his village has been destroyed, he seeks only vengeance. He is but a youth, slender and faster than any in his tribe. Adept with either hand, he fights with two hatchets, a whirling display of speed and coordination.

ATTRIBUTES

Awareness	Intelligence	Personality	Willpower
8	7	8	9
Agility	Brawn		Coordination
11	9		13

FIELDS OF EXPERTISE

Combat	2	Movement	3
Fortitude	1	Senses	1
Knowledge	—	Social	—

STRESS AND SOAK

- **Stress:** Vigor 9, Resolve 9
- **Soak:** Armor —, Courage 1

ATTACKS

- **Two Throwing Axes (M):** Reach 2, 4🦅, 1H, Thrown, Vicious 1
- **Knife (M):** Reach 1, 4🦅, 1H, Hidden 1, Improvised, Unforgiving 1
- **Sling (R):** Range M, 3🦅, 1H, Stun, Volley
- **Savage Glare (T):** Range C, 2🦅 mental, Stun

SPECIAL ABILITIES

- **Forest-Born:** While in a home forest, Togquos may reduce the Difficulty of any action relating to stealth or movement by one step.
- **Savage Glare:** When making a Threaten attack, Togquos can spend 1 Momentum to gain the Vicious quality.

THE GHOST OF THUNDER RIVER

ETHETAY, PICT TRACKER (TOUGHENED)

Her name is "Good One", and she is well-liked amongst the Raven tribe. Though it is uncommon for Raven women to hunt, her skill is undeniable, and she is the most successful of the tribe's hunters. Her mother was also a great hunter, and taught Ethetay to follow the spoor and tracks of animals through the most difficult terrain. She is generally quiet, though sharp-tongued when provoked. Her half-cloak is covered with bone rings, and she prefers to use obsidian and flint weapons, despite access to bronze or iron weapons taken from Aquilonian settlers and soldiers.

ATTRIBUTES

Awareness	Intelligence	Personality	Willpower
11	8	8	8

Agility	Brawn	Coordination
11	9	11

FIELDS OF EXPERTISE

Combat	2	Movement	3
Fortitude	1	Senses	2
Knowledge	1	Social	—

STRESS AND SOAK

- **Stress:** Vigor 9, Resolve 8
- **Soak:** Armor 1 (Leather Cape, Torso/Arms), Courage 1

ATTACKS

- **Flint Knife (M):** Reach 1, 4🗡, 1H, Hidden 1, Improvised, Unforgiving 1
- **Bow (R):** Range C, 5🗡, 2H, Volley, 2 loads
- **Savage Glare (T):** Range C, 2🗡 mental, Stun

SPECIAL ABILITIES

- **Forest-Born:** While in a home forest, Ethetay may reduce the Difficulty of any action relating to stealth or movement by one step.
- **Savage Glare:** When making a Threaten attack, Ethetay can spend 1 Momentum to gain the Vicious quality.
- **Accuracy:** Ethetay can reroll 1🗡 when making a successful Ranged Weapons attack.

ON THE RED SPOTTED TRAIL

Night has fallen on this fall day, and the few remaining leaves are brown and black, the ground littered with a thick, rich carpet of the fallen. The moon is exceptionally bright, almost eerily so, and the animals, birds, and insects of the marshy forest are almost subdued. Breath steams in the cold, and the ground is slightly wet with a recent rain. Tracking the foreign devil has been made easier by the ground cover, and his fleeing path has led the war-party to a place outside Raven territory, where they do not often go: the Place of the Whispering Fog.

This is an ancient part of Pictland, generally avoided, but of no particular religious significance to the Picts. Any Pict making a successful Average (D1) Knowledge test will know a bit about the Place of the Whispering Fog. It is not as old as their ancestors from the time before the great floods that enveloped the world, but from more recent times, tens and tens of generations past rather than thousands. No game is found here: animals avoid it, and there is nothing but old ruins full of things the Picts have no use for. Sometimes shamans and witches come here for visions or to cultivate strange herbs, but generally it is left alone.

Any of the war-party making a successful Average (D1) Survival test will follow the man's bloody trail into the center of these old ruins, and should they follow, they will notice that the area is shrouded with thick streams of mist that seem to emanate from the ground, shifting as if in undetectable breezes, moving lazily and lit almost lambent by spears of moonlight through the trees. Sounds of wildlife grow quiet, but no obvious source of menace presents itself. However, the overall experience of being in the place — so different from the Picts' familiar territory — requires an Average (D1) Discipline test, with a failure costing 1 ♆ mental damage and increasing the Difficulty of all Personality or Willpower actions by one step.

THE TOMB OF THUMOCRIS

The Picts do not know this, but this is the living tomb of an ancient Acheronian sorcerer named Thumocris. When this dying sorcerer saw the downfall of his empire around him and the extermination of the Acheronians by their former subjects, he fled north and using his magic, built a stronghold against the primitive Picts of the time. Thumocris grew old in this isolation when he sensed the approach of death, he wrought a mighty enchantment to ensure renewed life when the conditions became right.

The walls of the stronghold have long since fallen, most of the chambers exposed and looted, and the underground labyrinth beneath the tomb collapsed long ago, filled with water, silt, and rock. All that remains is a large plaza, once the courtyard of Thumocris' stronghold and now the center of his tomb. The chamber around the tomb itself has similarly crumbled, and only the central sepulcher is left.

The Pict characters examining these ruins notice several towers that have fallen, and that the expanse and level of complexity marks this as a large fortress, like those of the Aquilonians and the Zingarans to the south. Other Pict tribes over the centuries — and even the lost Ligureans — have made their marks on this place, with (now mouldering) savage tribal offerings to the strange gods that once held sway over this place. Vegetation has choked much of the ruins, blocking passage, but the most visible place is the center, a peaked building that is mostly intact, roughly the size of a large hut. It is to this place that the blood-spattered trail leads.

As the Pict war-party approaches, should they choose to scout the area they will see that the structure has only a single entrance, a wide slab that once sealed it having fallen askew in the entry. Other entrances seem to have been buried with the collapse of the fortress around it, and moss and vines indicate an inevitability and solidity to this last place. The roof, however, seems to be partially collapsed, and with areas apparently open to the moonlit sky above.

A smudge of a bloody handprint is visible on the light stone, showing the passage of the trespasser. The walls are thick enough to muffle any sounds, and inside is darkness, the entry apparently gained through a short passage that leads immediately to one side, then inside. Any Pict attempting to climb the outside can do so with a successful Average (D1) Athletics test, and will get the same view as entering the chamber, though from a different vantage.

Any Pict entering the sepulcher will come around the corner of a short, dark passage, emerging into a large and oddly-shaped chamber, with smaller branches off the main chamber. Part of the high ceiling has fallen in, overburdened with growth and weakened by antiquity. Stone blocks, broken and intact, lay heaped and strewn on the floor. Light shines in from the moon, above, but shadows and darkness remain in many places. Vines hang down. Puddles of water and moss are everywhere. Unlike the rest of the ruins, this place has not been entirely looted. Set into niches in the walls are stone jars and other boxes made of clay and metal, each fitted perfectly to the alcove. Among them are a great many skulls and bones set with metal and gems. Carvings on the walls depict a variety of demonic or otherworldly creatures and entities.

> *'Who knows what gods are worshipped under the shadows of that heathen forest, or what devils crawl out of the black ooze of the swamps? Who can be sure that all the inhabitants of that black country are natural?'*
>
> — Valannus, "Beyond the Black River"

In the center of the room, however, looms an impressive sight: a huge sarcophagus with the bed set at an angle. Strange carvings decorate the sides and the lid, which lies on the ground as if pried open. It is empty, with no sign of the inhabitant. As the Picts approach, the gamemaster should call for an Average (D1) Observation test, with success indicating that they hear something moving in the chamber, in one of the shadowy side-alcoves.

OUT OF TIME

From these shadows steps a strange figure, his skin bright in the moonlight, pale as that of the despised settlers. A headpiece or helmet of some sort entirely encloses his head, neck, and upper shoulders, concealing his face entirely save for eyes that glow through narrow eye-slits. Upon his arms, hands, and torso are pieces of some sort of ceremonial armor, made up of mottled silver and set with enamelled plates. He radiates a wave of dread, forcing a Challenging (D3) Discipline test, causing 1 Wound and 1 Trauma, with failure immediately causing any within the area — including those outside — to feel preternaturally nauseated and afraid, adding one step of Difficulty to all physical and mental skill tests.

At this point, the Picts will probably either attack or try to flee. The gamemaster should spend enough Doom to allow the figure to move at the beginning of the turn, and his first action will be to gesture, casting an instantaneous spell that causes the stone slab of the sepulcher to rumble and close fast, using an alternative effects version of *Dismember*, *No Door May Bar My Path!* as described on page 177 of the **Conan** corebook. As he does this, he speaks in a language that seems to have a physical sensation greater than just sound. Moving into the light, he appears even more terrifying, his skin pale and cadaverous and his bodily movement unnatural and possessing an eerie, inhuman grace. This is Thumocris, risen from his sarcophagus, seemingly angry at the trespassers.

Should the Picts attack Thumocris, he stands as if uncaring of the force of their assaults, his armor impermeable and his exposed skin absorbing the force of the Picts' attacks. The gamemaster may even allow the Pict characters the sensation that they might win, then having the figure shrug off injury and react to devastating effect. He absorbs the initial attacks, then begins moving on his own, grasping at weapons and using Doom to disarm the Picts where he can, laying hands upon them and hurling them about the interior of the sepulcher as if they were rag-dolls, his inhuman strength evident, speaking in that strange and terrible tongue all the while. If they do not attack, he will attempt to use the *Dismember* spell against them, moving onto another victim when one is disabled.

Any Picts that enter the side-passage the figure emerged from will see a curious sight: the naked mummy of a pale-skinned man laid to repose, with arms laid at his side. Anyone attempting to disturb these remains will incur the wrath of the strange figure, who will attempt to defend it at all costs. On the ground near the corpse is a leather string of human ears, relatively fresh, clearly taken from Picts. Of the Bossonian the Picts trailed into the tomb, there is no sign.

Though the Picts are easily outmatched and will inevitably fall to Thumocris within a couple of rounds of combat, he will not kill them. He is actually trying to keep them alive and unconscious, if bloody. If Thumocris is able to grapple with any of the Picts, he will instead try to subdue them, for use later.

If any of the Picts did not enter the tomb, the gamemaster can allow them to describe their actions, watching what happens from their vantage point outside, whether observing from a hole atop the tomb or waiting outside the now-sealed door. As the point of view shifts to the outside world, the gamemaster may end the encounter with the lingering, terrified scream of the last of the Pict war-party inside, leaving their fates uncertain.

At this point, the gamemaster should describe the exterior of the sepulcher once more, noting that the wildlife outside, which had risen to a fevered pitch during the encounter, quiets, and eventually the thrum and chitter of natural forest life return. Soon, it is as if nothing had happened, and the forest is as it was, still as it has been for thousands of years. Any survivors can flee at this point, carrying the dreadful news back to their tribe.

THUMOCRIS (NEMESIS, HORROR)

Born in ancient Acheron, Thumocris was mighty amongst the sorcerers of that land and era, a master of life and death and the transition between. Thousands died at his hands in his diabolical experiments, and his name was not spoken save in fearful whispers. During an atavistic voyage across the eons, he saw that his empire would fall, and that the barbaric tide that opposed it would raze the ruins of Acheron to the ground, and use its rubble as a foundation to build their own cities. To escape this, he took his household far to the north, through howling wilderness into fathomless woods, and there Thumocris built a stronghold in which to continue his work.

The Picts of the area soon learned to stay away, and eventually Thumocris wearied of his unnaturally-extended life and his isolation. He cast enchantments upon himself to enter a torpor that would last millennia, until the time was right for him to rise again and exert his will upon the world. The wards upon his sepulcher were such that when an Bossonian renegade and Pict-killer named Magnus stumbled across his tomb, and sought refuge, his long dormant spirit woke, seizing control of the man's mind and inhabiting Magnus' body. Thumocris laid his own desiccated remains in an alcove nearby, and donned his garments of old, the signs of his power, and it is at this point the Pict war-party arrived.

His current goal is to keep his real body intact and collect enough human sacrifices among the civilized folk to re-create his former stronghold and to return his body to life, re-inhabiting it and abandoning Magnus' mortal clay. To this end Thumocris has cast considerable magic to render Magnus' body proof against magic, bargaining with demonic entities for greater sacrifices yet to come.

ATTRIBUTES

Awareness	Intelligence	Personality	Willpower
12	14	13	14
Agility	Brawn		Coordination
10	14 (1)		10

STRESS AND SOAK

- **Stress:** Vigor 19, Resolve 18
- **Soak:** Armor 3 (Orichalcum Armor, Head/Torso/Arms), Courage 2

FIELDS OF EXPERTISE

Combat	2	Movement	1
Fortitude	4	Senses	3
Knowledge	5	Social	2

ATTACKS

- **Hammerlike Fists (M):** Reach 1, 7 ◈, 1H, Grappling, Knockdown, Stun
- **I Will Take Your Heart! (R):** Range C, 7 ◈, Intense, Piercing 3, Vicious 2.
- **Sorcerous Might (T):** Range M, 8 ◈ mental, Area, Intense

SPECIAL ABILITIES

- Doom-Herald
- Dread Creature 3
- Fast Recovery (Vigor 2)
- Inhuman Brawn 1
- **Sorcerer:** Thumocris is a skilled sorcerer, and can use spells such as *Dismember*, *Enslave*, *Fury of the Elements*, *Haunt the Mind*, and *Venom on the Wind*, and will later use a variant of *Raise Up the Dead* to reinvigorate his body to its former fullness.
- Inured to Pain

DOOM SPENDS

- **Acheronian Sorcery:** In addition to the spells described above, Thumocris knows Acheronian sorcery and is able to achieve a variety of effects that defy the known limits of magic. To simulate this, the gamemaster should spend Doom in a proportionate amount when Thumocris wishes to achieve a particular sorcerous effect, with minor Doom spends (1+ points) required for minor effects, up to larger effects requiring more Doom to achieve (5+ points).

> *Beyond the river the primitive still reigned in shadowy forests, brush-thatched huts where hung the grinning skulls of men, and mud-walled enclosures where fires flickered and drums rumbled, and spears were whetted in the hands of dark, silent men with tangled black hair and the eyes of serpents. Those eyes often glared through the bushes at the fort across the river.*
>
> — "Beyond the Black River"

DEATH AT THEIR HEELS

After this initial encounter is played out, the gamemaster should have the players return to their normal player characters, and here their adventure begins. The gamemaster can read or paraphrase the following information to the players.

> *Velitrium, in Aquilonia's Westermark, is a settlement alongside the Thunder River, a trade center and market for the other forts and communities. The inner fort is surrounded with palisade walls, though some farms and outer buildings have been built south of the garrison along the bank of the river. You have each come to Velitrium for reasons of your own, but following a daring series of Pict raids in nearby lands, the garrison commander has summoned all able-bodied men and women to aid in the defense of the town. You have answered his call, and have been newly deputized to defend the town.*

The player characters stand outside the garrison commander's house on a crisp winter afternoon, a few weeks of snow having formed a brittle crust underfoot, and light flakes drift lazily down. Baron Trebellius, the garrison's commander, has just finished a speech. The Baron is an Aqulionan, overconfident and arrogant. He is seemingly bored by this duty, taken solely to look after the lands he holds adjacent to the outpost, and the speech was one given several times over the last few days, and he expects to repeat it again in the days to come.

After a preamble about the dangers and the necessity of defense of the frontier, Trebellius informed the player characters that they would be paid in accommodations, board, and coin equivalent to 1 Gold per week, and that all of those present are instructed to report to the ale-hall for their evening meal before a pre-nightfall sojourn out along the river to scout for signs of Pictish incursion. The gamemaster may wish to ask the players to each describe what brought their character to the region, if they do not already know one another, and why they answered the baron's call. If desired, the gamemaster can assume that others are standing alongside the player characters, similar mercenaries, wanderers, and opportunists seeking fortune at the edge of the civilized world, or the player characters might be the only ones who have answered the summons this day.

If the player characters have been around for more than a few days, they are aware that the garrison has been run fairly ragged, and its forces are in poor spirits, the last few weeks taxing them to their utmost. Normally it is relatively quiet here, with the occasional settlers and traders passing through, or some few bands of mercenaries seeking to claim bounties on Picts paid by some of the other forts, but Velitrium takes no part in such trade, and has been left alone for the most part. However, in recent weeks assaults by the Picts have increased dramatically, and Velitrium is full of farmers and settlers driven back from up and down the banks of the Thunder River, as well as from the other side. All of these folks tell of several tribes of Picts attacking in numbers, more organized and destructive than ever before.

Finished with the player characters, Baron Trebellius turns to his aide and begins examining a dispatch, likely from Tarantia, Aquilona's capital city. As the player characters decide what to do next, a great cry is heard from the wooden palisade walls surrounding the garrison. Guards manning the northern wall and gate have become interested in something happening outside, and are scrambling for a vantage spots either on the observation towers, the gate itself, or pressing their faces against the logs of the palisade wall to peer through the gaps.

Should any of the player characters join them, clambering up the ladder to observation points behind the rough wooden stake-walls, peering between gaps in the palisade, or going to the gates, they will see the cause of the commotion. At the edge of the great clearing to the north of Velitrium is tree a wall, and from it, two men emerge, clearly garbed as some of Velitrium's scouts. One is half-carrying the other, who is barely able to walk, his feet dragging, head down, and one arm hanging limply. A successful Challenging (D2) Observation test reveals that both men are wounded, and that several arrows protrude from the half-unconscious one. The first is holding a hatchet at the ready as he tries to drag his friend forward. One of the men on the wall shout their names — Hauk and Titus — both veteran woodsmen.

They move several yards into the clearing, and then turn and head back the way they came, away from the river-bank, just as a mob of Pict warriors charge out of the tree-line at an angle, trying to cut them off from the fort and safety. One of the Picts glares at the fort and brandishes a captured sword, and with a whoop, turns back and joins his war party pursuing the men into the trees. As this happens, some of the men in the fort fire arrows at the Picts, though the range is so great the Difficulty is increased by two steps, their arrows missing or striking to minimal effect.

Trebellius orders the gates closed and a full watch on the walls, with archers ready to defend the garrison if there are more Picts. As he does so, a great cry goes out from the wall and gate guards to assist the scouts. Trebellius balks, seemingly frozen by indecision. If he orders troops out, he could lose them, giving the Picts an opportunity to attack the garrison, and if he lets them die, the Picts will be even further emboldened, and morale will suffer.

Time is of the essence, as those in the garrison hear the distant echoes of footsteps crashing through the trees and the whoops of the war-party. If the player characters wish to intervene and volunteer to go out after the scouts, they must succeed in an Average (D1) Persuade test to convince him to order the gates opened so they can head out. Or they can attempt an Average (D1) Command test on the gate guards directly, against Trebellius' orders, though he will only protest weakly.

If the player characters do not wish to take part in any rescue attempts, other volunteers will go out and eventually bring them back, but in much worse shape. Their fate is revealed in *Council of Fear* on 82.

THE DEADLIEST PREY

Hopefully, the player characters will rally and be willing to venture forth into the wilderness in search of the pursued woodsmen. The gate guards will ready themselves, then open the door briefly to allow the player characters and any other search parties to go out quickly, racing across the clearing and going into the trees in pursuit of the Picts. Depending on the player characters' plans, some other scouts and garrison guards will volunteer to go out and search for the missing woodsmen, forming several parties.

In the chaotic, well-trod snow, it is an Average (D1) Survival test to find and follow the initial tracks of the woodsmen, and to distinguish their buckskin boots from the moccasins worn by the Picts. Examining the trail, it is apparent that the woodsmen managed to escape the Picts temporarily by covering their tracks, and that the Picts broke up into two groups of roughly a half-dozen apiece. A Complication on this test may indicate that the area has more Picts than those the player characters saw from the garrison walls — many more, grouped into small parties of the same size.

While the player characters are out in the wild, should they attempt to avoid notice by the Picts, they must succeed in struggles pitting their Stealth versus the Picts' Observation to move without notice, and a struggle of Survival versus Survival skills to keep the Picts from picking up their own trails! Failure on the Stealth tests reveals their location to a band of Picts, which will use Stealth to attack, or will simply race out of the trees in a running assault, hoping to overwhelm the soft civilized folk quickly. Failing the Survival test means the player characters are so intent on camouflaging their tracks that they become lost. Any Complications could mean that the player characters are lost, and must find the path again, or that they stumble inadvertently onto a group of Picts.

Finding Hauk and Titus requires either a successful Daunting (D3) Survival test to track them once it becomes obvious they've tried to conceal their path, or a Challenging (D2) Observation to hear the sounds of a distant skirmish, off some distance in the rough terrain to the north of the fort, just near the bank of the Thunder River. They have concealed themselves in a rocky corner of what was once a creek gully, and one round before the player characters find them, they are found by one group of Picts, who try to force them out of the cleft they've hidden in.

When the player characters arrive, they will find Hauk attempting to defend the now-unconscious Titus, and circled by a group of Picts. There are Minions equal to the number of player characters and at least one Toughened Pict for every two player characters. Hauk will continue to fight, but cannot use Momentum from the group's pool, nor does he add to it. Titus has only one remaining Wound and is unconscious, beyond revival at this time. The Picts will either fight to the death or flee if vastly outmatched.

When the Picts are dealt with, Hauk thanks them, and retrieves his wounded friend. He asks for help carrying him, as Hauk is already bleeding from a few wounds. There is no time for medical treatment, however, as the howling Picts are everywhere around them, and they should try to return to the safety of the garrison before they are discovered once more.

Depending on how successful the player characters are at avoiding conflict, they can either make their way back to the garrison without incident or they can encounter additional bands of Picts. The number of Picts in the area is growing rapidly, and there is no shortage of the threat they present. The gamemaster should determine the relative size and frequency of remaining Pict war parties, and adjust any encounters as desired.

THE GHOST OF THUNDER RIVER

PICTS ON THE WARPATH (MINION, TOUGHENED)

In the weeks since Thumocris rose from his crypt, he has brought with him members from various tribes of Picts, in an attempt to drive the civilized interlopers out of Pictland. Gwaweli, Hawk, Snake, Tanengi, and even survivors of the Raven tribe are arrayed against Velitrium, painted and feathered as if for war, fiercely eager to strike back against those that threaten their land.

Parenthetical values are for Toughened Picts: these elite warriors also add +1 🜚 to their physical and mental attack damages.

ATTRIBUTES

Awareness	Intelligence	Personality	Willpower
9/10	7	7/8	9/10

Agility	Brawn	Coordination
10	9/10	10

FIELDS OF EXPERTISE

Combat	2/3	Movement	2
Fortitude	1/2	Senses	2
Knowledge	—	Social	—

STRESS AND SOAK

- **Stress:** Vigor 5 (10), Resolve 5 (10)
- **Soak:** Armor —, Courage —

ATTACKS

- **Hatchet:** Reach 2, 5 🜚, 1H, Vicious 1
- **Knife:** Reach 1, 4 🜚, 1H, Hidden 1, Thrown, Unforgiving 1
- **Bow:** Range M, 4 🜚, Volley
- **Javelin (R):** Range 2, 4 🜚, 1H, Fragile, Piercing 1, Thrown (Medium)
- **War Cry (T):** Range C, 3 🜚 mental, Stun, Vicious 1

SPECIAL ABILITIES

- **Minions:** Picts are defeated after one Wound or Trauma. It's up to the gamemaster if this means they're dead, playing dead, cowering, fleeing, or unconscious. They roll only 1d20 each for skill tests normally.
- **Mob:** Picts will use the mob rules for Minions, as described in the **Conan** corebook on page 305.
- **Forest-Born:** While in a home forest, a Pict may reduce the Difficulty of any action relating to stealth or movement by one step.

DOOM SPENDS

- **Seize the Initiative:** Picts can act before a player in a turn if the gamemaster pays 1 Doom point for each Pict.

HAUK THE GUNDERMAN (TOUGHENED)

Born in Gunderland, Hauk is a sturdy and even-tempered veteran scout and seasoned Pict-fighter, slow in speech but reliable in deed. He has the tawny hair and rangy build bespeaking the purity of his Hyborian bloodline, clad in well-worn buckskins and woollens, with harness of leather and a ragged blue kerchief knotted about his neck in the fashion of the frontier.

ATTRIBUTES

Awareness	Intelligence	Personality	Willpower
10	8	7	9

Agility	Brawn	Coordination
10	10	10

FIELDS OF EXPERTISE

Combat	3	Movement	2
Fortitude	2	Senses	2
Knowledge	1	Social	—

STRESS AND SOAK

- **Stress:** Vigor 10, Resolve 9
- **Soak:** Armor 1 (Leather Jerkin), Courage 1

ATTACKS

- **Hatchet (M):** Reach 2, 6 🜚, 1H, Thrown, Vicious 1
- **Shortsword (M):** Reach 1, 6 🜚, 1H, Parrying
- **Dirk (M):** Reach 1, 5 🜚, 1H, Hidden 1, Parrying, Thrown, Unforgiving 1
- **Steely Glare (T):** Range C, 2 🜚 mental, Stun

SPECIAL ABILITIES

- **Frontiersman:** A seasoned ranger out of Gunderland, Hauk can add an additional +1d20 to any test related to survival while in the wilderness.

COUNCIL OF FEAR

Back in relative safety in Velitrium, the player characters can talk further with Hauk, who is being treated in the long-house where the scouts and guards are quartered. Baron Trebellius orders the gate and wall guards doubled, and the guards peer anxiously at the surrounding tree-wall, wondering if the Picts are out there watching.

Titus is still gravely injured, and any player character wishing to assist in treating him may do so. Otherwise, the outpost's healer will tend to the man's wounds, removing the arrows from his body and bandaging him. He does not wake up, and will be unconscious for quite a while. Hauk's injuries, on the other hand, are less critical, and he is able to talk while the gashes and cuts he suffered are cleaned and sewn closed. Other foresters and soldiers crowd around them while Hauk relates his tale, directed at his commander, Trebellius, as well as the player characters if they were the ones to rescue him.

Trebellius has his aide taking notes, ostensibly for a message back to the Aquilonian king in Tarantia, seeking support and additional troops that will not come. (Note that at the beginning of Conan's career, this would be King Vilerus, while later it is Namedides. Both kings are neglectful of the frontier, and have contributed to the precarious situation through their inattention.)

THE TALE OF HAUK

Along with another scout named Rolf, Hauk and Titus were ranging the banks of the Thunder River, north-west of Velitrium, scouting the aftermath of the recent spate of Pict attacks. Normally the Picts burn the farms of the settlers they attack and take heads of those they kill, but not this time: they are taking prisoners — farmers and other settlers — and bringing them back into Pictland. The three scouts came across dozens of Pict canoes set along the bank, with at least a half-hundred Picts of various tribes in some sort of heated discussion. They concealed themselves and observed.

The Picts were led by a figure that seemed oddly incongruous, a white-skinned man, his face concealed under an ornate masked headdress. Even at a distance, there was something disquieting about the figure, and the Picts seemed unusually obedient to him, almost as if they served him in fear. He spoke to them in a language that none of the foresters could understand, but they seemed to comprehend his meaning. Hauk understands enough of the Pictish tongues to know that they called him "The Ghost".

The foresters watched as the Picts brought forth a settler family — husband, wife, and two children — trussed tightly and gagged. There was some disagreement about who got them, but the Ghost indicated that they belonged to the Raven Picts, and would go with them. As the Ravens made to put their captives into canoes to take across the river, Titus drew back his bow and fired an arrow into the masked figure, hoping the loss of their leader would dishearten them. The arrow struck the man right in the heart, but to no effect. He pulled the arrow from his white-skinned breast, and a moment later, gestured at the place where the three men were concealed.

With a howl, the Picts surged after them, and all three broke their cover and ran pell-mell, trying to escape. Rolf was caught by the Picts, and as he was dragged down, he urged Hauk and Titus to warn Velitrium. From then, it was all-out flight, and the Picts chased Titus and Hauk down the river bank for almost ten miles, until they arrived at Velitrium and were rescued.

ARGUMENTS AND DELIBERATIONS

Once the tale is told, the room erupts into debate about what to do next. Trebellius is content to leave the farmer family and Rolf to their fate. There is, he argues, no way to know where they were taken, and in all likelihood they will long be dead before anyone can find them. All hands, instead, should be on hand for the defense of Velitrium, and he forbids anyone to put any more thought into another course of action. At this, many of the soldiers avert their

THE GHOST OF THUNDER RIVER

eyes and the woodsmen show their open disdain for the practical cowardice of their garrison commander.

Should the player characters decide that this situation is not to their liking, they may attempt Persuade tests in a struggle against Trebellius' Discipline 8 (Expertise 2, Focus 1). If he is convinced to change his mind, he will allow the player characters to go, but cannot be convinced that it would be in the best interests of the garrison to allow anyone else. At this, Hauk stands, re-tying his neckcloth and shrugging back into his tunic. He says he will go. He knows where the Raven village is, and can lead others there.

Another potential reason to cross the river in pursuit is to see if they can kill the strange white man, the "Ghost", and put an end to this particular Pictish incursion, hopefully fragmenting this temporary alliance. At the very least, the player characters can help scout where this Ghost is based out of, so that a larger group can be mobilized and sent against him in force. If a larger party goes in, they will be noticed immediately and will never make it against the combined efforts of multiple tribes of Picts.

If the player characters do not volunteer for this task, Hauk still will. The garrison commander will be convinced by this show of bravery, and he will offer the player characters a purse of Aquilonian lunas (about 5 Gold apiece) to be split evenly among those who return with the captives or proof of their fates. Should the player characters have absolutely no interest in helping captive farmers or in aiding the garrison in discovering the identity of the Ghost, Baron Trebellius will be indifferent to them. They are expected to report for duty and help guard the walls and gates with the others. See *The Ghost Walks* sidebar on page 85 in this case.

If and when the player characters agree to go on the rescue mission across the Thunder River, into Pictland, they are given a short time to equip and ready themselves. They may requisition any harness, armor, and weapons they wish from the armory that stands as a part of the garrison's inner fort, and are provided with ample dried food, if they need it. They can upgrade to better weapons, get additional loads of ammo, healing poultices, and so on, but will be warned that these do not help overmuch for stealthy infiltration of wilderness areas. The trade of the ability to move quickly and with stealth for some modest degree of protection is a bargain few seasoned woodsmen would make.

Pleased that they are going along, Hauk readies a couple of canoes for the player characters to use. If it is not obvious to the player characters, he suggests that the best course of action is to wait until nightfall and then to coordinate with the gate-guards, who will send out a sortie to draw out and engage the Picts gathered outside Velitrium. Simultaneously, Hauk and the player characters can slip off to the south of the fort, heading into the woods with the canoes, running quickly to the water-side where they can cross the river's span and make their way under cover of darkness.

> **DISOBEYING ORDERS**
>
> If the player characters do not attempt (or fail) to convince Baron Trebellius to allow a rescue party, they may simply choose to strike out on their own, climbing over the walls or sneaking through the gate in defiance of orders. Similarly, if they are not part of any plan to rescue the farmers and the captured scout, the player characters will encounter Hauk, later in the morning, as he readies himself for the attempt. In this case, the player characters may even find themselves stealing canoes and fighting guards as they attempt to leave the fort, striking out into the unknown despite being forbidden to do so. The guards may look the other way, if the player characters are sufficiently convincing, wishing them good luck.
>
> In either case, the gamemaster should use the guards from the CONAN corebook on page 317.

The need for stealth and distance is obvious. The Picts are surely watching Velitrium. Crossing Thunder River in full view of any hidden Picts will turn the group into targets, their bodies riddled with Pict arrows long before they reach the other bank.

SOULS DOWN THE RIVER

If he has been spurred into action, when night falls an hour or so later, Baron Trebellius orders several groups of bowmen, foot-soldiers, and scouts to the front gate. They make a show of marching out as if to search along the northern bank of the Thunder River and going to the outlying farms to bring in any needed settlers or survivors. Meanwhile, at the southern end of the fort, the canoes are lowered over the palisade walls, and the player characters and Hauk with them. There will be one canoe for every two player characters and Hauk, with enough space to handle at least five additional characters (the family and Rolf). The plan is to carry the canoes several miles downriver, towards Fort Tuscelan, and then launch once they are safely out of sight of the Picts, crossing the Thunder River there. Once they have landed, they are to strike inland to the Raven village, then returning, they will signal to Velitrium, which will send an escort to bring them safely back.

The gamemaster should call for each player character carrying the canoes to make an Average (D1) Athletics test to carry the canoe successfully at speed through the uncertain footing in the darkened forest to the south-west of Velitrium, and another Average (D1) Stealth test to avoid making any noise. A Complication rolled during either of these tests might alert Picts to the player characters, while two Complications might indicate that they stumble into a Pict ambush, or may fall down, creating a commotion. The gamemaster should use the Picts described on page 81 if necessary, in groups of three or four Minions, with one Toughened Pict. Alternate encounters might involve frightened settlers (no write-ups needed), scouts from Fort Tuscelan (use the write-up for Hauk, or the Guards on page 317 of the **Conan** corebook), or even wild animals.

The passage down the bank should go relatively quickly — unless any incidents occur — and the player characters will be able to put the canoes into the river and begin paddling across. If the gamemaster would like to interject some drama or another conflict at this juncture, the gamemaster may allow them to be readying the canoes when a group of Picts rushes at them from the dark forest, or even attempts to clamber onto the canoes, having seen them and swum a short distance in ambush.

> *Once dark-skinned men had built their huts where that fort stood; yes, and their huts had risen where now stood the fields and log-cabins of fair-haired settlers, back beyond Velitrium, that raw, turbulent frontier town on the banks of Thunder River, to the shores of that other river that bounds the Bossonian marches. Traders had come, and priests of Mitra who walked with bare feet and empty hands, and died horribly, most of them; but soldiers had followed, and men with axes in their hands, and women and children in ox-drawn wains. Back to Thunder River, and still back, beyond Black River, the aborigines had been pushed, with slaughter and massacre. But the dark-skinned people did not forget that once Conajohara had been theirs.*
>
> — "Beyond the Black River"

THE RIVER CROSSING

Crossing the Thunder River can be as uneventful as the gamemaster desires, requiring an Easy (D0) Sailing test for the designated "pilot" of each canoe, and an Average (D1) Stealth test to avoid making too much noise while crossing the river. Canoes are described on page 139 of the **Conan** corebook, should the gamemaster need more information.

Again, this is an instance where the gamemaster should determine if an action scene is needed, and can add spice to this simple passage with a water-based combat encounter, having several Picts in canoes and kayaks see them and move to engage, pulling up alongside once arrows and javelins have been launched. Fortunately for the player characters, the opposite shore of the Thunder River does not have any Picts in waiting, so any Picts on the river will be forced to handle them alone.

The gamemaster should judge the relative strength of the player characters when determining how many Picts. There are two Picts per canoe. An equal number of Minions to the player characters is a sufficient challenge, given the complexity of the encounter. One or more Toughened Picts can be added to the canoes to bolster this encounter, if desired.

Following are some quick guidelines for handling a combat on the water:

- The gamemaster should increase the Difficulty of Sailing tests to reflect the challenge of maneuvering them defensively (or offensively).

- A successful Sailing test should be required to maneuver alongside a Pict canoe so that battle may be engaged.

- The uncertain footing will increase the Difficulty of all combat and movement-related actions by one or more steps, with the pilot of each canoe able to spend Momentum to reduce this penalty on a one-to-one basis.

- A Complication might send the a combatant overboard, with a successful Challenging (D2) Athletics test needed to stay on the canoe, or to catch the edge before falling entirely into the river.

- Two or more Complications might pitch the entire canoe over, causing everyone to make a Challenging (D2) Athletics test to hold onto the canoe rather than plunging underwater haphazardly.

- Fighting underwater increases the Difficulty of all melee tests by an additional step, and the use of any weapon other than a knife becomes problematic. Swinging a weapon underwater is useless, and normally, spears are only useful in still water or for fishing. This is a time for grappling and knife-work, and if engaged in combat while submerged, a character — player or Pict — will need to make a successful Average (D1) Athletics test to keep from sinking.

Additionally, the gamemaster might want to introduce additional challenges in the form of a rocky outcropping, low-hanging tree branches, or treacherous shallows, with a relevant expenditure of Doom.

Once on the other side of the river — whether passage was red-soaked or quiet — the player characters can tie their canoes off and make their way inland, through likely-deserted farmland and across the North Creek, all the way to the Raven village.

COMBING THE WILDERNESS

Once the player characters leave their canoes, they need to pass overland, going into the north Conajahara territory into the area where Hauk knows the Raven village lies. He suggests they head there immediately, rather than trying to track their quarry from the riverbank opposite the place he, Titus, and Rolf encountered the gathering, as this would expose them to too many potential risks. It is a gamble, assuming that the Ravens took the captives to their home village, but it seems the most reliable of options.

It takes a Challenging (D2) Survival test to find the way to the Raven village, with Hauk providing expertise. If none of the player characters are able to track successfully, Hauk can lead them, using his own Senses Field of Expertise, aided by his Frontiersman special ability. Along the way, the gamemaster may choose to throw additional encounters in with Picts, using the guidelines presented earlier. This is normally Raven land, but the Snake, Gwaweli, Hawk, and Tanengi are all present, drawn by the Ghost's call. Avoiding such run-ins requires a successful Struggle, with the player character group's Stealth tests pitted against the Picts' Senses Field of Expertise.

Despite the presence of settlers, here on the other side of the Thunder River, threats other than Picts abound, and if the gamemaster wishes to avoid too many Pict-based encounters, alternate encounters might include bears, wolves, or giant snakes from the **Conan** corebook. Varied enemies might include a Chakan (described in the **Conan** quickstart adventure *To Race the Thunder*, available free online), or other fiendish menaces. However, gamemasters should avoid varying these threats too widely, however, as the focus of this adventure is on the threat posed by the Ghost — Thumocris — and distracting elements might lead the player characters along false trails trying to decipher some alternate threat.

Anywhere they find signs of civilization, such as farmland or trails, they will find destruction, with farms that have been ransacked (but not burnt) and the dead. However, it should become clear that some settlers have been taken alive, with no signs of their passing other than the trail leading into Raven territory.

THE GHOST WALKS

In the event that the player characters choose to remain in Velitrium and do not pursue the Ghost across the Thunder River to rescue his innocent captives, rather than having the adventure end abruptly with this display of un-heroic apathy towards the fate of others, the gamemaster can bring the problem to them. Later that night or the next night, while they are in the long-house sleeping, a veritable horde of Picts will storm Velitrium, led by the Ghost. The Ghost uses sorcery to tear down the front gate. The Picts, surge inside, taking men, women, and children of the settlement prisoner, and setting fire to the palisade walls and wooden buildings of the settlement during their raid.

If the player characters remain unaware of the raid, or are slow to respond, they will be captured by the Picts — or subdued and awaken in bonds — and taken across the Thunder River to the site of Thumocris' sepulcher. There, they will face the threat of being sacrificed to renew his life-force and awaken his body, so that he might return to his own flesh. In this case, should the player characters be unable to free themselves and make a stand, Hauk will arrive stealthily and set them free, sawing through bonds and arming the heroes with captured Pict weapons.

THE VILLAGE OF THE RAVEN

Hauk can lead the players directly to the Raven village or can provide guidance to its location, deep within the increasingly marshy forest. As the player characters approach, the gamemaster should have any trackers in the group attempt an Average (D1) Survival check, with success yielding the knowledge that a great many tracks lead out of the village, and few lead back in. The surrounding wall is intact, but a successful Average (D1) Observation test reveals the tell-tale signs of fire on the logs that made up the wall. A single gate stands wide open, no sign of any watchers. The village itself was a traditional one, a dozen or so huts and a larger gathering hall, likely the chief's dwelling, but now everything has been burnt to ruin, deserted.

The player characters should be able to walk openly into and around the ruined village — likely an unusual experience — without any sense of danger. Nothing is left of value here. Food-stores have been emptied and useful tools and weapons are all gone, even items that would have survived the fire. It looks as if the fire happened relatively recently, within the last few months.

> *Beyond the river the jungle rose like an ebony wall. The distant screech of a panther broke the stillness. The night seemed pressing in, blurring the sounds of the soldiers outside the blockhouse, dimming the fires. A wind whispered through the black branches, rippling the dusky water. On its wings came a low, rhythmic pulsing, sinister as the pad of a leopard's foot.*
>
> — "Beyond the Black River"

The Sigil Out of Time

As the player characters look around, the gamemaster should ask any with 1 or more points of Focus in Sorcery to make an Average (D1) Observation test. Any player characters searching for anything out of the unusual will also find it with a successful Challenging (D2) Observation test. Success gives a sensation of something unsettling, and the source of this feeling quickly becomes obvious: a strange sign scratched on some sort of wooden post in the center of the village, a single, lonely spar of wood jutting upward. It has been untouched by the flames that claimed the rest of the village.

Freshly scratched into the wood, as if by a sharp knife or claw, this mark gives those looking at it overlong an unsettling sensation. It is unreadable, but clearly has some occult significance, and any character succeeding in a successful Challenging (D2) Sorcery test will recognize the language as one of the many magical scripts used in ancient Acheron, though out of place here. A successful Average (D1) Lore test confirms that the dread empire of Acheron had its heyday thousands of years ago, spreading as far north as Aquilonia and Nemedia, south to the border of Stygia, and as far east as Koth. This fearsome empire, driven by sorcery, was crushed by wave after wave of enemies, Stygians foremost among them, and it fell, its people scattered, its cities shattered and forgotten.

Any player character foolhardy enough to touch the emblem will trigger a minor bit of Acheronian sorcery, a harmless use of the spell *Atavistic Voyage*, giving the subject a vast and cosmic vision of the benighted gulfs above and beyond the veil of the sky, and a sense of the presence of fearsome and terrible creatures dwelling in the dark between stars. The vision shifts to the Earth once more, and displays in abstract fashion the spread and fall of the empire of Acheron, focusing on one man who saw it coming, a tall and pale-skinned man with lambent eyes, wearing a masked head-dress and ornaments of strange mottled silver and jewels. His name is whispered, as if by a thousand ghosts…"*Thumocris*". He beckons to the viewer, as if in a summons, and the vision ends with his eyes burning the viewer's sight, as if the player character had inadvertently stared at the sun for a moment too long.

The experience, though seemingly taking several moments, is over in an instant, and those observing the person touching the sigil will see them stiffen and hear the faintest whisper of that name, even if they are not touching it. Any player character experiencing this vision must make an Average (D1) Discipline test, with failure resulting in 1 ☠ of Despair. Hauk will have no part of it, and any wild animals will steer clear of the sigil if they are brought near it.

Should the player characters avoid the Raven village altogether, the gamemaster may wish to introduce the sigil at some other point, perhaps carved into a ceremonial border pole, or even onto the trunk of a tree in the woods surrounding the village, to be encountered while the player characters are on their way to the ruins.

Hot on the Trail

After this, the player characters can examine the ground for tracks, or Hauk can continue to aid them. Finding the trail of the group that took Rolf and the settlers requires a successful Average (D1) Survival test, and it will also become apparent that other small bands of Raven Picts came through here recently with other captives, made obvious by their footwear. Oddly, they are accompanied by another figure wearing boots, like those a soldier or warrior might wear. The group stopped in the village and waited for a short time, forcing the prisoners down on the

THE GHOST OF THUNDER RIVER

ground, then dragging them to their feet to continue on the way. The trail will lead the player characters through the northern marshlands to the Place of the Whispering Fog, several hours away from the village.

The gamemaster can spice up the trip there with encounters (or the threat of near-encounters) with Raven or other Picts on the hunt, Chakan, wild animals, or more long-ranging scouts out of Fort Velitrium, but generally, the closer they get to the ruins, the less activity they will see. If no encounters are desired, the gamemaster can have the player characters arrive in the Place of the Whispering Fog without incident.

THE PLACE OF WHISPERING FOG

Trailing the Raven Picts and the Ghost from the Raven village back to the Place of the Whispering Fog requires a successful Average (D1) Survival test. The thick forest grows quiet, almost sullen as they near it, and at this point, the player characters begin seeing elements of the ancient ruins, fashioned in the style of old Acheron. A successful Daunting (D3) Lore test will reveal the source of these ruins from the shattered, time-worn remnants visible here. The gamemaster should refer to *Prelude: A Torch Shines Across the Aeons* on page 71 for the description of the Place of the Whispering Fog, noting that with the near-revivification of Thumocris and his sorcerous exertion, the place itself seems more active, the mists that permeate it moving more noticeably. There is an almost muffled hum in the air whose origin cannot be placed.

The Picts have lit torches and placed them about the ruins, and the sepulcher has been cleaned of vines and foliage, much of the rubble dragged away and cleared. Some effort has been made to reorganize the place, to ready it for a sorcerous ritual that will call upon entities from the Outer Dark to restore Thumocris' body to life so that he might leave the body of the Bossonian mercenary and Pict-hunter, and re-enter his own flesh.

Outside the sepulcher are a number of Raven Picts equal to the number of player characters, waiting for the ceremony to begin, with them are two of the captives, the settler children, a young boy and girl, bound and gagged. They are sitting on the ground next to one another. The girl is whimpering in terror, while the boy is unconscious. The gamemaster should use the Minion versions of Picts on the Warpath from page 81, supplementing them with one or two Toughened foes. Any approaches to the sepulcher require a successful Struggle pitting Stealth against the Picts' Senses Field of Expertise.

Unless they are all dealt with immediately, at least one of the Picts shouts to alert those inside, or races into the interior of the sepulcher to alert the others. Once alerted, some of the Picts inside rally to protect Thumocris while a number of Minions equal to the number of player characters rush outside to slay the hated interlopers.

Should the player characters spend the time to speak to the children, Mallea, the 10-year old daughter will tell them that her parents are inside, along with the scout, Rolf. Her brother Silus, aged 6, fainted along the way here. She has seen the Ghost without his mask, and she says that he's "like us", a white-skinned Hyborian, although there is something strange about his eyes. He speaks no language she's ever heard before.

THE RITUAL OF REVIVIFICATION

From outside the sepulcher, the player characters will easily be able to hear a chant uttered in the Acheronian language. Inside the main chamber of the sepulcher, the player characters will see Rolf and the two settler parents — Nelius and Glorina, both Aquilonians — bound and on their knees. The interior is lit by sputtering torches and braziers filled with strange-smelling incense, and smoke fills the upper half of the room, drifting out through the holes in the ceiling.

The Ghost stands before a large sarcophagus, its bed at an incline to display its inhabitant, a withered mummy. Holding onto the intended sacrifices is a small group of Picts: those that the players portrayed in the *Prelude: A Torch Across the Aeons*. Any Pict that died in that initial encounter with Thumocris will not be present, and should be replaced by a Toughened Pict (page 81). Like their brethren, they have been *Enslaved* by the Acheronian sorcerer, acting from the inhabited body of Magnus, the Bossonian Pict-killer they trailed into the ruins. They are fanatically loyal to him, and will be so until his destruction.

Should the player characters have dallied overlong before entering the interior of the sepulcher, one of the captives will have been sacrificed (the gamemaster should determine which one). The Ghost holds a shallow bowl of bronze and a dagger, and is using a fingertip to paint blood onto the chest and face of the mummified figure in the sarcophagus. If the player characters arrive in time to stop him, he will be readying the bowl and a ritual dagger for this purpose. Hauk will have no part of witnessing his fellow scout or either of the settlers murdered, and will do whatever he can to stop the ritual from taking place, regardless of how the player characters proceed, even if it means foolhardily leaping into the midst of the sepulcher and fighting the Ghost single-handedly.

If the ritual is interrupted, the Ghost orders the Picts against the player characters, frantically attempting to complete his invocation to the gods of the Outer Dark, asking these horrific entities to restore his desiccated mortal remains to renewed life. He kills each of the captives in rapid succession, taking three rounds for each (killing them, draining their blood, and then painting the mummified corpse with that blood), and then on the tenth round, completes the ritual, opening a rift from which the entity of the Outer Dark can manifest, granting him his wish. Though the Picts are no strangers to diabolical rituals and grisly magic, this is outside anything they have experienced. They, like the player characters and all others witnessing this sight, must attempt a Challenging (D2) Discipline test, with failure inflicting 2 ❂ mental damage, and they must make tests against their Fortitude, suffering one step of Difficulty on all actions for a number of rounds equal to the Resolve lost. Depending on the situation, the Picts may flee outright.

If the ritual is completed, the Ghost removes the headpiece, revealing himself as a Hyborian, brown-haired and likely from the Bossonian Marches, from appearance, though his eyes gleam strangely, seeming to catch the light as if at night-time. He breathes outward, a glimmering wisp of energy emerging from his mouth, and the light disappears from his eyes. The Bossonian collapses and the wisp enters the mouth of the corpse, returning it to life. If the player characters are able to affect this immaterial form, it has only Thumocris' Resolve and Trauma.

Once awakened, the ancient sorcerer's flesh strengthens and life returns to his withered limbs, the chest rising as breath enters it, and his eyes open wide and terrible, his lambent hate-filled glare. If the body rises, it has Thumocris'

> *For as they watched, an awful transmutation became apparent. The withered shape in the sarcophagus was expanding, was growing, lengthening. The bandages burst and fell into brown dust. The shriveled limbs swelled, straightened. Their dusky hue began to fade.*
>
> *— The Hour of the Dragon*

THE GHOST OF THUNDER RIVER

full attributes as described on page 77. It attacks using the same techniques described in the Prelude, but fights without any intention of capturing or subduing his foes.

CONCLUSION

Once Thumocris is defeated, the player characters can free the surviving captives. Depending on the player characters' actions, the sorcerer's defeat may send any remaining Picts retreating back into the woods and eventually to their village, relieved to be free from his domination. Alternately, they will attack in fury, dying to a man. To prevent that possible massacre, the player characters can be joined by late arrivals from Velitrium or scouts from Fort Tuscelan that followed their trail. A small force of armed soldiers or scouts striking quickly after a battle in which the Picts' leader has fallen will break their morale and send them scattering, eager to depart this shunned place.

EXPERIENCE AND REWARDS

Successful completion of the adventure — including the defeat of Thumocris and the cessation of Pict unrest — should be worth roughly 200 experience points for each player character, adjusted by the gamemaster based on roleplaying, problem-solving, and other factors.

Searching the ruins of Thumocris' sepulcher reveals a wealth of items of potential value, ranging from gem-set bones; carvings of wood, ivory, and bone; pieces of occult paraphernalia such as spells etched onto sheets of emerald and other indestructible surfaces; weapons and accoutrements of meteoric iron (mostly rusted), orichalcum, adamantine, and other metals and alloys whose making is long-forgotten. There are skulls, horns, bone, and tusks from animals that no longer roam the world, and have not for millennia. A player character with some knowledge of alchemy might be able to find phials of ancient substances useful in that practice, though many will have dried up or become inert over the ages.

Still other items of value are the offerings made by the Picts and Ligureans over the years, ranging from staves and wands set with sea-shells, flutes and musical instruments made of carved bone, skulls flensed and painted with ornate glyphs, and a wide variety of other items that may be of interest to collectors or sorcerers, but would likely be shunned by civilized folk. The question of how to transport this find back through Pict territory presents a challenge, and the gamemaster may wish to gloss over such logistics and provide the player characters with an amount of Gold commiserate with their efforts, with 2–5 Gold for opportunistic looting on the way out, to 5–10 Gold for a thorough sacking of the place, or even more if the material finds its way to the hands of collectors, rare item dealers, sorcerers, or alchemists.

If word spreads of the player characters' role in this resolution, the gamemaster should award each of them 1 point of Renown. Additionally, if the player characters remain in Velitrium for their Upkeep phase, they will find all costs reduced by 1 Gold and any relevant tests reduced by one step of Difficulty.

CHAPTER 5
THE THOUSAND EYES OF AUMAG-BEL

> *"Your ancestors were men, though strange and monstrous — but gods, ye have become in ghastly fact what my people called ye in scorn! Worms of the earth, back into your holes and burrows! Ye foul the air and leave on the clean earth the slime of the serpents ye have become!"*
>
> — Bran Mak Morn, "The Worms of the Earth"

When a precious amulet is stolen from them by a gang of children, the player characters must pursue the thieves into a strange, subterranean palace. There they encounter hideous creatures born as the result of terrible sorcery. Only after braving these terrifying and deadly encounters will they come face-to-face with the devious Aumag-Bel, prevent the dreadful ritual he seeks to enact, and free the city of his villainous influence.

PROLOGUE

There have been many ages of the earth. Some linger, almost forgotten, but impossible to eradicate. Beneath the city where the player characters have indulged their desire for strong drink and warm company, one might find the remnants of a far more ancient place. The modern over-city has been constructed on top of the ruins of an ancient kingdom, where once lived an abhorrent, worm-like race of sorcerers.

The final remnant of this deadly species is the dark, ominous presence of Aumag-Bel. No one is quite certain how long he has lurked in the darkness, sending forth his juvenile thralls to do his bidding and his armored guards to murder any who would seek to intrude upon his lair. But now, the player characters have arrived in his city, the kind of men and women who just might be able to break his ruthless hold on the surface world.

ARRIVING IN THE CITY

The city in which the player characters arrive is a bustling, mercantile city and the player characters' arrival should reflect that. Perhaps they arrive as the guards of a caravan, having recently completed an adventure. Drunk with success, they come to a settlement looking to carouse and recover from the harshness of battle and the rigors of life in the wild.

Whatever the player characters have been through, they should head to the taverns and brothels of the city, drawn by tales of reckless debauchery and the legendary talents of the local whores — of all genders. Allow the player characters to spend their gold, slake their lusts, and recover their vitality.

Once the player characters have completed their carousing activities, perhaps have them gather in a tavern to nurse their hangovers and prepare for another expedition into the Stygian wilds or the sewers of Aquilonia.

Before the player characters can begin to debate where they should go and what they should do, an arrow thunks

THE THOUSAND EYES OF AUMAG-BEL

THE AMULET

The adventure can be used at any time over the course of a long running campaign — simply initiate it immediately after a period of carousing (See pages 288–289 of the CONAN corebook). If the adventure is run as a one-off, have the player characters meet in a tavern after an epic debauch, or even to discuss an upcoming heist before the opening events discussed below...

However, at this point, it is important to emphasize that one of the player characters possesses a treasured amulet. It is not a new thing — the player character was given it by a deceased parent or an aged mentor, or perhaps it was gained in the character's first coming-of-age adventure — the legendary raid on an Aquilonian outpost or something equally worthy of renown. A gamemaster consciously crafting an epic campaign might like to introduce the amulet as a treasure won from a strange cache during an earlier adventure. It is important to ensure that the player characters will not simply forget about this item should it be taken from them — emphasize either its great sentimental value or its enormous value, or both. Even mention that it bore a vague magical aura — maybe people have expressed an interest in it before, antiquarians recognizing the symbology of an ancient race, long though extinct.

In reality, this amulet is a magical talisman crafted by the hideous worm-like race of whom the titular Aumag-Bel is the only survivor. This talisman, inscribed with a strange, geometric "eye" symbol, is the means by which the worm people prolonged their lives, as the traces of the Outer Dark which cling to the amulet warp the human form in such a way as to make it habitable for the worm-creatures.

Aumag-Bel, withered and ancient now, has been searching for this amulet for a long time. With it, he can finally achieve his transition from his dried, husk of a body to the new one he has chosen. Having sensed that the amulet is within his grasp, Aumag-Bel has kidnapped the person he intends to become: a fierce young woman who is the heir to an immense mercantile fortune.

The player characters know none of this initially, but their ignorance will not last for long.

---

into the center of the table in front of them, sending splinters of wood flying. A group of armed and armored men stand at the entrance to the tavern, one with a nocked bow, the others with weapons drawn.

"Give us the amulet!" they demand. *"Give it to us and Aumag-Bel shall let you live!"*

At the sound of this name, the other patrons in the tavern immediately try to escape, pushing their way through the rear exit. The armed men, guards of Aumag-Bel, single out the player characters. There are a number of guards equal to the number of player characters plus two. They will fight until they are overpowered, and will try to flee if they are clearly going to lose, scattering as quickly as possible.

A Complication in this scene is likely to lead to one of the player characters slipping on a pint of spilled beer and ending up prone — giving an opponent an extra d20 on one of their attacks. Alternatively, an extra guard standing outside in order to prevent anyone from entering the tavern might abandon his post and join the fight.

GUARD OF AUMAG-BEL (TOUGHENED)

Bought with gold, promises of power and the opportunity to exploit both of these, the guards of Aumag-Bel are loyal to the sorcerer and prepared to carry out his orders to the letter. Of course, their association with the sorcerer also leaves them aware of what happens to those who cross him. For this reason, they can appear to be fanatically loyal. In truth, they are simply terrified, but this terror manifests itself in much the same way. Each has a strange geometric symbol tattooed upon his wrist, the "eye" of Aumag-Bel.

ATTRIBUTES

Awareness	Intelligence	Personality	Willpower
9	7	7	7

Agility	Brawn	Coordination
9	9	9

FIELDS OF EXPERTISE

Combat	1	Movement	1
Fortitude	—	Senses	1
Knowledge	1	Social	—

STRESS AND SOAK

- **Stress:** Vigor 9, Resolve 7
- **Soak:** Armor 2 (Brigandine), Courage 2

ATTACKS

- **Spear (M):** Reach 3, 🔱5, Unbalanced, Reach 3, Piercing 1
- **Shield (M):** Reach 2, 3🔱, 1H, Knockdown, Shield 2
- **Steely Glare (T):** Range C, 2🔱 mental, Stun

SPECIAL ABILITIES

- Inured to Fear
- **Terror of Aumag-Bel:** The guards will not surrender and will not allow themselves to be taken prisoner. They would rather die than betray Aumag-Bel and, if captured will impale themselves on their own weapons or otherwise seek to end their lives.

AFTER THE FIGHT

At the end of the fight, the owner of the tavern tries to hurry the player characters out of the door.

"Get out, get out...killing his men in here...I'll not last till night fall..."

If the player characters try and quiz the landlord, he tells them what little he knows:

"Aumag-Bel... he rules this city... everyone is his... and if you've got something he wants... you're best running until your horse dies under you or your feet fall off... And if he wants that there amulet of yours... well, you're better just giving it to him. He'll get it one way... or the other."

THE THOUSAND EYES OF AUMAG-BEL

The player characters can't persuade the landlord to say anything else because he doesn't know anything else. Threats, cajoling or bribery won't work — this is all he knows.

Examining the corpses of the guards reveals little, except tattoos of a strange geometric depiction of an eye on both wrists, found on an Average (D1) Observation test — similar to that found on the amulet the player characters possess, but little else.

A RETURN TO THE STREETS

Outside the tavern, any passersby conspicuously avoid the player characters. Words travels quickly in the city, and the player characters have earned the attention of Aumag-Bel. The door of the tavern has been marked with a savage, red geometric eye shape, the same as that tattoo found on the guard's wrist. It is this that is making strangers in the street give the player characters a wide berth. If the player characters attempt to accost any of those veering wildly away from them, or making apotropaic signs at them to try and ward away the malice of Aumag-Bel, they are quickly shunned and even pushed back by a crowd who do not want to be associated with those who have earned the ire of the city's shadow ruler.

The gamemaster should emphasize the player's sudden pariah status. People mutter *"You are cursed!"* at them beneath their breath. The streets themselves are thronged with people, all carrying an impossible assortment of goods and produce between them, and all of them making their own lives much more complex and difficult by giving the player characters a wide berth. They are all heading for a central market which the player characters can ascertain the location of on an Average (D1) Observation test — the sound of a thousand or more people all haggling and exchanging coin is difficult to mistake.

The player characters can attempt to leave the city at this point, or they can choose to head toward the market in an attempt to find out more about Aumag-Bel.

THE ROBBERY

If the player characters take the advice imparted to them by the barman who threw them out of his establishment and attempt to leave the city, use the following scene. If they ignore the advice and head into the city, or for the market, the gamemaster can reserve this scene for later.

As the player characters head for the nearest gate which leads out from the city, back into the untamed lands beyond, a small group of street urchins approaches. The children seem innocent but poor, ragged, and dirty. They are playing games with one another, perhaps tossing a small ball of leather strips from one to the next with effortless dexterity. At the fringes of the city, there are fewer people around, most already headed to the market in order to trade and haggle. There are a few beggars and the odd drunk, weaving unsteadily to their squalid residence. The children approach the player characters quite boldly and say something like: *"Please can we have the icon which belongs to our master?"*

Depending on what the player characters do at this point, any one of a number of different events can occur:

- If the player characters speak with the children, they will not get much from them beyond the request repeated. If they ask what Aumag-Bel needs with the amulet, one of the children shrugs and say *"So he can change again, of course!"* This is the extent of the information which the children divulge and all they can honestly reveal.

- If the player characters try and push past the children, to grab one of the children, or to attack, the children dodge, but immediately try to steal the amulet. The children are highly skilled thieves and use whatever means they can to obtain the amulet. The children have accomplices hidden behind the player characters — which the very observant might be able to notice on a Daunting (D3) Observation test — while those children before the player characters are distracting them, those behind are quickly arranging themselves for a quick raid on pockets and coin pouches; spotting a child sneaking in from behind requires a player character to make a Dire (D4) Observation test. Even if this fails, the children are highly nimble and light-fingered. Preventing them from gaining the amulet requires a Dire (D4) Awareness or Thievery test. If the thief-children manage to gain the icon, then the chase begins below.

- If the player characters manage to avoid the children's attempts to filch the amulet, another cadre of Aumag-Bel's guards appear, to reinforce the children's attempts. During the chaos of brutal combat, one of the children may get another chance. Alternatively, one of the guards may sacrifice an attack to pluck the amulet from a player character's neck or belt and throw it to a companion, before being skewered.

Complications in this scene might revolve around the player characters being tripped or deceived by the children they encounter — losing weapons, gold, treasured belongings, and anything else they take their eye off! If more guards arrive, a Complication might result in them managing to surprise the preoccupied player characters.

Perhaps by now the player characters are curious about the nature of Aumag-Bel, or simply irritated by his incessant attacks upon their person, so as to try and hunt him down. If the player characters seem to think that upon reclaiming the amulet, their adventure is concluded, then have them hear of the kidnapped daughter of the wealthy local merchant.

"Aumag-Bel has taken her" say the whispers in the marketplace. They also do much more than whisper about how wealthy the merchant is, and that his daughter is both beautiful and enormously popular amongst the people. There will be great rewards for those who rescue her…

A CHASE IN THE MARKET PLACE

If the player characters choose to head into the city, they will almost inevitably end up heading to the market. There are any number of places they might choose to head, but the people they speak to in those locations will be evasive and non-committal. The very bravest refer to the children as being connected to Aumag-Bel and following them may lead them to greater revelations. If asked where the children are to be found, they will always indicate the market.

If the player characters follow this advice and head to the market, they are not directly accosted by the children, and can spend some time exploring the stalls. There are an enormous number of strange and exotic things to find and — if the player characters have any gold left from their debauches — buy. The breeze in the crowded marketplace smells of roast meat and rich, cloying spices. Men and women from every corner of the continent thrust their goods under shopper's noses, demanding that they inspect them or buy them. There are conversations in every language and coin of every variety. The narrow pathways between market stalls are thronged with shouting, gesticulating people and the hectoring tones of merchants and their customers are almost deafening, bartering over the price demanded for any and every item. The place is alive with chatter and the chink of gold.

The player characters might use the opportunity to do some research on who, or what, Aumag-Bel is or even to sell the amulet. If asked about Aumag-Bel, the player characters may be directed to a few sellers of rare scrolls or other esoteric lore. These people, with names such as Harslan of Koth, Briseis the Philosopher, or Lentila of the Order of the Scroll, are the primary potential sources of information about the city and about the amulet. As far as the amulet is concerned, no one will buy it. A few brave and extremely curious antiquarians may examine it, but as soon as they see the geometric eye pattern they will thrust it back at the player characters and refuse to countenance exchanging money for it. They will however, quietly, tell the player characters what they know of Aumag-Bel:

- The strange geometric eye symbol has been found in this area long before the city was even founded. It is associated with the immortal Aumag-Bel, a powerful sorcerer who remained alive through the use of an amulet.

- Some stories, recorded in ancient records which the antiquarian has seen in the vast, sinister libraries of Stygia, maintain that this symbol was associated with the ancient, tyrannical ruler of a kingdom whose palace once stood beneath the foundations of the city the player characters are now within.

- Although the kingdom fell, the image of the eye never disappeared, and the name of Aumag-Bel is still whispered through the alleyways of this city, a secret ruler, eternally present and ever watchful.

This, in various different versions, is all the player characters are able to learn from the itinerant scholars who attend the market; however, they will be told that Aumag-Bel's children stalk the market, stealing gold or food and occasionally marking victims who are taken and never seen again. What happens to those unlucky enough to fall into the clutches of Aumag-Bel's guards is uncertain, but there are whispers of screams in the darkness beneath the city. The vendors may also mention *"The thousand eyes of Aumag-Bel"* and point the player characters to a place where the geometric eye shape has been carved into a wall or even into the ground.

THE THOUSAND EYES OF AUMAG-BEL

Once the player characters have finished exploring the market, the gamemaster should have one of them attempt a Daunting (D3) Observation test. If the player character doesn't notice, then the child-thieves steal the amulet on a Challenging (D2) Coordination test. Once the amulet has been stolen, the player characters can make an Average (D1) Observation test to notice the children running away and their prize with them. A Challenging (D2) Observation test determines what has been stolen.

If the player characters do pass the initial Observation test, the player characters notice two children creeping towards them, concealing themselves beneath the table-stalls laden with the assembled produce of the world. If the player characters notice the children, then half a dozen children suddenly rush them from all directions, emerging from under other tables and slipping between members of the crowd. At this stage, the gamemaster should run the theft scene detailed in the previous section (See *The Robbery*, page 93).

THIEF-CHILD (MINION)

Small, dressed in rags and clearly used to life on the streets and the hardships which that necessitates, these children may initially look as though they can be simply discounted. What else does one do with the flotsam of the city? But, be careful. These children are wily, cunning, and driven by their fear of Aumag-Bel and their need for food. This is a powerful combination.

ATTRIBUTES

Awareness	Intelligence	Personality	Willpower
9	6	7	7

Agility	Brawn	Coordination
9	6	9

FIELDS OF EXPERTISE

Combat	1	Movement	3
Fortitude	1	Senses	3
Knowledge	1	Social	—

STRESS AND SOAK

- **Stress:** Vigor 3, Resolve 4
- **Soak:** Armor —, Courage 1

ATTACKS

- **Punch (M):** Reach 1, 2 🦅, 1H
- **Thrown Rock (R):** Range M, 3 🦅, Improvised, Stun

SPECIAL ABILITIES

- **Agile:** Each thief-child gains 1 bonus Momentum on any Movement test.

LET'S OVERTURN THESE TABLES

If the thief-children manage to procure the amulet, they instantly break away from the confusion and hubbub they have caused and flee from the player characters as quickly as they can, with their prize. The gamemaster decides how many thief-children the player characters need to keep track of (although any more than six is likely to make the gamemaster's life more difficult). The gamemaster could use a token to keep track of which thief-child has the amulet, or each time a thief-child is caught, the gamemaster can roll at random to determine if that one has the amulet.

The thief-children work together to avoid the player characters, passing the stolen item from one to another. Keeping track of this should be a difficult task. Each time the player character nearest to the thief-child with the item might conceivably witness it being passed along, the player character must make an Average (D1) Observation test. If that fails, then the next time a switch is made, the Difficulty is elevated by one step, to a maximum of Dire (D4). If the player characters manage to capture the thief-child carrying the item, the thief-child throws the item to a nearby companion. Plucking the item from the air requires a Daunting (D3) Coordination test. If the player characters manage to apprehend the thief-child and retrieve the amulet, the gamemaster should skip the rest of the chase scene and move directly to the *Den of the Black Lotus* (see page 97).

As the thief-children dash through the marketplace, the player characters can attempt to follow and catch up with them. The marketplace is extremely crowded, with a number of obstacles which the player characters have to overcome as they pursue the thief-children.

The thief-children know the market as though they had a map of it tattooed on their skins. If the player characters want to keep up, they have to negotiate their way through the maze of different stalls, shops, and other, less salubrious areas of the market and its surroundings. In each scene, for every Momentum the player character generate, they may spend 1 Momentum in an attempt to grab one of the thief-children on a Daunting (D3) Athletics or Melee test.

A Complication in this scene can mean that the player characters are accosted by one of the stall holders demanding payment for some goods damaged during the chase. This should delay the player characters and prevent them from making a grab for one of the thief-children during this turn. Alternatively, a newcomer to the city might confront the player characters for chasing children (not realizing that these children are the servants of a powerful sorcerer).

The gamemaster should treat each of the following areas as separate scenes, with its own set of Complications. Momentum spent to avoid one Complication cannot be used to avoid one encountered in the next scene.

A Slave Trader's Chain of Human Wares

Manacled about the throat and feet, these slaves obstruct the player characters as they try to close the distance between themselves and their quarry. They have to be agile as a panther to avoid becoming tangled in lengths of chain, leaping over the long chain links or knocking the overseer down as he tries to restrain the unfortunates under his control.

Player characters must succeed in a Challenging (D2) Acrobatics test in order to avoid the unfortunate slaves as they crowd the path. If the player characters fail, then the player characters lose 1 point of Momentum generated during the chase. If one of the player characters takes the time to break the slaves' chains on a successful Challenging (D2) Brawn test, or with a 2 point Momentum spend, the gamemaster may choose award to the player character 1 Fortune point.

A Blacksmith's Forge

The thief-child darts under the black iron anvil, slipping through a rack of poorly-made swords and between the legs of the amazed smith. The player characters must dodge around the forge entirely or squeeze themselves awkwardly through the close, dingy space, requiring an Average (D1) Athletics test.

This is the easiest way through the smithy. However, if the player characters choose to simply avoid the obstacles, they forgo the chance to catch the thief-children ahead of them. Player characters who are particularly athletic might attempt to leap the forge, requiring a Daunting (D3) Athletics test. A successful vaulting of the forge immediately allows the player characters a chance to grab one of the children on a Daunting (D3) Resistance test. A failure, however, inflicts 3 damage to the player characters as the intense heat of the forge burns them.

Ambush!

The thief-children dart into a narrow alleyway, the entrance of which is shrouded by a particularly dense collection of market stalls. As the player characters follow them, exerting every ounce of energy they possess to close the distance, rocks suddenly begin to rain down upon them! It is a trap! Allow the player characters a Daunting (D3) Observation test to see if they notice the ambush the thief-children are leading them into. Those who succeed have the opportunity to dodge the first fusillade of sling stones and mud bricks that are slung at them. Those who fail do not get the chance to avoid the rocks and are hit by a fistful of small rocks, doing 1 (after armor and Soak).

Passing through the alleyway in such a way as to avoid any further deluges of rock or firing back at the attacking thief-children lets the thief-children get further away, meaning that any chance to grab one of them is lost. Spending 1 point of Momentum allows a player character to barrel through a second hail of stones, in order to make a grab at one of the thief-children — doing so, however, means that the player character loses the opportunity to dodge and is hit by a handful of stones at 1 per handful.

The Priests of Mitra

In every city, there are men and women seeking to make others believe as they do. It is no different here. What is more unfortunate for the player characters is that a group of devotees of Mitra, clad in the traditional robes of their god and swinging the incense holders which purify the air so that Mitra may deign to look down upon the unworthy, make a difficult obstacle for anyone, especially burly warriors. The thief-children, upon reaching the Mitrans, do not attempt to simply slip past them. Instead, they incline their heads piously, receiving a brief benediction and a pat before they are let go. However, when attempting to get past the priests, the player characters are beset by supplicatory hands, asking for donations to the Temple of Mitra, or conversion to his worship.

Pushing their way roughly through the priests alienates the crowd in the marketplace and may even bring the curses of Mitra down upon the player characters. If the player characters do attempt to simply shoulder through the priests or otherwise react violently, the gamemaster should earn a Doom point. If the player characters speak with the priests and explain their predicament and the righteousness of their mission, on a Daunting (D3) Persuade test, the Mitran priests are convinced to apprehend one of the thief-children as they slink away and may even help the player characters persuade the thief-child to assist the player characters — allowing player characters to make a Persuade test reduced by one step of Difficulty.

> ### CATCHING A THIEF
>
> If the player characters manage to catch one of the thief-children, convincing them to betray Aumag-Bel (whom they, quite rightly, fear) and their fellow thieves (the only family they know) should not be an easy task.
>
> The player characters can go about it in a number of ways — a noble or aristocratic player character might be able to Command a child to assist them, on a Daunting (D3) test; given a suitably impressive speech of course. Alternately, with a successful Daunting (D3) Lore test, a player character might be able to persuade a thief-child that the player characters truly have the means to defeat Aumag-Bel, referring to the legend and history.
>
> The gamemaster is encouraged to let the player characters come up with imaginative means of ensuring the thief-child's help, or if all else fails, the player characters can secure it at the cost of 2 points of Doom.

THE DEN OF THE BLACK LOTUS

The thief-children disappear into the fug-filled confines of an underground drug den, concealed within which is also the entrance to Aumag-Bel's under city: the remains of the ancient palace upon which this city has been founded. Alternately, a captured thief-child leads the player characters into the enclave, cautiously, her fear of Aumag-Bel only just superseded by her fear of the player characters who have caught her.

The Den of the Black Lotus is a series of cramped, squalid rooms. A thick, pungent fog fills the air, concealing the way ahead and making every movement enervating. After a few minutes within the Den, each player character must make a Challenging (D2) Resistance test, or suffer 1 of mental Stress from the addictive nature of the Black Lotus. The thick fug of lotus smoke however makes visibility difficult and, as a result, all Difficulty checks relating to sight should be made at one step higher than would otherwise be the case.

The addicts who populate these rooms are of disparate ages and origins — the black lotus is indiscriminate in whom it enslaves — but are uniform in their dishevelment and hopelessness. The player characters can see the dead lassitude which lurks behind their eyes. Open mouths with few teeth try to form words, but fail more often than not. These unfortunates are the wreckage of humanity and, if the player characters do demand information from them, they gaze, bewildered and impassive, straight at them. If the player characters resort to violence in order to coerce answers from the docile figures sprawling in the detritus of their own habits — curled and flaking lotus leaves, the residue of sap clinging to the walls, the husks of burnt petals — they simply apologize and assume a fetal position. They are long used to abuse from Aumag-Bel's guards and are too broken and cowed to offer anything beyond vague apologies and beg for more lotus. An offer of an extra hit of the Black Lotus can procure stammered directions to the tunnel, leading below the Lotus Den.

If the player characters managed to capture one of the thief-children, she scarcely glances at the atrophying forms, huddled in rags at the edges of the corridors. Only if one of the lotus-eaters gets in the way of the child or the player characters — perhaps clawing at their legs and importuning them for more lotus — the thief-child treats them contemptuously, kicking at the wretched form and berating him fiercely.

Further on, the squalid rooms of the Lotus-eaters become squalid rooms lined with blankets, where Aumag-Bel's thief-children sleep, and, judging by the rotting food and feces in the room, do everything else that nature requires.

> ### THERE BUT FOR THE GRACE OF MITRA...
> A gamemaster committed to drawing out the strain of dark humor which infects Howard's work might imply that the lotus-addicts show signs of having been thief-children themselves at some time, perhaps they have been branded as thieves, or have other distinguishing features which suggest they were once caught and punished; the only escape from the life Aumag-Bel subjects his followers to ends in addiction, ruin, and death. Ridding the city of him will be a genuine civic service. Though, how the player characters feel about being useful members of society will vary from group to group...

There are only a few thief-children in the three chambers which constitute their quarters. The rest are out plying their trade. The few who are here are too surprised by the player characters' presence to do much. If the player characters are being guided by one of their number, the thief-children watch the characters warily and may answer a few questions before assuming a watchful silence. If the player characters have found their way to these quarters unaided, one or two of the thief-children attempts to raise an alarm. The player characters can stop this via physically clamping a hand across the child's mouth on a Challenging (D2) Athletics test to leap across the room, followed by a Challenging (D2) Resistance test to restrain the child and prevent him or her for calling out. A player might also be able to persuade a child not to call for the guards on a Challenging (D2) Command or Persuade test.

If the player characters cannot prevent the children from raising an alarm, then their cries draw the guards from the next section away from the entrance to the under-city. They fight the player characters in the thief-children's quarters, leaving unguarded the tunnel the player characters are searching for.

If the player characters do manage to silence the thief-children before the guards are summoned, then they can persuade them to help (see the *Catching a Thief*, page 96) and elicit some information from them about Aumag-Bel and the dangers they have yet to face.

What the Children Know

- Aumag-Bel lurks below, in his palace, at the end of the long dark tunnel.
- The thief-children never go into the dark tunnel. Strange things lurk there, hideous creatures which feast on human flesh. Sometimes they can hear them, shambling in the darkness and once, just once, they

A SUBSTITUTE SACRIFICE

If the player characters have already retrieved the amulet from the child-thieves at this stage, the thief-children imply that the young woman was kidnapped, as far as they could tell, as a stand-in for the amulet. Reclaiming the amulet has not ensured that Aumag-Bel's threat is stymied, far from it. Instead, the methods by which Aumag-Bel intends to achieve his unguesle aims have simply become grislier than might previously have been the case!

glimpsed terrible twisted, inhuman features in the flicker of torchlight.

- Guards protect the entrance of the tunnel but within, there is no torchlight.

- Sometimes, people are taken into the darkness of the tunnel to meet Aumag-Bel. Very few return. Those that do join the black lotus devotees who inhabit the remoter chambers of the Den.

- Quite recently, the guards were sent into a frenzy of activity by Aumag-Bel's commands to seek the precious amulet that had "returned" to the city.

- The guards also returned a day or two ago with a young woman they had kidnapped. The thief-children remember this vividly as the young woman fought the guards bitterly before being dragged into the tunnel, biting and punching and grasping at the guards' weapons. This kind of passionate will to live is something the thief-children have not seen in many years.

During this scene, the gamemaster might have one of the docile drug-addicts suddenly rear up, clutching at one of the player characters, leading to a brief scuffle. Alternatively, the player characters might breathe in too much of the black lotus and suffer a Stunned effect for the next round of combat they become embroiled in.

PASSAGE TO THE UNDER-PALACE

This scene starts the descent into Aumag-Bel's subterranean kingdom and sets the player characters on the final path to their confrontation with the arch-sorcerer who has caused them such difficulties. At the end of a long narrow corridor, leading away from the children's quarters, a tunnel slopes away into darkness. Despite a few guttering torches, the light in this area is poor. The darkness emanating from the tunnel seems to drain light from the air around the player characters. The corridor is filled with shadows in which the player characters might conceal themselves, but which make certain tasks much harder — for this scene, all tests are one step of Difficulty higher. The stone and exposed, hard-baked earth that compose the tunnel are decorated with the strange geometric eye symbol which the guards have tattooed on their wrists. At the entrance to the tunnel are six guards, each lounging confidently against the tunnel walls, waiting to be relieved.

If the player characters did not manage to prevent the thief-children from raising the alarm in the previous scene, then the there should only be one guard left who flees from the adventurers, as detailed below.

If the player characters managed to secure the help of one of the thief-children in the previous scene then he or she leads them to the entrance of the "long dark tunnel" which leads to Aumag-Bel and of which the children are so afraid. The child warns the player characters about the waiting guards if the player characters have sought to comfort or reassure the child, or if the player characters are prepared to spend a point of Momentum. If so, then the player characters need only pass an Average (D1) Stealth test to launch a surprise attack upon the indolent guards.

If the player characters didn't manage to persuade the thief-children to assist them, then the presence of a black tunnel appearing at the end of a corridor ought to be something of a hint of the next steps. If the player characters have not been warned about the guards, then initially, have each player make a Dire (D4) Observation test to see if they notice the guards ahead. The murkiness of the corridor accounts for the difficulty of this test. Should the player characters fail, then the player characters must pass a Daunting (D3) Athletics test to see if they have managed to avoid making enough noise for the guards to be able to pinpoint their location and launch a surprise attack of their own. If the player characters do notice the guards at a distance, have each player make a Daunting (D3) Stealth test. Any failures alert the guards and remove the possibility of a surprise attack; the fight should then proceed as normal.

The guards are identical to those the player characters have already fought, and act in much the same way, with one exception. Once the guards are reduced to the final combatant, this last man standing stares at the player characters wide-eyed and frightened for a moment, as if considering continuing to fight. He then throws down his spear and flees into the tunnel. If the player characters try to chase him down, let them proceed into the mouth of the pitch-black tunnel hot on his heels, but they won't be able to catch him in the darkness.

Once the player characters have entered the tunnel, have the player characters each make a Challenging (D2) Awareness test. Should they pass, they can hear the guard running somewhere ahead of them. There is an abrupt

THE THOUSAND EYES OF AUMAG-BEL

gasp, a wet gurgling noise, and the crunch of bone and sinew. Then silence. Have the player characters make a Challenging (D2) Discipline test at this point, taking 1⚅ of mental damage on a failure.

A Complication might lead to player characters becoming disarmed, or even falling into the pitch darkness of the tunnel, keeping them out of the fight for every turn they cannot pass a Daunting (D3) Observation test.

THE DARK LABYRINTH

The tunnels which connect the city above and the abandoned, forgotten palace below are long and dark and hard to navigate. The blackness is virtually impenetrable. Even with torches, all tasks and tests are carried out at 1 higher difficulty if done at close range, three levels of Difficulty higher at medium range, and all tests beyond medium range are performed at an Epic (D5) level of Difficulty. A player character succeeding in an Average (D1) Insight test can ascertain that this darkness is more than natural. The sorcery of Aumag-Bel may have allowed him to survive these many centuries, a foul cancer at the heart of the city built upon what was once his, but it is beginning to warp the world around it; stone walls twisting into strange geometries and the earth rupturing as though from some tremendous pressure beneath.

As the player characters progress through the darkness, have them make regular awareness tests on an Average (D1) or a Challenging (D2) level of Difficulty. Successes draw their attention to ugly, sucking, rasping noises in the darkness or the sound of shuffling feet. The walls are coated in something that feels like mucus. It drips in hideous globules from the ceiling, and it oozes from the walls.

After a while, the gamemaster should emphasize that the player characters are losing all sense of direction, unsure which way is forward and which would lead them back to the Den of the Black Lotus. They are hopelessly lost, and their only hope is to press on. Upon making this revelation, have the player characters make a Challenging (D2) Discipline test, with 2⚅ of despair as they are forced to confront the apparent hopelessness of their position.

Finally, after the player characters begin to feel as though they are lost forever in the impenetrable darkness of the tunnels, on an Average (D1) Observation test, the player characters notice a light beginning to flicker ahead of them. The closer they get, the stronger the light becomes, although within the darkness of the tunnel, it still appears weak and trembling even as the player characters draw nearer.

The player characters emerge from the darkness into the first room of Aumag-Bel's palace and, more importantly, into sudden blazing light. The supernatural darkness which infested the tunnel falls away, and the resurgent light is dazzling. And then something moves…

A Complication might lead to player characters walking hard into a wall or losing their footing and taking 2⚅ of physical damage.

THE TWISTED SERVANTS OF AUMAG-BEL

The shambling, hideous forms which emerge from narrow apertures set into the walls of the chamber the player characters have entered are those guards who have been in Aumag-Bel's service too long. As soon as the player characters enter the chamber, they are greeted by a chorus of low animal moans. The Servants of Aumag-Bel stir and begin moving towards them.

The horrific powers which the sorcerer has used to keep himself alive over many hundreds of years warp the world around him and have a terrible effect on those nearby. The magic which Aumag-Bel draws from the Outer Dark twists and distorts nature in various, hideous fashions. Most of the guards in Aumag-Bel's service are not aware of the hideous transformation which awaits them, and very few survive the metamorphosis. Those few that do are Aumag-Bel's watchdogs, their minds destroyed by prolonged exposure to the raw stuff of the cosmos, their bodies misshapen. All they can do is attack those whom their ablated senses do not recognize as being under their master's protection.

The first glimpse the player characters have of the creatures is a horrific revelation of the cost that magic extracts from those unlucky enough to confront it. Any who witness this must make a Daunting (D3) Discipline test or else suffer 1⚅ Despair from this revelation.

The Servants of Aumag-Bel are slow, weak, and stupid, but they attack in numbers. They clutch at the player characters with arms which have become tentacles, ridged with corrupted flesh. Many of them seem to lack heads, these having somehow descended into the rest of the pulpy mass of torso from which stunted legs with an assortment of toes and claws and bone extrude. The Servants cannot be reasoned with and are immune to any psychological effects. They are almost entirely mindless — once human creatures who have been reduced to a single focused hunger which Aumag-Bel uses on his enemies and those unfortunate enough to stumble into his clutches.

The fight can take place across a number of the chambers which make up Aumag-Bel's subterranean palace. The player characters can use ancient statues and the remnants of other art for cover, or even push them over onto the Servants for 5⚅ on a successful, Daunting (D3) Brawn test. The palace chambers are illuminated with a series of torches mounted in sconces and iron chandeliers which hang from the ceiling. All of these can be used against the Servants quite effectively (see page 152 of the **Conan** corebook).

Fortunately for the player characters, their efforts have already thinned out the ranks of the guards whom Aumag-Bel can call upon, so none arrive at the sounds of the raging battle. Instead, once the player characters have dispatched the Servants, they are finally within the limits of Aumag-Bel's hidden palace and almost able to reclaim the amulet that Aumeg-Bel stole from them and is about to use for a truly dreadful purpose.

As a Complication, the gamemaster might have a Servant reanimate (though with only 1 Wound left), or have one of the Servants catch on fire accidentally and set one of the player characters on fire as a result.

If the player characters examine the corpses of the Servants, a successful Challenging (D2) Insight test reveals that they are, or rather were, Aumag-Bel's guards once. Magic has twisted them into this hideous, blasphemous form. Whatever power it is that Aumag-Bel wields is dark and dangerous, and it must be stopped. The torches light the way along a series of corridors, all of which lead toward the center of the palace.

> The Lion strode through the Halls of Hell;
>
> Across his path grim shadows fell
>
> Of many a mowing, nameless shape —
>
> Monsters with dripping jaws agape.
>
> The darkness shuddered with scream and yell
>
> When the Lion stalked through the Halls of Hell.
>
> — Old Ballad, "The Scarlet Citadel"

THE SERVANTS OF AUMAG-BEL (TOUGHENED)

Broken, warped, and racked by exposure to the most hideous of sorceries — these creatures were once Aumag-Bel's guards, and, some of them at least, were once the child-thieves who procured the gold with which the sorcerer bought his power and continued survival. Now, they are a mass of extrusions, ruptured flesh. Hideous to behold, the mindless creatures hunger for the flesh of those who are as they once were.

ATTRIBUTES

Awareness	Intelligence	Personality	Willpower
5	3	—	12
Agility	Brawn		Coordination
6	10		9

FIELDS OF EXPERTISE

Combat	3	Movement	—
Fortitude	3	Senses	1
Knowledge	—	Social	—

STRESS AND SOAK

- **Stress:** Vigor 10, Resolve 12
- **Soak:** Armor 2 (Leathery Skin), Courage 2

ATTACKS

- **Flailing Blow (M):** Reach 1, 4 🗡, Grappling (see *Dragged Under*, below)

SPECIAL ABILITIES

- **Dragged Under:** If three or more Servants surround a single player, then the Servants gain the Grappling quality.
- **Inured to Fear and Pain**

THE FORGOTTEN PALACE

On the way to confront Aumag-Bel, the palace complex through which the player characters wander is riddled with thick, unnatural mold which falls from the walls in sodden clumps. A viscous, gelatinous substance drips from cracks in cyclopean stone walls. There are more stone statues, some depicting men and women of great beauty, others depicting wizened, hybrid things with protuberant eyes and flabby, reptilian tongues. An Average (D1) Observation test reveals a series of mosaics hidden behind the thick, rotten vegetation which descends from the ceiling. The mosaics tell a strange, disjointed story from which portions are missing. The main elements seem to consist of a strange race of hideous, worm-like beings (possibly those depicted in the statuary but it is quite difficult to tell) who emerged from the earth and established a kingdom on the surface. A ferocious war is then depicted, one fought between the worm-beings and some sort of primitive human race.

The gamemaster should emphasize the difficulty of determining whether these primitive human forms are simian or ophidian. All that is obvious is their humanoid form and their use of weapons in a fashion which the worm people could not stand against, although the hideous casualties which the worm-beings managed to inflict are depicted in horrifying detail. The final intact mosaic depicts the worm-beings withdrawing from the world and burrowing back into the earth.

The city through which the player characters wander is unsettling and beautiful in equal measure. The architecture is vast and ancient and incredibly sophisticated. Even those bits which have crumbled after the slow work of probing roots and millennia show evidence of impressive masonry techniques and advanced technology. What is unsettling are the strange statues and reliefs which leer down at the player characters from the walls. There are also holes bored into the walls and floor, about the thickness of a man's arm and, for any player who wishes to stick his or her arm in there, slippery with some strange, iridescent substance. Beyond this, however, the holes are too narrow to go further into and too narrow to see down into.

In every room and corridor, the most common symbol the player characters see is the geometric eye sigil tattooed on the guard's wrists. It is ubiquitous here and, while some of the sigils are clearly recent and crudely etched into the stone, others have been carefully inscribed and bear beautiful detail.

As the player characters traverse the city, touch on the unearthly beauty of the sculpted ceilings and walls which surround the player characters as they pass into areas of even greater, though spoiled, luxury. Bas-reliefs now replace the statues and mosaics. These depict the same odd combination of worm-beings and beautiful human beings which the statues represent. Sprawling roots and earth cover everything, but the beauty of the decoration is still obvious.

The tracks of their quarry are not hard for the player characters to follow — an Average (D1) Survival test lets the player characters know they are on the right trail. Clearly the guards (or the children) who brought Aumag-Bel's amulet did not believe they would be followed, and their footprints are extremely clear and easy to track. A Momentum spend lets the player characters recognize the tracks of another set of guards, who came through, quite recently, plainly carrying a burden — the young woman the children, or the merchants in the market, mentioned?

After the player characters have spent enough time amongst the ruins of the Palace, have one of them make a Challenging (D2) Observation test. A success alerts the player characters to the sounds of intense activity, heavy footsteps, and an unusual, keening chant from somewhere up ahead. If the player characters do not manage to hear this and instead stumble into Aumag-Bel's altar unprepared, then their opponents get to attack first without the need for the gamemaster to spend any Doom points for the privilege.

IN THE LAIR OF AUMAG-BEL

As the player characters enter the vast altar-chamber, they behold the vast ziggurat of stone which rises from the floor, almost thirty feet in height. All four sides of the ziggurat are staggered into stairs. The ceiling in the room is almost too high to be seen but on a Challenging (D2) Observation test, the player characters can make out a vast, elaborate carving which seems to depict the worm-beings seen in the earlier mosaic, sliding down a man's throat. Fires in massive braziers blaze in every corner of the room and the walls of the chamber, unlike the rest of the palace, are blank save for a single image — the geometric eye symbol, etched into the stone in enormous dimensions.

An Average (D1) Observation test also allows the player characters to identify, for the first time, Aumag-Bel. Atop the ziggurat, a shambling, shadowy form is moving around slowly and awkwardly. Shuffling from a stone table on which are placed a number of cruel looking obsidian tools, the sorcerer bends over the prostrate form of his intended victim, a young beautiful woman with lustrous dark hair. She is well-dressed and, though unconscious and chained to the altar, seems unharmed. Aumag-Bel is hooded and only a pair of wizened hands can be seen extending from a long, crimson robe.

At the sound of the player characters' entrance, Aumag-Bel glances toward the chamber entrance and issue a low keening whistle, quite unlike anything the player characters have ever heard: wild and shrill and inhuman. At this sound, eight of the hideous, twisted Servants of Aumag-Bel begin to clamber ponderously from pits dug into the ziggurat. The Servants cannot go far; chains force them to remain on the ziggurat but they are hard to dodge should the player characters begin to ascend it.

Around the bottom of the ziggurat are eight of Aumag-Bel's guards. If the player characters heard the activity in the chamber and proceeded stealthily, then the guards who are stationed around the base of the ziggurat are caught unawares and unprepared, allowing the player characters to gain a surprise attack should they choose to take it. If the player characters failed to detect the activity in the last scene, then the guards are ready for them and rush them as soon as they enter.

In the midst of the combat, the player characters should again be made aware of a low keening chant, becoming ever more frenzied and ever stranger in its tone and content. Half-formed, half-remembered words can now be discerned amongst the noise, stirring strange notions and images in the player's minds — visions of strange cities threaten to fill their minds and the taste of cold earth swamp their mouths. If a player character is not in the midst of combat, he must make a Fear test or take 2 ◈ of mental damage. Player characters who are in the midst of combat must also make a Fear test as these tainted, racial-memories flit through their minds, but they only take 1 ◈ of mental damage, as they are otherwise engaged.

Once the guards have been dealt with, the player characters can now begin to ascend the ziggurat, readying themselves for the final confrontation with Aumag-Bel. The ziggurat is steep and, of course, patrolled by the lumbering forms of the Servants. There are eight Servants of Aumag-Bel who descend the stairs to engage with the player characters, as soon as they mount the ziggurat. The Servants keep close to Aumag-Bel, acting as a bodyguard and attempting to drive the player characters away, as the ritual

THE THOUSAND EYES OF AUMAG-BEL

approaches its climax. They will also attempt to block any ranged weapon directed at Aumag-Bel, flinging themselves in front of arrows, darts or slung stones. Whenever a player character seeks to fire a ranged weapon at Aumag-Bel, the nearest servant will automatically perform an Athletics test to intercept the projectile. The gamemaster should spend Doom points freely to represent the extra vitality which the Servants possess, being so close to their magical source — it may have corrupted them, but it also serves to invigorate them.

Any player character that suffers 3 or more points of physical damage in a single attack from one of the Servants must also roll a Challenging (D2) Coordination test to avoid being knocked down the stairs to the bottom of the ziggurat for a further 2 🜚 of physical damage.

As they reach the pinnacle of the ziggurat, the player characters should ready themselves to meet their nemesis.

A Complication might lead to a player character sustaining a bleeding wound, which costs 1 point of Vigor for each round it goes untreated by a Challenging (D2) Healing test. Alternatively, a weapon might shatter or a bow string might break.

THE DREAD SORCERER, AUMAG-BEL

Aumag-Bel turns to face the player characters once they reach the top of the ziggurat. He lowers his hood to reveal the face of a withered, twisted old man. He is completely bald, and it seems as though the skin stretched over his skull is about to burst apart, revealing white bone. His face twists into a snarl as the player characters draw near, and he spits his defiance at them.

If the player characters lost the amulet, Aumag-Bel lifts it up, letting it twist and dangle in the torchlight, announcing to the intruders:

"You have pursued this talisman with admirable tenacity… it would not have availed you, you know. It is a thing of my people and only we can use it. And I am the last of them. I am the last of my race and I must survive, surely, that we may rise again and claim your world as our own, as your claimed ours as your birth right. Back, dogs, or feel the ancient power of my race!"

If the player characters managed to keep hold of the amulet and have secured it somewhere far away from Aumag-Bel, he will say the following:

"You have taken the ancient relic of my people. The last sacred object which bound me to them. It matters not. The ritual can still be completed without it. I will not die here and neither will the ancient, noble race of whom I am the last."

With these defiant words, Aumag-Bel heads directly towards the unconscious woman on the altar. He should be holding a strange obsidian device, something like a wide tube. A Daunting (D3) Observation test should allow a player to notice what looks horribly like tooth marks bitten into the stone itself. This is the means by which Aumag-Bel, in his true, real form, intends to transfer himself into a new host.

Aumag-Bel is a parasite, one of the ancient worm creatures depicted in the various works of art decorating the palace complex. He has survived by attaching himself to a number of human hosts which he uses to sustain himself, using the last vestiges of his people's magic to assemble a criminal empire in the heart of the city he lives beneath. At this point, Aumag-Bel's current host is beginning to crumble and fail. Despite this, however, the magic and energy of Aumag-Bel still renders the host a formidable opponent. Aumag-Bel hopes to transfer himself into the healthy body of the young, unconscious woman on the altar. Aumag-Bel's magic is extremely powerful, but he is loath to use it, in case he should exhaust himself before he has a chance to complete the ritual which allows him to survive and be reborn.

Aumag-Bel initially heads for the woman on the altar, trying to complete the ritual as quickly as possible. As soon as the player characters launch an attack, however, he turns on them and attacks savagely, at first with the melee weapons he is holding and later with his magic.

A Complication might lead to a player character freezing in horror and dropping to their knees, aghast at the power of their foe, missing their turn. The earth might shift beneath their feet, leaving them prone.

THE HOST OF AUMAG-BEL (NEMESIS)

The fleshly form of Aumag-Bel is a formidable sorcerer and foe. Although this form has begun to wither, the strain of his dark magic proving far too much for poor mortal flesh to withstand, he remains capable of the most terrifying feats of sorcery. The power which resides in Aumag-Bel is capable of pushing even the decrepit host body to the limits of human abilities. Defeating him will require strength, fortitude, and no small amount of luck.

ATTRIBUTES

Awareness	Intelligence	Personality	Willpower
5	13	8	14

Agility	Brawn	Coordination
10	9 (2)	10

FIELDS OF EXPERTISE

Combat	2	Movement	3
Fortitude	1	Senses	3
Knowledge	3	Social	—

STRESS AND SOAK

- **Stress:** Vigor 12, Resolve 15
- **Soak:** Armor 2 (Ritual Jewelry), Courage 2

ATTACKS

- **Obsidian Knife (M):** Reach 1, 4 🦅, 1H, Vicious 1
- **Obsidian Ritual Tube (M):** Reach 1, 4 🦅, 1H, Stun

SPECIAL ABILITIES

- **Host:** While encased (or "mounted") within the host, Aumag-Bel suffers no impairment from Wounds but the visible marks inflicted are gruesome and horrific. Every time a Wound is dealt, the gamemaster should mark it off as normal. The host can only suffer 4 Wounds before being maimed. At this point, the gamemaster should immediately have all player characters roll fear as if Aumag-Bel had just revealed its true form to them. Otherwise consider Aumag-Bel to have the *Inured to Pain* ability.

DOOM SPENDS

- **Weird Magic:** Aumag-Bel can spend Doom as a standard action in order to cast the abilities listed below. He will only begin to use these abilities once he has suffered 2 Wounds.
- **Hypnotic Stare (2 Doom):** Aumag-Bel fixes a target with his eyes, transfixing them with the dreadful intensity of his glance. The transfixed player character must pass a Daunting (D3) Discipline test or suffer 2 🦅 mental damage and act as though Stunned for the next turn.
- **The Clutch of Earth (4 Doom):** Using his people's elemental connection to the earth, Aumag-Bel draws the dark, moist loam up through the narrow gaps between the stones in the floor and the ceiling, trapping the target in place and crushing them beneath the torrent of soil. A player character must succeed with a Dire (D4) Agility test or be unable to move or attack for a turn (he may defend against subsequent attacks, however) and suffer 2 🦅 from the falling earth.
- **The Embrace of the Worm (4 Doom):** With more than human flexibility, Aumag-Bel wraps himself about a player character, clamping himself to them and drives his teeth into the exposed throat of the entrapped foe. Aumag-Bel must make a successful Movement test to carry out this attack. If successful, the victim suffers 4 🦅 physical damage and 2 🦅 mental damage from the savagery and strangeness of the attack. Anyone witnessing this attack must also pass a Daunting (D3) Discipline test or suffer 2 🦅 mental damage.

THE FINAL HORROR

As the final blow is delivered to Aumag-Bel, the player characters should have a moment to savor their victory and narrate how the mangled husk of his body slumps to the ground. However, before the player characters have a chance to begin to free the woman chained to the altar, the corpse of Aumag-Bel suddenly rears back up, on to its feet and stands swaying. The head of the corpse hangs uselessly backwards, until the skin of the throat begins to contract and expand like a bullfrog's throat. Then, the flesh rips apart and a hideous worm creature, encrusted with dozens of blood-shot, constantly staring eyes, erupts from the hideous wound it has left in the man it used as a host. The worm writhes about for a moment, like a hideous tentacle, jutting out of the ruined neck.

The player characters should make a Resolve test. Any player characters who fail instantly take 2 🦅 mental damage, ignoring Soak, as they witness something so unutterably hideous.

THE THOUSAND EYES OF AUMAG-BEL

The worm regards them through its unblinking, unwavering eyes and then leaps forward towards its intended host. The worm form of Aumag-Bel launches itself directly at the chained woman on the altar and tries to burrow into her through any exposed flesh — her mouth, throat, or stomach are all options for it. It is fairly weak and pathetic without its human host, but can be dangerous if not stopped quickly. If the worm should manage to come into contact with the chained woman, the player characters have three combat turns to remove it, or the worm has found a new host. If this happens, the player characters must fight the reanimated Aumag-Bel, in the body of the new host (the gamemaster should use the same stats as for the original Aumag-Bel).

If the player characters unchained the woman from the altar, then the revenant Aumag-Bel can move about freely from the get-go. If the player characters did not have time for this, then Aumag-Bel spends his/her first turn using *Clutch of the Earth* to shatter the chains on a successful Challenging (D2) Willpower test and appropriate Doom spend.

Once the player characters have slain the worm (hopefully before it has attained a new host), they have slain Aumag-Bel and the quest is complete. If the player characters claim the amulet from his corpse and do not choose to keep it, it can be sold for a good sum to a disreputable scholar, but is otherwise without use. The last creature on earth who understood its power lies slain beneath the player characters' swords. Beyond this, there is little to claim from the subterranean palace, although there is the young, beautiful woman to be rescued (if they managed to prevent Aumag-Bel claiming her body as his own).

A Complication might result in dropped weapons or, more dangerously, the worm managing to reach the prone woman without the player characters being able to stop it immediately.

THE WORM WITHIN, AUMAG-BEL'S TRUE FORM (NEMESIS)

The true form of Aumag-Bel, finally revealed, is a pathetic, hideous creature. Wriggling, abandoned, and almost useless without a host, the creature is the last remnant of a race that was had a mighty empire. Now it rages, futilely, against the vast darkness of extinction.

ATTRIBUTES

Awareness	Intelligence	Personality	Willpower
9	13	9	14

Agility	Brawn	Coordination
8	4	8

FIELDS OF EXPERTISE

Combat	2	Movement	1
Fortitude	1	Senses	5
Knowledge	1	Social	—

STRESS AND SOAK

- **Stress:** Vigor 5, Resolve 15
- **Soak:** Armor 2 (Horror), Courage 1

SPECIAL ABILITIES

- **Fear 2**
- **Frail:** Aumag-Bel is a creature of unknown provenance. Its final form is quite weak and only has 1 Wound. When reduced to this form, Aumag-Bel immediately suffers a Trauma.
- **Weird Magic:** It still has access to the abilities of the Host of Aumag-Bel (see *Host of Aumag-Bel*, page 104) but must buy them at 1 extra Doom per use.

THE JOURNEY'S END

The young woman is Dergar Sheev, and she is the daughter of a wealthy and famous merchant prince of Vendhya. If the player characters were forced to kill her in order to stop Aumag-Bel, then the adventure ends here. Heading back up to the city above, the player characters are treated generously by the populace and offered free room, board, and beer for several nights as the locals thank them for taking care of the sinister figure of Aumag-Bel who has plagued them and stolen from them for so long.

The gamemaster might consider beginning their next adventure with the player characters pursued by Dergar Sheev's father, the wrathful Murghen Sheev. Perhaps the distraught father has sought supernatural help in order to enact his vengeance against the player characters, convinced of their complicity in his daughter's disappearance, or instead has kidnapped and enslaved them as they slept, drunk, after another debauch.

If the player characters managed to rescue Dergar Sheev, then the ending of the adventure is somewhat brighter. Once awakened from her sorcerous slumber by the death of Aumag-Bel and freed from her constraints, she grasps the arms of each of the player characters in a martial grip and thanks them for their aid. Once above ground, she leads the player characters to her father and offers lavish encomia to their martial skill, bravery, and honor.

Grinning and delighted with the safe return of his beloved daughter, Murghen Sheev firmly embraces the player characters himself and promises them a night of feasting, carousing, and pleasures of proportions beyond even their lustiest dreams. If the player characters are otherwise inclined, he offers them assistance in these other pursuits. He also hints at the possibility of work as guards for his legion of caravans, or aboard his many ships. A gamemaster can definitely parlay this ending into the opening for adventures set almost anywhere, in any nation of the Hyborian Age.

Whatever happens to the player characters next, whether they are hunted by Murghen Sheev or employed by him, they have rid the city of Aumag-Bel and, at least in this corner of the land, they will be remembered as heroes. Or they will be dead, in a city deep beneath the earth and forgotten entirely...

EXPERIENCE

All the player characters who emerge, more or less intact, from the under-city of Aumag-Bel should be awarded 300 experience points apiece. The gamemaster might consider awarding 50 extra experience points to the characters who:

- Caught one of the child-thieves *before* they reached the Den of the Black Lotus.
- Killed the Aumag-Bel host form.
- Prevented the worm form of Aumag-Bel from infecting Dergha Sheev.
- The gamemaster might also reward extra experience to any players who were particularly engaged in the story or who roleplayed with special enthusiasm.

Ideally, the gamemaster should not allot any more than 100 additional experience points to any of the player characters. This means that the characters develop at roughly the same rate.

"A devil from the Outer Dark," he grunted. "Oh, they're nothing uncommon. They lurk as thick as fleas outside the belt of light which surrounds this world. I've heard the wise men of Zamora talk of them. Some find their way to Earth, but when they do, they have to take on earthly form and flesh of some sort. A man like myself, with a sword, is a match for any amount of fangs and talons, infernal or terrestrial."

— "The Vale of Lost Women"

CHAPTER 6
THE RED PIT

"What do I know of cultured ways, the gilt, the craft and the lie?

I, who was born in a naked land and bred in the open sky.

The subtle tongue, the sophist guile, they fail when the broadswords sing;

Rush in and die, dogs — I was a man before I was a king."

— "The Road of Kings"

PROLOGUE

On the western marches of Koth, in the bleak hills near the border with Argos and Ophir, lies an ugly scar in the earth that men call the Red Pit. From its depths, slaves hack blocks of fine rose-hued limestone from the ground — stone ultimately bound for the palaces and villas of Khorshemish. The slaves who are sent here rarely last a season. They live at the whim of the elements, toiling beneath the blazing sun by day and huddling together in their rags for warmth by night. Despite all this, some still have dreams — dreams of freedom — though most dream only of the rich red froth of vengeance.

For the purposes of this scenario, the player characters begin as slaves, naked but for a twist of cloth around their loins and armed with only their wits, their fists, and a handful of makeshift weapons. Regardless of their origins, they face the same fate: to scrape and scrabble at the rock until Death comes for them.

Unless they can wrest their freedom from the Master of the Pit.

That Master is a brutal man called Abidaal, a eunuch deep in the confidence of the Kothian king. A cadre of his countrymen, Pelishtim mercenaries from western Shem, prowls the edges of the Red Pit, ever watchful. But inside the quarry, Abidaal employs a gang of slave drivers to keep the other slaves in line. Nazarus the Whip is their overseer. The last member of Abdibaal's retinue is a nameless Stygian, tall and gaunt, whose sole task is to care for the eunuch's prized pet: an *a'ghama*, a 300-pound carnivorous lizard he keeps caged near the edge of the Pit.

SYNOPSIS

The adventure begins as the slaves' workday draws to a close. The brazen horn has sounded and Abdibaal orders Nazarus and his slave drivers to tally how much stone each slave grubbed forth, collect their tools, and mete out punishment to those who missed their quota. Only after will they receive their meagre ration of hard bread, water, and a wooden bowl of herb stew.

A lucky few — the player characters among them — who have demonstrated a willingness to work and who have "kept their noses clean" have their irons removed for the night... a luxury calculated to make the balance of the slaves work that much harder. For the moment, however, the player character's legs are free, and they stand closer to the sweet taste of freedom than they have in months.

The player characters start with only their fists against Nazarus' whip and the other slave drivers' truncheons. However, should the player characters sweep aside the slave drivers and their chief, they might secure mining tools to wield in their defence or even spur a general slave uprising. No matter how they begin, their revolt does not pass unnoticed. Abdibaal astride his horse, up at the lip of the mine, orders his archers to target the player characters along with any other slaves foolish enough to join them. Through this hail of arrows, the player characters must rush to the base of the only scalable cliff, atop which the Master of the Pit, his guards, his archers, and his monstrous pet lizard await.

Once they reach the relative safety at the foot of the Pit wall, they must gather their strength and make for the surface. Impetuous player characters may choose to scale the face of this cliff barehanded, with nothing but raw courage and Mitra's blessing between themselves and the archers' deadly shafts. Craftier player characters might release the Pit's massive stone-hauling basket, letting it plummet to the quarry floor to provide a rope straight to the surface. Most likely, the player characters scurry up twin rope ladders hanging from a rocky outcropping high on the wall, a formation called the Eunuch's Ear.

As the player characters ascend from the Red Pit to the Eunuch's Ear, Abdibaal does not sit idle. He exhorts his archers to maintain their barrage. If need be, he lowers a few of his mail-clad Pelishtim to the Eunuch's Ear with orders to cut the ladders before the player characters reach the outcrop's surface. Should the player characters take and hold the Ear, the remaining mercenaries rain down havoc with their broad-bladed spears. Finally, if all else fails, Abdibaal orders the grim and silent Stygian to unleash the mighty *a'ghama*. Maddened by the reek of spilled blood, the beast claws its way into the Red Pit, bent on slaking its hellish appetite.

The hammer falls; with it, the rust-pitted iron manacles that have been the symbol of your enslavement clatter to the ground. The sudden release from their chafing weight elicits a low and dangerous chuckle from the back of your throat — like the cough of a leopard that has caught the scent of its prey.

The gap-toothed slave driver squints up at you, then over his shoulder at that hulking fool, Nazarus. "Don't get used to it, swine!" the Kothian overseer bellows. "You've done well, aye, and Master Abdibaal rewards those who keep their backs bent and their noses clean. But you're not free, you hear me? Tomorrow, those go back on." Grinning, he cracks his whip for emphasis. "Now move, ere I lose my patience with you, slave!"

THE RED PIT

> *But you don't move. You stand, shoulders squared, your lungs expanding as you draw in a deep breath of hot, rancid air. The sheer walls of the Red Pit rise above you — an open-air prison that your captors swore would break you. "No one like you can live long as a slave!" they gloated. But what do they know of people like you, men and women who have trodden a thousand blood-mired paths — from the deck of a Zingaran galley, heeling in the froth of slaughter, to the dank alleys of the East, where a razor-edged whisper augurs death? A slave? By the gods, you've been a slave and more besides!*
>
> *It has not been easy to get to this moment. You've bided your time, swallowed equal measures of anger and pride. You've danced to the tune Nazarus and his mangy pack have played, kowtowing to his whip and to their endless jibes, all under the watchful eye of the overseer, Abdibaal, and his swarthy Pelishtim mercenaries. You've played your part. But no more.*
>
> *Now, it's your turn to call the tune.*
>
> *With a bellow of maniacal fury, you snatch the gap-toothed slave driver by his throat. Corded muscle writhes along your blade-scarred forearm as you haul him aloft. Iron fingers convulse, crushing the life out of him. Spitting in contempt, you hurl his scrawny corpse at his mates before whirling to face the slaves at your back — men you have toiled alongside, starved with, and bled with.*
>
> *"Bloody kindred of the chain!" you roar. "Would you lick the boots of those who would grind you into dust... or would you be free? Aye, rise up and slay the dogs!" And with a shout that shakes the foundations of heaven, the gods of blood and slaughter descend upon the Red Pit to once more claim their own...*

Enslaved and condemned to die in Koth's most infamous quarry, the player characters must overpower their jailers, evade a withering hail of arrows, and defeat a vicious man-eating lizard as they scale the Red Pit's sheer walls. Even death is no price to pay, in order to taste the air of freedom again!

AND SO IT BEGINS

The player characters' goal is simple: fight tooth and nail to reach the surface and gain their freedom. There are no intrigues, no ulterior motives; this tale is pure action, a bloody, bare-knuckled contest for survival — will they die as slaves under the brutal summer sun, or break out and triumph, freeing themselves from a dreadful bondage. The goal of the non-player characters is equally simple: stop the player characters and restore the status quo to the Red Pit.

THE LAY OF THE LAND

The action begins at *The Entry to the Red Pit* (see page 110), with a scrawny, gap-toothed slave driver hammering an iron awl-punch through the rivet securing the player characters' pitted leg manacles... and granting them a slim chance of escape. A second slave driver waits here as well, holding a woven basket to take the pitted iron chains.

Adjacent to the player characters, in the slave flats (page 114), nearly 120 slaves stand and watch, shuffling and clanking. In the feeding area (page 112), Nazarus sits at a massive table laden with baskets of bread and a huge pottery urn of still-warm herb stew. He oils his whip, while his merry band of thugs (nine additional slave drivers) stands by and wagers their night's ration of bread on which shirker will next suffer their chief's wrath.

Two additional areas — the euphemistically-named "billet" and the scree-field (page 114) — stand between the player characters and the scalable eastern wall of the Pit (page 114).

Forty feet up the eastern wall juts an outcropping called the Eunuch's Ear (page 115). Here Nazarus and his slave drivers sleep, in a cave that reeks of sweat and rancid meat. There's shelter beneath the outcropping from any archers on the Red Pit's rim. Two rope ladders lead up from the quarry floor to the top of the Eunuch's Ear.

Adjacent to this outcropping, just off its southern edge, hangs the giant stone-hauling basket (page 117). This triple-woven hopper is suspended from a cable-thick rope that runs to the surface, where its control mechanism and counter-weight are located.

Lastly is the surface of the Red Pit (page 118). In it stand the twelve Pelishtim mercenaries — three archers

DON'T WANT TO BE A SLAVE?

If the gamemaster does not like the idea of the player characters starting as slaves, have them instead in the bottom of the pit, having been captured by slavers and about to have their manacles put on. This scenario is designed to be a way for player characters to first meet one another, to give them a bond which can endure any adversity. It can even be used as the starting point of a campaign — what can be more dramatic than starting as a wretched slave and ending as a king or queen?

However, if the gamemaster wants to bring the player characters down a notch or two, this adventure can serve that purpose as well: have them sold into slavery during a period of carousing and beginning from there...

The adventure should serve the gamemaster's purpose, just as these rambunctious slaves should be serving Abdibaal!

and eight spearmen and their captain — that make up Abdibaal's personal guard. The Master of the Pit perches here, as well, his thick bulk astride a chestnut mare. His pet, an *a'gham*a, waits in its iron cage: a nightmarish lizard like something dredged from the bowels of the River Styx, slavering and agitated. A gaunt Stygian in the ragged robes of a former priest tends the beast.

Once the fighting breaks out, the scenario offers two paths to reach the cliff face. The scree-field (page 114) leads through their fellow slaves and across a field covered in scree, the detritus of limestone chips hacked from larger blocks. On the one hand, this scree-field proves difficult and hazardous to navigate. On the other, it provides a near limitless supply of fist-sized stones for throwing.

The second route through the slave flats winds among the many rough five-foot by five-foot limestone blocks recently extracted from the quarry walls. These provide cover, but slow movement, and may prolong the player characters' exposure to ranged attacks. The gamemaster should leave the choice, ultimately, to the player characters and should not be afraid to adjust the number of opponents they have to face or the difficulty of the challenges ahead of them. Player characters in **Conan** rarely die in situations not worth immortalizing in songs and epic poems. The gamemaster should remember this when running the adventure.

LET MY PEOPLE GO

The player characters are present along with two slave drivers (see *The Entry to the Red Pit* below, for additional details). While the terrain here is clear — with no outstanding obstacles and no cover — the player characters cannot leave this area without either killing or incapacitating the two slave drivers, or Persuading or Commanding the slaves in the billet to let them pass.

The summer sun is low in the west, creating pools of shadow extending from the western wall of the Pit, across the entry to the Red Pit to roughly the outer edge of the feeding area. The shadows require a Challenging (D2) Observation test (or the Senses Field of Expertise for nonplayer characters) for anyone trying to distinguish the player characters from among the other slaves at distances beyond Medium.

The Entry to the Red Pit

The attempt to escape from the Red Pit starts when the player characters stand up against the two slave drivers at the entry to the Pit. These two — along with Nazarus and their nine cronies in the feeding area — must eventually be incapacitated or killed. The only question is how soon Nazarus responds to the player characters' opening bid to escape.

The Red Pit

1. Entry to The Red Pit
2. Feeding Area and Billet
3. Slave Area
4. Scree Field
5. The Eunuch's Ear
6. The Eastern Wall
7. The Stone Hauling Basket
8. The Pit's Edge

THE RED PIT

One of the slave drivers in this area holds a spoil basket containing the player characters' recently removed iron manacles. If recovered, the spoil basket may be used as a makeshift shield. The other slave driver holds a small hammer and an awl-punch, which, together with the iron manacles, make passable weapons if recovered.

If the player characters eliminate the two slave drivers at the entry to the Pit during the first combat round, the shock of their revolt affects Nazarus and his other slave drivers exactly as if the player characters staged an ambush. The gamemaster should allow the player characters an opposed test of Stealth versus Nazarus' Senses Field of Expertise. Only one player character can make this test, but the players may choose the player character with the highest score in the appropriate attribute. If it succeeds, the player characters receive 1 bonus Momentum for their pool. If the test fails, Nazarus is too quick, and the gamemaster may spend 1 Doom to advance the slave drivers to the top of the initiative order for the second turn.

Without leaving the entry to the Red Pit, the player characters may make a Daunting (D3) Persuade or Command test to convince the other slaves to join them in revolt. Unless the player characters succeed on this test or a related test, the slaves refuse to surrender their tools — more small hammers and spoil baskets. However, if the player characters manage to generate 1 or more success, the slaves will stand aside to let them pass as they attempt their escape. If the player characters generate no success when talking with their fellow unfortunates then they will not only refuse to join the revolt, they will also refuse to move, which transforms the billet into Difficult terrain. See *Brothers Before the Lash* (page 113) for additional details.

As soon as Nazarus can act, he orders his surviving slave drivers to subdue the player characters. Nazarus, however, remains in the feeding area while his minions do his dirty work. The turn following the player character attacks, the archers on the lip of the Red Pit notice the fight and attempt to shoot the player characters down from Extreme range.

The Slave Driver Flees

The gamemaster may wish to spend 1 Doom to grant one (and only one) of the slave drivers at the entrance more of a fighting chance, allowing him to act before the player characters and scurry back to his chief's side.

Everyone Except Nazarus is Shocked

In the event the player characters win the opposed test for an ambush, the gamemaster should consider spending 2 Doom to increase Nazarus' reaction time. He alone moves before the player characters and enters the area to attack, while shock delays his remaining drivers. In this event, the archers at the edge of the Red Pit begin firing the round following Nazarus' attack.

IMPROVISED WEAPONS

Ingenious or resourceful player characters will likely be able to lay hands on a number of items suitable as weapons. The following are suggestions for improvised weapons that might be easily obtained, while others might be described using the rules provided in *Improvised Weapons* on page 152 of the CONAN corebook.

- **IRON MANACLES (M):** Reach 2, 3🔥, 1H, Improvised
- **SPOIL BASKET (M):** Reach 1, 2🔥, 1H, Improvised, Shield 1
- **HAMMER (M):** Reach 1, 4🔥, 1H, Improvised
- **AWL PUNCH (M):** Reach 1, 2🔥, 1H, Unforgiving 1

SLAVE DRIVER (MINION)

Like their comrades in the Feeding Area these are slaves elevated to positions of authority by Abdibaal. They eat better, sleep out of the elements, and are experienced shirkers where hard labor is concerned. They're consummate bullies, using force and intimidation to bend others to the Master's will. If they survive the initial onslaught, the slave drivers wade into the player characters with their truncheons, dropping anything else they are carrying. They fear Nazarus more than anyone and fight to the death.

ATTRIBUTES

Awareness	Intelligence	Personality	Willpower
8	7	7	7

Agility	Brawn	Coordination
9	8	8

FIELDS OF EXPERTISE

Combat	1	Movement	1
Fortitude	—	Senses	1
Knowledge	1	Social	—

STRESS AND SOAK

- **Stress:** Vigor 4, Resolve 4
- **Soak:** Armor 1 (Light Mail), Courage 1

ATTACKS

- **Truncheon (M):** Reach 2, 3🔥, 1H, Stun, Knockdown

SPECIAL ABILITIES

- **Strength in Numbers:** A successful attack by a slave driver inflicts an additional +2 ⚔ damage against any creature that has already been attacked this round.

NAZARUS THE WHIP

The terrain is clear, save for the massive table occupied by Nazarus and surrounded by his thugs. Fully ten feet long and six inches thick, three trestles support this slab of aged and weather-hardened oak. Its gouged and pitted surface holds six woven reed baskets filled with hard bread, wooden bowls, a huge earthenware pot of tepid herb stew, and the rolled parchment scrolls of the Pit's slave ledgers.

The Feeding Area

If the player characters remain in the entry to the Red Pit, Nazarus and his slave drivers leave this area and lumber in, truncheons flashing, to attack the player characters. If the player characters move into the feeding area, the slave drivers engage them and Nazarus leaps to the top of the table as a Response Action. When he lands, he shakes but does not spill the towers of bread and soup. The teetering towers of food rivet any slaves who have not attacked the slave drivers and — even mid-revolt — the gamemaster should narrate the anger that flashes at the prospect of losing their meager meals. This also means, however, that the gamemaster must spend 2 Doom per slave driver in order to change their position in the order of combat.

From atop the table, Nazarus wields his whip, first against any player character who spoke out against him, then against the player character with the highest Brawn. While fighting from this perch, Nazarus gains 1 bonus Momentum to every attack against any foe on the ground.

If the player characters attack and other slaves do not join them, this exposes the player characters to archery from the edge of the Red Pit. Nazarus and his slave drivers are known figures that stand out, despite the distance. With the cover and confusion provided by their fellow slaves, it requires a Doom spend for a non-player character to accurately target a player character. When arrows miss, the gamemaster is encouraged to describe them hailing down but striking only inanimate objects, or even other slaves.

Attacking Nazarus

Player characters that attack Nazarus must join him atop the table and risk spilling the slaves' meals. If some of their fellow slaves are already in the fight, they avoid Nazarus and his whip like the plague, leaving him free to assault the player characters. The gamemaster may wish to describe Nazarus using his whip to choke the life from any slave personally known to the player characters, or else taking sadistic delight in the wound he inflicts on any he can reach with the lash.

Whether or not the player characters convinced a substantial number of the slaves to revolt, anyone who ruins the food stacked on Nazarus' table — especially the herb soup — incurs their wrath. Combatants, including Nazarus, must succeed on an Average (D1) Acrobatics test to **not** splash through the food while fighting atop the table.

Six of the hungriest slaves immediately attack anyone who knocks over the food.

If the player characters incited a general revolt and *then* Nazarus spills the food, gamemasters should consider setting a pack of slaves on him all at once, then simply narrate the overseer vanishing, screaming, beneath a pile of enraged men — the spray of his blood, his unseen death rattle. The whip, handle stained with gore, lands beside the nearest player character for retrieval.

While engaging Nazarus atop the table, player characters may spend 1 Momentum to knock him off. They may spend 2 points of Momentum to force Nazarus to stumble into the slaves' food, potentially incurring their wrath as described above.

THE RED PIT

The table itself proves a useful defence against arrows from the edge of the Red Pit. Success on an Average (D1) Athletics test allows any player character to tilt the table on its side and seek cover behind it. It requires a minimum of two characters and success on an assisted Challenging (D2) Athletics test to lift and carry the table like a massive shield. The table acts as a shield providing 4⚡ cover Soak. Player characters carrying the table in this fashion are encumbered, which increases the Difficulty of all physical actions by one step. Additionally, player characters carrying the table treat all areas they move through as Difficult terrain, but this does not increase the challenge posed by terrain that is already Difficult.

Corpses also make good shields, whether of slave drivers or fellow slaves. For that matter, live slaves also work. If the player characters do not think of it themselves, succeeding on an Average (D1) Insight test gives them the idea.

Carrying a corpse is encumbering, increasing the Difficulty of all physical actions by one step. The corpse will act as cover, providing 4⚡ cover with the Fearsome 1 Quality (any Effects rolled inflict 1 mental damage on the wielder as they become covered in gore). The gamemaster can add +1⚡ to this by spending 1 Doom. Carrying a hostage also encumbers a character, increasing the Difficulty of all physical actions by one step. As a shield, a hostage slave provides 5⚡, Shield 1, Fearsome 1, and has Vigor 4 (absorbing any damage inflicted upon it). The slave must be grappled first and will try to escape each round (using only a single 1d20). Doom can be spent to add d20s to this test.

The adversaries in this area are slave driver Minions, as described on page 111. There are double the number of slave drivers as there are player characters.

If any player character engages Nazarus atop the table, the gamemaster might spend 2 Doom to force *them* to spill the food and draw the immediate attack of six slaves. Unlike Nazarus, however, the player characters are capable of avoiding this bloody combat with a Challenging (D2) Persuade test. Whatever happens, this tactic instantly frees Nazarus to engage a different player character.

Additionally, after the player characters defeat Nazarus and his slave drivers, the gamemaster might spend 1 Doom to allow the Master's troops on the Red Pit's rim to act before the player characters' next turn.

NAZARUS (NEMESIS)

Squat and powerfully built, this vicious Kothian brawler is overseer of the Red Pit and Abdibaal's right-hand man. The Red Pit is his fiefdom and he rules it with an iron fist. Those who cross him can only pray for death as he strips the skin from their backs and adds it to his trophies. If the slaves do not revolt *en masse*, Nazarus seeks to subdue and re-shackle the player characters. Otherwise, he tries to slay them.

ATTRIBUTES

Awareness	Intelligence	Personality	Willpower
8	9	7	10
Agility	Brawn	Coordination	
10	12	8	

FIELDS OF EXPERTISE

Combat	2	Movement	1
Fortitude	—	Senses	1
Knowledge	1	Social	—

STRESS AND SOAK

- **Stress:** Vigor 12, Resolve 10
- **Soak:** Armor 2 (Brigandine of Human Skin), Courage 2

ATTACKS

- **Whip (M):** Reach 3, 6⚡, 1H, Fearsome 2, Grapple
- **Punch (M):** Reach 1, 5⚡, 1H, Stun, Knockdown
- **A Thousand Angry Curses (T):** Range C, 3⚡ mental, Stun, Area

SPECIAL ABILITIES

- **No Mercy:** Identical to the talent described on page 73 of the **Conan** corebook.

BROTHERS BEFORE THE LASH

In the billet, a relatively empty area adjacent to the feeding area where slaves can rest before going back to work, the broken-spirited and apathetic slaves crouch in fear, still chained, their near-naked bodies wracked with exhaustion. As a result, the billet counts as Difficult terrain unless the player characters succeeded on a Persuade or Command test to secure their fellow prisoners' support. The twelve slaves in this area might be adversaries or potentially won over as allies to the player characters.

Due to inches-thick gravel left from mining the quarry walls, this area is Difficult terrain.

The Tower of Babel

Gamemasters who wish to increase the difficulty of the Persuade or Command test to incite a slave riot should consider spending 2 Doom to change the slaves' languages to ones no player characters speak.

Complications When Fomenting Revolt

If the player characters generate a Complication while Persuading or Commanding the slaves, the gamemaster may consider a more personal form of Complication. For example, one of the slaves might recognize the player character as the reason for their enslavement. Instantly, this person calls out the player character's crime and seeks vengeance. Even if the player characters successfully foment a slave result, this Complication causes 3 🦅 slaves to attack the player characters.

If the player characters generate a Complication while failing their Persuade or Command test to incite revolt, the gamemaster should add one step to the Difficulty of all future Persuade or Command tests.

Slave (Minion)

The slaves of the Red Pit are a varied lot — native Kothians, gaunt from hunger; Shemites with wild eyes and unkempt blue-black beards; tawny-haired Argosseans who pine for the sea; and proud Ophireans who cling to their arrogance in spite of their station. Despite their differences, they fight with the feral persistence of a pack of wild dogs. These slaves use the same statistics as the slaves encountered earlier in the adventure. Slaves use the same statistics as slave drivers, however, they fight without weapons, using the rules for fighting empty-handed, described in the **Conan** corebook on page 73.

THE SLAVE FLATS

The three archers on the rim of the Red Pit shoot repeatedly at anyone who enters this area, which counts as Medium range for them. However, this is also where the slaves spend their days toiling to chip massive cubes of limestone from the quarry walls. These scattered five-foot by five-foot limestone blocks provide 4 🦅 cover Soak to any player character succeeding with an Acrobatics test to dodge arrows. Once the player characters take cover, they may then make an opposed Stealth test against their opponent's Observation to deny the line of sight to the archers on the Red Pit's rim.

THE SCREE-FIELD

Here, slaves shovel the fist-sized chunks of debris left from whittling down the limestone blocks of the slave flats to fit the stone-hauling basket. As a result, this area is both Difficult and Hazardous terrain, but its jagged detritus may prove useful as weapons. The three archers on the Red Pit's rim shoot repeatedly at anyone who enters this Zone, which counts as Medium range for them. This area offers no cover from the hail of arrows, until player characters reach the base of the wall beneath the Eunuch's Ear.

If the player characters enter the scree-field without improvising something to cover their feet, they cut themselves on the foot-deep shards of limestone that coat the zone like quicksand and take 1 🦅 damage. Success on an Average (D1) Craft test with an object like a spoil basket

allows them to avoid this damage. If the player characters fail the Athletics test required to navigate this zone, they take an additional point of damage from the limestone scree and will need to make an additional Average (D1) Athletics test to cross the zone.

Finally, as a Minor Action, any player character may stoop and retrieve two hunks of jagged stone debris suitable for throwing.

> ### JAGGED STONE DEBRIS
>
> Whenever a player character or non-player character searches for a handy improvised weapon while in this area, the gamemaster can either pick from the list below or roll a d20 to see what comes to hand.
>
> | ROLL | RESULT |
> |---|---|
> | 1–5 | Large hefty rock. 3 🦅 |
> | 6–10 | Sharp sliver of rock. 3 🦅, Vicious 1, Fragile |
> | 11–15 | Fist-sized chunk of blunt rock. Range C, 2 🦅, Improvised |
> | 15–20 | Fist-sized chunk of shell-filled limestone. Range C, 2 🦅, Improvised, Fragile |

BY TOOTH AND NAIL

Player characters can reach the base of the Pit wall by exiting the slave flats or the scree-field. For the purposes of climbing the wall directly to freedom, the ground near the eastern wall counts as Difficult terrain. However, the area also possesses a special point of egress, located directly below the Eunuch's Ear. Player characters must first get to the base of the eastern wall before exiting onto the rope ladders of the Eunuch's Ear, described on page 116.

The Eastern Wall

Player characters who decide to climb the cliff wall, avoiding the Eunuch's Ear may do so. However, the cliff wall is Difficult terrain, and climbers endure constant archery fire from the rim of the Pit. Moreover, climbing the cliff wall is a three-story climb, requiring success on three consecutive Athletics tests. The Difficulty of each test is equal to the floor of the climb — Average (D1) for the first floor, Challenging (D2) for the second, Daunting (D3) for the third. Player characters can use Momentum to get to a higher level in the same turn.

Additionally, each Injury sustained while climbing forces a Resistance test. On a failure, player characters are knocked from the wall. The Difficulty of each test is equal

THE RED PIT   115

to the amount of damage sustained while climbing. Player characters that fall from the wall take 1+2💀 damage per story fallen.

Alternately, player characters may go to the eastern wall directly beneath the Eunuch's Ear and achieve complete cover from the archers on the rim of the Pit, who may no longer shoot at them. This respite proves temporary as the player characters must either scale the cliff itself or emerge from cover to scale the rope ladders if they wish to progress further. It is impossible to climb over the outcrop to the top of the Eunuch's Ear any other way. See *The Eunuch's Ear* (page 115) for additional details on scaling the rope ladders.

Player characters that start climbing the cliff wall from directly beneath the Eunuch's Ear outcrop remain completely protected from archers for the first of their three consecutive Athletics tests. They must emerge from beneath the overhang to finish the climb, facing archery fire as normal during the latter two tests.

Finally, after the player characters enter the area near the wall, Abdibaal orders three of his eight Pelishtim spearmen lowered on ropes to the surface of the Eunuch's Ear with orders to cut the rope ladders. See page 116 for more information.

If the player characters ignore the Eunuch's Ear and successfully climb the cliff wall to the surface, as they near the top, any Pelishtim spearmen remaining on the Pit's edge will attack them. Being poked with spears during the final Daunting (D3) Athletics test of their climb is part of why it *is* a Daunting test. However, characters who take an Injury from the Pelishtim spears during this last leg of the climb — whether or not they succeed at the final Athletics test — must make an *additional* Average (D1) Resistance test or be knocked from the wall.

On the second of the three Athletics tests used to climb the wall, ascending player characters may spend 1 Momentum to clamber from the cliff face into the giant stone-hauling basket (described on page 117), which also provides complete protection from the archers.

Finally, player characters might use Fortune points to accelerate their climb.

It's Raining Slaves

If any slaves survived the battle with Nazarus and his Drivers, the player characters' bold ascent inspires them to follow. Some prove swifter climbers than the player characters and, at any given time, gamemasters should consider narrating them as above or below the player characters scaling the Pit wall. This allows the gamemaster to spend 1 Doom or a Complication plucking a slave off the cliff face — perhaps after taking an arrow to the face — and smashing the hapless slave into a player character. Player characters hit by a falling slave must succeed at an Average (D1) Acrobatics or Resistance test or also fall from the cliff.

Checking Their Ascent

If the player characters *rapidly* ascend the cliff face — for example, using Momentum or Fortune points — the gamemaster might spend 2 Doom to place three Pelishtim mercenaries into the stone-hauling basket and lower it to the climbers' level. These mercenaries add their spear attacks to the hazards of the ascent.

THE EUNUCH'S EAR

The Eunuch's Ear is an outcrop of rock jutting from the side of the Red Pit halfway between the surface and the floor. From above it resembles an ear, thus the moniker. This is also where Nazarus and his slave drivers sleep, away from their fellow slaves. Each night, they retreat up two rope ladders, pull them up behind, and retire for the evening. The Master of the Pit even granted Nazarus the privilege of chipping a small cave into the cliff wall.

Neither the Ear nor the cave constitutes Difficult terrain. However there is only one way to enter the Eunuch's Ear: characters must succeed on an Average (D1) Acrobatics test to climb the rope ladders to the top.

An Ear to the Grindstone

The moment the player characters draw near, the Master of the Pit orders three of his Pelishtim mercenaries lowered on ropes to the top of the Ear. Abdibaal has the ropes withdrawn after depositing them. Armed only with falchions — they left their other equipment on the edge of the Red Pit — the mercenaries have orders to cut the rope ladders.

If the player characters get close and, on their very next turn, began climbing the rope ladders into the Eunuch's Ear, then they reach the top just as the mercenaries begin to cut the ladders from their moorings.

An opposed test pits the climbers' Acrobatics against the mercenaries' Brawn and determines whether the player characters reach the top seconds before the mercenaries cut the ladders — or seconds after. Treat each ladder as a separate skill test.

If the mercenaries win either opposed test, they cut the rope ladder in question and anyone on it falls to the bottom of the Pit, taking 4 ♆ damage.

The first player character to reach the top of a ladder before it is cut must succeed on an Average (D1) Acrobatics or Melee test to leave the ladder and gain a foothold on the Ear. Success also allows allies behind them to leave the ladder without making this test. However, during the round in which the first player character up the ladder attempts to gain a foothold on the Ear, the defending Pelishtim receive 1 bonus Momentum to all their attacks.

Once the player characters gain a foothold on the Ear, they must battle any surviving mercenaries while still being under fire from the archers on the Pit's rim. Their deadly skills with the bow are no longer impeded by distance. If the player characters defeat their better-equipped Pelishtim foes, they secure real armor and weaponry for the first time since their captivity.

Anyone entering the small cave carved into the cliff finds complete safety from the archers in the Red Pit's rim. Clever player characters might drag corpses into the cave and don defeated foes' equipment. Within the cave, among the slave drivers' filthy bed rags, they can also discover two oil lamps. Success on an Average (D1) Alchemy test allows player characters to construct crude explosives — Exploding Oil Lamp (Range C, 2♆, Incendiary 2).

Finally, when it becomes clear that the player characters will win the battle for the Eunuch's Ear, Abdibaal orders his Stygian servitor to release the imprisoned *a'ghama* (see page 119).

The wall between the top of the Ear and the surface at the Red Pit's rim is Difficult terrain, and it requires success on a Daunting (D3) Athletics test reach the surface. Player characters may spend 1 Momentum from the Climb test struggle to not only reach the top before the ladders are cut, but also to exit the ladder and gain a foothold on the Ear, unopposed.

Player characters fighting the mercenaries at the top of the rope ladders may spend 2 Momentum or a Fortune Point to grab an enemy and hurl him to his death on the stone shards below.

Half a Ladder is Better than No Ladder

If a player character wins the opposed test to climb a rope ladder before the Pelishtim cut them loose, the gamemaster might choose to spend 1 or 2 Doom to allow the Pelishtim to successfully cut one of the two legs off the ladder. This sends the cut ladder swinging wildly into the other ladder.

Anyone on the now-swinging ladder must succeed at a Challenging (D2) Acrobatics test or fall to the floor of the Red Pit, taking 4 ♆ points of damage. Player characters may spend 1 Momentum from this Acrobatics test to leap to the more stable ladder, to the stone-hauling basket, or to the outcrop of the Ear itself.

Any player character who leaps from a ladder to cling to the stone outcrop of the Ear cannot climb horizontally or vertically from this precarious perch. Instead, on their next turn they must succeed at a Daunting (D3) Acrobatics test to leap to any remaining ladder or into the stone-hauling basket. If all of these means of escape are severed, the player characters can still clamber up, from level to level, via the walls of the Pit. This requires a Dire (D4) Athletics test for each climb.

Deadly Hail of Arrows

The gamemaster might spend 1 Doom to grant the archers on the edge of the Red Pit an additional d20 while firing at the player characters — especially if the player characters avoided taking damage from archery up to this point.

Vertical Dominoes

Gamemasters might spend 2 Doom to break a rung of the ladder. After a rung breaks, player characters must succeed on an Average (D1) Acrobatics test to hold onto a rung or plummet into the next climber below. A player character slammed by the falling body of his ally must succeed on a Challenging (D2) Acrobatics test to retain his grip on the ladder and may spend 1 Momentum to catch and hold his falling friend.

If more than one person plummets down the ladder in this fashion, increase the difficulty of the subsequent Acrobatics tests by one step of Difficulty for every additional falling friend. No one clinging to a ladder may catch more than one falling friend at a time, forcing them to choose when struck by more than one falling person.

Anyone who falls off the ladder to the bottom of the Red Pit takes 4 ♆ points of damage.

THE RED PIT

PELISHTIM (TOUGHENED)

The Pelishtim of western Shem, with their hooked noses and curled blue-black beards, are famed throughout the Hyborian kingdoms as disciplined fighters and archers without peer. They frequently offer their skills to whatever king or noble rogue can meet their price — for these sons of the South do not sell themselves cheap. Pelishtim prefer to fight in units of three spearmen where possible.

ATTRIBUTES

Awareness	Intelligence	Personality	Willpower
9	8	9	8

Agility	Brawn	Coordination
10	9	9

FIELDS OF EXPERTISE

Combat	1	Movement	1
Fortitude	—	Senses	1
Knowledge	1	Social	—

STRESS AND SOAK

- **Stress:** Vigor 9, Resolve 8
- **Soak:** Armor 3 (Mail Shirt and Helmet), Courage 1

ATTACKS

- **Sword (M):** Reach 2, 4 ⚔, 1H, Parrying
- **Spear (M):** Reach 3, 4 ⚔, 2H, Piercing 1
- **Bow, Shemite (R):** Range L, 3 ⚔, 2H, Piercing 1, Volley

DOOM SPENDS

- **Seize the Initiative:** Pelishtim can act before a player in a turn if the gamemaster pays 1 Doom point for each Pelishtim.

THE STONE-HAULING BASKET

This massive rope and leather basket hangs by a hemp cable thicker than a man and connected to a winch at the lip of the Red Pit. Powered by oxen, the device hauls limestone boulders to the surface. It is large enough to hold six humans. When this adventure begins, a femur-thick iron peg locks the winch mechanism in place. The basket dangles halfway down the cliff face, a few feet above the surface of the Eunuch's Ear and far enough from the edge of the Ear that neither Abdibaal nor his minions believe anyone foolish enough to leap for it. Those at the bottom of the Red Pit cannot easily spot the iron peg, nor ascertain details of the winch mechanism until they are closer.

Player characters who wish to send the stone-hauling basket plummeting to the bottom of the Pit must remove the iron peg locking it in place. This is only possible when no one is in the basket or climbing its massive cable, as weight on the device jams the peg.

To knock the iron peg free, player characters must first spot it. From the floor of the Red Pit, this requires succeeding on an Epic (D5) Observation test. For player characters on the surface of the Eunuch's Ear this becomes a Daunting (D3) Observation test. Once spotted, inflicting a cumulative 6 points of damage on the iron peg knocks it free and sends the stone-hauling basket crashing to the floor of the Red Pit.

If recovered, the iron peg makes a serviceable weapon — Crude Iron Peg (Reach 2, 4 ⚔, 1H, Improvised, Stun, Knockdown).

Player characters who wish to leap from the Eunuch's Ear into the stone-hauling basket (or onto the cable) must sprint and succeed on a Daunting (D3) Acrobatics test, which hurtles them across the gap and inside the basket (or onto the cable) in a single move. Once within the leather and rope cocoon of the basket, its depth provides complete protection from archers on the lip of the Red Pit.

Leaping into the basket (or onto the cable) from anywhere in the area requires having already succeeded on the first of the three tests required to climb the cliff bare-knuckled (see The Eastern Wall, page 114, for additional details) and only then succeeding on an Epic (D5) Acrobatics test to leap laterally and reach the cable or the basket interior.

Once in the stone-hauling basket, climbing the basket's hemp cable to the surface is easy, requiring success on a single Challenging (D2) Acrobatics test. Anyone climbing the cable in this manner becomes a priority for the Red Pit's guardian archers, who unleash a volley before the climber reaches the surface.

Provided the gamemaster deems it reasonable, the player character who delivers the final damage and knocks the iron peg free from the winch may spend 1 Momentum to smash the falling stone-hauling basket into anyone climbing the wall or land it on anyone in the slave flats or the scree-field.

> "Well," said Conan harshly, "is it not better to die honorably than to live in infamy? Is death worse than oppression, slavery and ultimate destruction?"
>
> — The Hour of the Dragon

What Would Abdibaal Do?

Chopping through a cable as thick as the one holding the stone-hauling basket requires more time than Abdibaal and his minions possess. Moreover, weight in the basket clamps the iron peg in place such that nothing short of sledgehammers will knock it free — and Abdibaal has none with him. Consequently, when one or more player characters enters the basket or reaches the cable, Abdibaal orders the *a'ghama* freed and driven below to hunt the climbers. See *The Pit's Edge* (page 118) for more details.

Alternately, after the player characters drop the stone-haul to the floor of the Red Pit, Abdibaal may order three of his fighters to man the winch and recover the basket. Drawing the basket back to the surface requires three men and three turns. Each turn spent at the winch draws the basket an additional zone's worth of distance from the floor of the Red Pit.

For example, at the end of the first turn spinning the winch, the basket ascends from the slave flats — where it was when it landed — to a Medium distance from the slave flats near the eastern wall. At the end of the second turn, the winch lifts the basket to a Long distance from the slave flats, but still near the eastern wall. If the basket is too far away from the player character attempting the jump, the jump is no longer possible.

Finally, player characters that succeed on a Challenging (D2) Stealth test may sneak inside the fallen basket unseen, perhaps to be drawn to the surface where they ambush the winch crew.

The gamemaster may wish to spend 1 Doom on player characters who enter the basket to set it swinging and spinning, increasing the Difficulty by one step. Any Complication renders everyone either in the basket or climbing the cable Dazed. Against player characters leaping into the basket, the gamemaster should consider spending 1 Doom so they reach only the lip of the basket and then dangle. On the following turn they must succeed on an Average (D1) Athletics test to haul themselves inside. This allows the archers on the Red Pit's rim to target the dangling player character an additional time.

If multiple player characters enter the stone-hauling basket, of if some player characters are fighting the *a'ghama* inside it, or if it will heighten the tension, the gamemaster should consider spending 2 Doom for Abdibaal to locate a sledgehammer. One of his minions may now attack the iron peg and, after inflicting 6 points of damage, will knock it free. The basket falls to the bottom of the Red Pit and delivers 2+4⚔ points of damage to anyone along for the ride.

Player characters climbing the cable when the peg pops free must succeed on a Daunting (D3) Athletics test to cling to the cable and ride to the bottom of the Pit unharmed. Failure means they flew off the cable and slammed to the bottom, also taking 6⚔ damage.

In the right hands, sledgehammers double as war hammers — Sledgehammer (Reach 2, 4⚔, 2H, Improvised, Knockdown, Stun).

THE SURFACE WORLD

The scenario ends when the player characters reach the surface and defeat any remaining foes. All defenders receive 1 bonus Momentum for attacks against characters climbing out of the Red Pit. They lose this bonus Momentum once the characters leave the Pit and stand on the level surface.

The Pit's Edge

The archers shoot their arrows (three reloads per archer) at the player characters. The Pelishtim mercenaries who did not descend to the Eunuch's Ear throw their spears at the player characters when they reach the Eunuch's Ear or after player characters attempt the second Athletics test required to climb the eastern wall.

As mentioned, once the player characters reach the top of the Eunuch's Ear or progress to within one skill test of reaching the surface, the Master of the Pit orders the Stygian to release the caged *a'ghama*. Once released, the barely-controlled lizard's first act is to eat the Stygian. Afterwards the threat of the Pelishtim spears, plus the smell of horse (which it despises), and the allure of dead

THE RED PIT

slaves together drive the creature into the Pit seeking easier prey.

Once the player characters reach the surface, any remaining Pelishtim cover the Master of the Pit's retreat, as he rides off for reinforcements. The rear guard troops include one sergeant, tougher than the rest.

Player characters may spend 1 Momentum or a Fortune Point to eliminate the bonus Momentum of the Pelishtim trying to stop them from exiting the Pit and reaching the surface.

Player characters may spend 2 Momentum earned during an attack against a Pelishtim spearman or archer to grab that foe and toss him down into the Pit. However, they may not use this tactic against the Pelishtim sergeant, who is too much a veteran to fall for it.

Player characters may spend 1 Momentum from an attack on the *a'ghama* to seize its dangling leash, giving it the Staggered condition. Spending 2 Momentum on any Melee, Athletics, or Animal Handling test allows the player character to mount the *a'ghama*.

Once riding the creature, a Daunting (D3) Animal Handling test as a Reaction prevents the creature from attacking anyone, while success on a Dire (D4) Animal Handling test allows the player character to ride the creature to the surface. Success on an Epic (D5) Animal Handling test allows a player character to ride the creature to the surface and also to force it to attack one foe (not including Abdibaal), before it throws the player character to the ground and flees.

If a player character foolishly grabs the *a'ghama*'s leash or attempts to leap onto its back, the gamemaster should consider spending 5 Doom points to send them both tumbling from the cliff face to smash onto the limestone below. Such a fall inflicts 3+6🩸 points of damage to both creature and rider. This might be made even more vicious by spending an additional 1 Doom to have the lizard land on its would-be rider, inflicting another 1+2🩸 points of damage to both of them.

Abdibaal's Departure

When the player characters reach the top, they find Abdibaal has escaped, seemingly into thin air, using whatever Doom is left to effect his retreat. He can, and should, be used as a recurring villain, perhaps unexpectedly appearing in a later adventure. Should the gamemaster wish to allow the player characters to defeat him, he can be treated as a Pelishtim Commander (Nemesis) described on the next page.

MIGHTY A'GHAMA (NEMESIS)

Who knows where Abdibaal found this beast, or by what sorcery he made it so huge and ravenous? Regardless, it is the terror that haunts the nightmares of the Red Pit's denizens. Its gaping maw and chisel-like teeth are no less fearsome than its dead, yellow eyes — eyes that only blaze to unholy life when it catches the scent of blood. The *a'ghama* is drawn by the scent of fresh blood. It will target characters who are already wounded first before going after any others.

ATTRIBUTES

Awareness	Intelligence	Personality	Willpower
9	3	5	8
Agility	Brawn		Coordination
12	14 (1)		9

FIELDS OF EXPERTISE

Combat	1	Movement	2
Fortitude	2	Senses	2
Knowledge	—	Social	—

STRESS AND SOAK

- **Stress:** Vigor 15, Resolve 8
- **Soak:** Armor 3 (Scales), Courage 3

ATTACKS

- **Cavernous Maw (M):** Reach 3, 7🩸, Intense, Vicious 1, only against prone targets
- **Lashing Tail (M):** Reach 2, 7🩸, Knockdown
- **Hissing Roar (T):** Range C, 4🩸 mental, Fearsome 1, Intense

SPECIAL ABILITIES

- **Fear 2:** This has been added into the Hissing Roar attack, above.
- **Feasting:** If the *a'ghama* kills a creature, it may spend a standard action to feast upon the remains. If it does so, it immediately recovers 5 Vigor or 1 Wound.
- **Inhuman Brawn 1**
- **Night Vision:** The *a'ghama* takes no penalties from darkness.
- **Sticky Feet:** The *a'ghama* is able to crawl up vertical walls as though walking along normal horizontal surfaces.

PELISHTIM COMMANDER (NEMESIS)

Tough, unyielding and loyal to the person who has paid for that loyalty, the Pelishtim commander leads his troops expertly — never compromising and never retreating. Any who oppose the Pelishtim always do so at the risk of their lives, though this risk increases severely once a trained commander steps in to lead his men into battle. His Pelishtim prefer to fight in units of three spearmen where possible, and he will always have three such fighters at his immediate command.

ATTRIBUTES

Awareness	Intelligence	Personality	Willpower
9	9	10	9
Agility	Brawn		Coordination
11	11		9

FIELDS OF EXPERTISE

Combat	2	Movement	2
Fortitude	3	Senses	1
Knowledge	1	Social	—

STRESS AND SOAK

- **Stress:** Vigor 11, Resolve 9
- **Soak:** Armor 3 (Mail Shirt and Helmet), Courage 2

ATTACKS

- **Spear (M):** Reach 3, 5🔥, Unbalanced, Piercing 1
- **Shield (M):** Reach 2, 3🔥, 1H, Knockdown, Shield 2
- **Falchion (M):** Reach 2, 5🔥, Unbalanced, Vicious 1
- **Shemite Bow (R):** Range L, 4🔥, 2H, Piercing 1, Volley
- **Steely Glare (T):** Range C, 3🔥 mental, Stun

DOOM SPENDS

- **Leadership:** The Pelishtim commander may spend 2 Doom to grant an additional +1d20 to all Pelishtim within Close range. This bonus die may be used on any skill test that group attempts before the end of its next turn.
- **Seize the Initiative:** The commander can act before a player character in a turn if the gamemaster spends 2 Doom.

EPILOGUE

The scenario ends when the player characters reach the surface and either dispatch or chase off the remaining foes.

LOOT

In addition to the equipment of their defeated foes, the player characters discover:

- 3 Gold each.
- Bedrolls and five days' worth of hardtack and watered-wine, left by the fleeing guards.
- A set of weighted ivory dice for cheating at games of chance. These "Cheat's Dice" provide 1 bonus Momentum to Thievery tests when used for gambling. An Average (D1) Observation test recognises that they are, in fact, weighted dice.

EXPERIENCE

Upon successfully escaping from their enslavement in the Red Pit, the gamemaster should award each of the player characters 300 experience points. The gamemaster should also feel free to award 50 or more additional experience points at her discretion, for particularly impressive roleplaying or for doing something especially ingenious. Other reasons for awarding extra experience points are detailed below:

- Freeing fellow slaves and exhorting them to rise up against their oppressors.
- Killing the *a'ghama* or Nazarus the Whip.
- Seizing the Eunuch's Ear and finding the path to the surface hidden there.

The gamemaster should try to ensure that no player character earns more than 100 additional experience points.

CHAPTER 7
THE SEETHERS IN DARKNESS

> *The thought of Set was like a nightmare, and the children of Set who once ruled the earth and who now sleep in their nighted caverns far below the black pyramids. Behind that gilded screen there had been no human body — only the shimmering, headless coils of a gigantic serpent.*
>
> — "The God in the Bowl

INTRODUCTION

The player characters have been hired by a loquacious scholar to accompany him on a quest for a lost ruin in the desert southwest of Zamboula — a ruin no one has ever seen or heard of before.

Unbeknownst to them, the scholar is actually a magically-disguised serpent person following an impossibly ancient and vague legend of a lost city of their ancestors "west of the great inland (Vilayet) sea". The "scholar" seeks the player characters' aid in reaching and finding the city, and has hired them as bodyguards, offering them virtually anything they may find in the ruins as additional payment for their services.

The city is buried beneath the sands. Hundreds of thousands of years ago, a community of serpent folk fled the burgeoning human population and went underground. Over millennia, their size and intelligence ebbed, until they became stunted, four-legged semi-intelligent lizards ruled by a few larger, smarter specimens of their race. Eventually, this lost race died out, but their mummified corpses and psychic energies remain in the dusty hallways and chambers of their buried, half-ruined city. When the serpent man scholar and the player characters arrive, they unwittingly awaken those psychic energies, and a long-dead race soon revives to defend its home.

THE ESTEEMED SCHOLAR AHMIN SELENI OF VENDHYA

Ahmin Seleni is a scholar and sage from Vendhya, a robust elderly man, short and stout, fast-talking and intelligent. He has traveled far from home seeking to hire a group of men to trek into the eastern desert of Turan. His voice assumes a low conspiratorial tone, as he adds that he seeks a ruined lost city rumored to be hidden somewhere in the desert. The player characters have never heard of such ruins in this area, unless succeeding in a Daunting (D3) Lore test, in which case they recall only vague and universally-discounted rumors. Seleni insists that his information — *"from obscure sources perhaps known only to a handful of persons in all the world"* — is accurate.

He hires the player characters for a week of travel, and pays each of them 2 Gold, a good wage. For this, they must agree to provide him service as guides and bodyguards, should the need arise. Further, Seleni says that any treasures found in the nameless city are theirs to divide among themselves, with one exception: he asks only that he be given first pick of any artifacts of special historical significance. If they press him (or if the players claim they would have, in retrospect), Seleni offers to give them the first day's pay to help outfit themselves for the trip.

Ahmin Seleni is actually a serpent man scholar, a member of a sect devoted to recovering lost secrets of their race's and sub-races' past. Using powerful lost magic, the sect transformed the serpent man into human form, that he retains until he or the priests reverses the spell. During the course of the adventure, Seleni's disguise can be detected with the *Astral Wandering* spell. Otherwise, a successful Epic (D5) Insight test may allow a player character to catch a glimpse of his true nature in moments of great stress — when fearful for his life, or in the face of mighty sorcery. If Seleni's true nature reveals itself, he cravenly begs for mercy, claiming to be a fugitive from a secret serpent folk sect, persecuted for stealing the secret of the lost city.

Should he be revealed, he'll admit that he is certain it is there, and will emphasize that he still wants the player characters to accompany him, under the same conditions as before, but he offers to double their wages with whatever he finds in the city. If necessary, the serpent man will use his sorcery to escape the player characters.

Ahmin Seleni dresses in fine but well-worn traveling clothes, and sports a walking staff and a scimitar hanging at his belt. He has his own camel and, if necessary, he might offer to buy one or two others for player characters that lack them. This consumes all of his funds, however, so their wages must now come from whatever is found in the lost city.

AHMIN SELENI (NEMESIS)

A sharp-eyed scholar whose eyes betray both age and vast intelligence, Ahmin looks fit for 62 his years but wearied by the long path that brought him there.

ATTRIBUTES

Awareness	Intelligence	Personality	Willpower
11 (2)	13 (1)	14 (2)	10 (2)
Agility	Brawn		Coordination
9	11		9

FIELDS OF EXPERTISE

Combat	—	Movement	1
Fortitude	—	Senses	4
Knowledge	2	Social	2

THE SEETHERS IN DARKNESS

STRESS AND SOAK

- **Stress:** Vigor 11, Resolve 12
- **Soak:** Armor (Scaly Hide and Heavy Clothing) 2, Courage 3

ATTACKS

- **Scimitar (M):**, Reach 2, 5 🜏, 1H, Cavalry, Parry
- **Venom-Tipped Staff (M):** Reach 2 or 3, 6 🜏, 2H, Knockdown, Persistent 1, Stun
- **Venomous Bite (M):** Reach 1, 3 🜏, Persistent 3

SPECIAL ABILITIES

- **Inhuman Attributes:** As modified above.
- **Inured to Poison:** Seleni is immune to all poisons.
- **Paralyzing Venom:** If the serpent-man's bite inflicts a wound, it numbs the limb with paralyzing venom. Any tests made using the numbed limb are two steps harder than normal. As a Standard Action, player characters can make a Daunting (D3) Resistance test to regain the use of the limb. A minimum of one such test must be attempted every day. Failure causes the player character to suffer 1 Wound as the numbness begins to affect the rest of the body. The venom will last until the affected player character succeeds in making the Resistance test. A fellow player character with the *Apothecary* talent (see page 67 of the **Conan** corebook) may assist in overcoming the venom's effects. As Seleni's human appearance is wholly illusion, he can make this attack in human form.
- **Sorcerer:** Seleni knows the following spells: *Haunt the Mind* and *Form of a Beast*.
- **Dread Creature 3:** Serpent-man form only.
- **Fear 2:** Serpent-man form only.

DOOM SPENDS

- **True Form Revealed!:** At the cost of 1 Doom, the serpent-man can reveal his true form, triggering the Fear and Dread Creature special abilities. If Seleni suffers 2 or more damage in a single round of combat, he automatically reveals his true form without the need to spend any Doom.
- **Slash and Bite:** For 3 Doom, the serpent man can make a scimitar attack and follow it up with a bite attack on the same target in the same round — performing this attack while in human form will automatically result in the reveal of his serpent form, without the need for the expenditure of Doom.

THE DEVOURING STORM

As the adventure opens, the player characters have been traveling in the desert for three days. At first, they followed the established caravan routes, but then they struck out southward into the trackless sandy waste. During the trip, Ahmin Seleni proves to be a knowledgeable and entertaining companion, telling all manner of historical, mythological, and fantastic tales. He talks so much that he may even irritate his companions. Seleni frequently consults the position of the sun and rides off to examine some random rock outcropping, no matter how distant. When asked, the scholar states he is looking for markings that might have been left behind by the city's inhabitants, eons ago. Seleni finally finds and reveals one such stone carving — faint hashes and squiggles, barely discernible on the ages-old stone. Seleni continues to consult the position of the sun, and then rides on to the next rock formation, searching for more signs so that he can triangulate the exact location of the ruins.

This goes on for two more days, when, in midmorning, the air turns deathly still — and unnaturally cool. In the south, the sky darkens ominously. A huge sandstorm is coming, filling the horizon with a purplish-black wall shot through with angry flashes of lightning. The player characters are far from shelter, save for the meager rock formations their companion fussed over during the past few days. Each member of the group must attempt a Challenging (D2) Animal Handling test to spur their horse or camel toward the nearest rock shelter. A failed test means the player character is caught in the storm before reaching shelter. A Complication indicates the rider takes 1 🜏 damage as the animal throws them and flees, leaving the poor soul to the mercy of the howling wind and skin-lashing sands. Ahmin Seleni's camel panics, bolting toward a distant rock ridge. A Daunting (D3) Observation test reveals that the scholar is apparently deliberately spurring his mount toward these rocks — but it's dangerous to try to follow him, requiring a Daunting (D3) Animal Handling test if someone tries, with results as above.

Those who reach the meager shelter of the nearest boulders need another Challenging (D2) Animal Handling test to secure their mounts, or the beasts bolt away after their riders have dismounted — taking any supplies, weapons, and other gear with them as they frantically race away. Any player character can use Momentum from successful tests to grab another's panicked mount.

Meanwhile, the storm thunders forward in an angry billowing cloud of sand. Ahmin Seleni is swallowed by the dark wall of the storm, along with anyone else who failed

AHMIN SELENI'S ROUTE THROUGH THE CITY

The dotted line on *Map 1: The City Beneath the Sands* shows Seleni's route through the subterranean city. He is at least a few minutes — perhaps a few hours — ahead of the player characters. His initial forays are tentative, since he doesn't know exactly where he's going. He initially encounters a handful of skeletal serpent-men that he quickly evades through speed and sorcery. On subsequent crossings into the Crypt areas, the spirits of the dead begin to recognize his true nature, and he is left unmolested. Eventually, Seleni makes his way to the temple area, where he manages to evade the monstrous Cave Horror (see *Cave Horror*, page 130) and enters the ancient fane of the long-dead serpent-folk.

It is here the gamemaster may wish to have the player characters find their wayward "companion", engrossed with studying the carvings on the temple walls, perhaps even copying some of them onto his own parchment. When the player characters encounter the Cave Horror outside the temple, Ahmin Seleni looks for a place to hide, heading for the Crypt of Kings. It is there that he discovers the Eye of Sephet, a treasure he makes every attempt to take for himself, either hiding it within the temple rubble or concealing it upon his person. If worst comes to worst, he may try to bargain with the player characters, offering to lead them out of the city if they'll just let him have the Eye — it will destroy any human that tries to use it anyway, he claims.

If Ahmin Seleni manages to elude the player characters, he'll try to exit the city the same way he came in. If he has the Eye of Sephet, he may show up again later in the gamemaster's campaign, perhaps seeking the *other* Eye of Sephet and whatever powers it might bestow upon the individual wielding both artifacts.

Player characters crossing Seleni's path into the city can follow his footprints with a successful Daunting (D3) Observation test. They must make similar tests at major intersections they come to, since the movements of the reanimated serpent-folk eventually cross and confuse the trail. The gamemaster should allow for three of these tests, as a general rule.

---

to reach the shelter of the boulders. Anyone caught in the storm must make a Daunting (D3) Survival test, with success indicating a loss of only 2 ⚔ damage from the stinging winds and choking sand and grit. A failed test inflicts 3 ⚔ damage, while any Consequences indicate the victim is smothered and buried in the sands, taking a total of 4 ⚔ damage and nearly suffocating before clawing their way free once the storm has passed.

Any player character bold enough and fast enough to follow Ahmin Seleni into the teeth of the storm sees the scholar abandon his camel when he reaches the clump of boulders he fled toward. A player character following to the boulders must make a Daunting (D3) Animal Handling test to keep their panicked mount from fleeing, as above. By the time the recalcitrant camel is dealt with effectively, the howling storm has engulfed the rock cluster, and all thoughts are to hunkering down as it passes.

Seleni, meanwhile, vanishes amid the rocks.

The raging sandstorm lasts for a few hours, leaving the player characters cowering amid their rocky shelters or horribly exposed out in the open. Sand gets in their eyes, noses, and mouths. Every nook and cranny of their clothing abrades with sediment. Lightning crackles within the shrieking winds. Finally, by mid-afternoon, the winds pass by, leaving the desert landscape rearranged with new dunes — some rock outcroppings nearly concealed, others newly exposed.

Should the player characters choose to leave at this juncture, without entering this mysterious city, the gamemaster may wish to use the rules for Fatigue from exposure to heat, as described on page 79 of the **Conan** corebook. They are free, of course, to exit and seek their own safety, but it will be rough going on the way back, arriving at civilization sunburnt and parched, with little to show for their efforts.

THE VANISHED SCHOLAR

Of their employer there is no sign. A Challenging (D2) Observation test follows the general direction his mount took him and there, among a clump of the graffitied stones Seleni sought, is a narrow cleft in the rocks — a passage snaking into the darkness below. Assuming the player characters decide to explore the mysterious passage, they now enter the city beneath the sands via the entry/exit marked "Z" on *Map 1: The City Beneath the Sands* (page 127).

Unfortunately, as soon as the group reaches the first north-south corridor, the ceiling several yards behind them collapses in a roar of falling stone and dust. The way back is utterly impassable — their only hope is to find another way out of the city. Luckily, their erstwhile employer left a trail of footprints through the ever-present dust (see *Ahmin Seleni's Route Through the City* sidebar).

THE SEETHERS IN DARKNESS

THE CITY BENEATH THE SANDS

The nameless city beneath the sands is eerie, oppressive, and dark. Without a light source, a poor soul is almost certainly doomed — likely to wander for days on end without discovering a way out, to say nothing of the possibilities of falling into a chasm or being swarmed upon by the city's former inhabitants. The city is eerily quiet, save for mysterious noises heard in the distant and not-so-distant darkness: skitterings, draggings, sounds of falling earth or stone, breathy wordless whispers or sighs, etc. The gamemaster should evoke the creepy, deadness of this lost civilization.

THE CITY'S GENERAL INTERIOR

Most of the passages are 6–7 feet high and barely that wide, chiseled right out of the solid stone. These passages are thick with the dust and cobwebs of millennia of disuse — except for signs marking the passing of Ahmin Seleni (see *Ahmin Seleni's Route Through the City*, page 124). Map 1: The City Beneath the Sands shows east-west and north-south hallways. The former are the living quarters or "galleries", while the latter are the "crypts". Both are described below. The shaded areas show where the ceiling has collapsed, rendering the passages totally blocked. There are also chasms where the stone has subsided and collapsed deep into the ground, again preventing or at least hindering passage. A chasm may be anywhere from five to one hundred yards across. The Xs shown on the map are suggested places for "Finds" that the player characters may come across as they explore the ruined city. See the *Finds* sidebar for a table of possibilities (page 126). The gamemaster may, of course, also introduce these discoveries when and where desired.

BEETLE SWARM (TOUGHENED)

Death in hundreds or thousands of glistening, black carapaces moving like angry oil.

ATTRIBUTES			
Awareness	Intelligence	Personality	Willpower
6	4	4	4
Agility	Brawn		Coordination
6 (1)	6		4

FIELDS OF EXPERTISE			
Combat	2	Movement	—
Fortitude	—	Senses	—
Knowledge	—	Social	—

STRESS AND SOAK
- **Stress:** Vigor 6, Resolve 4
- **Soak:** Armor 4, Courage 4

ATTACKS
- **Biting Swarm (M):** Reach 1, 3 🜂, Area (Close), Piercing 3

SPECIAL ABILITIES
- Inhuman Agility

DOOM SPENDS
- **They're Coming Out of the Walls:** For each Doom spent, the gamemaster can increase the damage done by the swarm by 1 🜂.
- **Swarm Initiative:** The gamemaster can spend 1 Doom to have a beetle swarm attack before the player characters in a given round. Otherwise, the player characters always make their attacks first.

THE CITY'S HISTORY

The city beneath the sands was built hundreds of thousands of years ago by a band of the serpent-folk, seeking refuge from the assaults of humankind. They retreated to the desert and built their city under the ground, digging through the solid rock when they could, and quarrying everything else they needed from the surface. Over time, the serpent-folk

FINDS

Roll	Effect
1–4	A single degenerate saurian skeleton, long-dead and inanimate (for the time being). Roll 1d20: On a roll of 1–10 the remains have a corroded short spear or shortsword, 11–20 there is nothing else of interest. Another roll of 1d20 with a result of 1–2 indicates the skeleton was wearing a fine weirdly-carved silver ring (worth at least 1 Gold), or a silver brooch with emeralds (1 Gold), or a pair of engraved copper bracelets (1 Gold for both).
5–6	The player characters encounter 1+1 🜲 remains identical to those described above. All are similarly armed/decorated.
7–8	As above, but 2+2 🜲 remains, all armed with spear or shortsword.
9–10	Entry 5–6 above, but molesting the skeletons unleashes beetle swarms (see page 125) equal in number to double the number of remains.
11–13	A pile of bones, broken and split as if gnawed upon.
14	A section of wall is pitted with finger-sized holes, and once the player characters pass by it, one beetle swarm per player character pours forth to devour the living (see page 125).
15	A section of floor collapses. Anyone failing a Challenging (D2) Athletics test plunges into the abyss, taking 3 🜲 and finding themselves trapped in the crypt mentioned below (another player character may spend 2 Momentum to catch a falling victim).
16–17	A section of ceiling collapses; anyone failing a Challenging (D2) Athletics test takes 3 🜲 damage. Armor protects against this damage, and any Complication indicates the player character is buried and trapped under the rubble, requiring a Challenging (D2) Brawn test to get free, or an Average (D1) Brawn test if assisted by others.
18	2+2 🜲 degenerate serpent-folk skeletons (see page 127), each armed or decorated as per entry 1–4, but one figure wears a bronze shortsword with a jewel worth 2 Gold in the pommel.
19–20	This encounter takes place in a crypt corridor only. A degenerate saurian spirit leaves its tomb and confronts the intruders. The lizard-ghost appears filmy and hoarsely shrieks its hate (Scare attack) or lashes out with the talons on its supernaturally long-reaching arms (Icy Talons attack). If it reduces a chosen target to 0 Resolve, the spirit possesses the target, and then uses that form to physically attack their companions, attempting to kill any living beings present. If the possessed is restrained, the ghost then engages another target continuing to do so until it is either brought to 0 Vigor or 0 Resolve and dispelled, or the intruders leave the current section of crypts.

became smaller and slightly less intelligent — mutating into saurians — and they feared the chaotic surface world whose hairy proto-human dwellers had driven them into hiding. Their civilization lasted for thousands of years, but eventually, they died in their nameless city beneath the desert.

ANATOMY OF A SEETHER

The creatures themselves became more saurian than ophidian in appearance. Their bodies were about four feet long, with tails the same length. Their blunted snouts were alligator-like, but their craniums were large. They were capable of upright movement, albeit in a hunched posture, but many crawled about on all fours — particularly later in their devolution. They used tools and weapons, primarily spears and shortswords fashioned from bronze, but had little experience with warfare. They subsisted on insects, bats, small animals, fish taken from underground lakes and rivers, and fungi grown in special chambers deeper underground. In the dark, they waited… and devolved further.

The rulers of this society were its larger and more intelligent members — rarities among their kind. These saurian kings were interred in a crypt beneath the great temple at the center of the city.

The saurians' life-forces still reside within their buried city. They have been dormant for thousands of years, but now that there are living intruders within their ancient home, their spirits whisper forth from their tombs, seething with hate, attempting to drain psychic energy from intruders. This energy is used to animate the corpses of some of the saurians, and these reinvigorated things crawl forth to slay intruders. The longer the intruders stay, the more defenders they will revive.

THE SEETHERS IN DARKNESS

DEGENERATE SAURIAN SKELETONS (MINIONS)

Too long-dead to be fetid, only the faint dust upon their bones stirs the nostrils as this throwback species of deceased saurians lurches in the creeping darkness.

ATTRIBUTES

Awareness	Intelligence	Personality	Willpower
8	7	7	9

Agility	Brawn	Coordination
6	9	6

FIELDS OF EXPERTISE

Combat	1	Movement	—
Fortitude	1	Senses	1
Knowledge	—	Social	—

STRESS AND SOAK

- **Stress:** Vigor 4, Resolve 5
- **Soak:** Armor 1 (Corroded Bronze Breastplate and Mummified Hide), Courage 6 (Dead)

ATTACKS

- **Short Sword (M):** Reach 1, 4 💀, 1H, Parrying
- **Short Stabbing Spear (M):** Reach 3, 4 💀, Piercing 1, Fragile
- **Bony Claws (M):** Reach 1, 3 💀, Vicious 1
- **Snapping Jaws (M):** Reach 1, 5 💀, requires a Doom spend (see below)

SPECIAL ABILITIES

- **Night Vision**
- **Unliving**
- **Flammable:** The brittle, dry, scaly hide of the saurians burns easily — attacks with the Burning Quality count as having Vicious 1.

DOOM SPENDS

- **Snapping Jaws:** For 1 Doom a degenerate saurian skeleton can make an additional Bite attack against a foe.

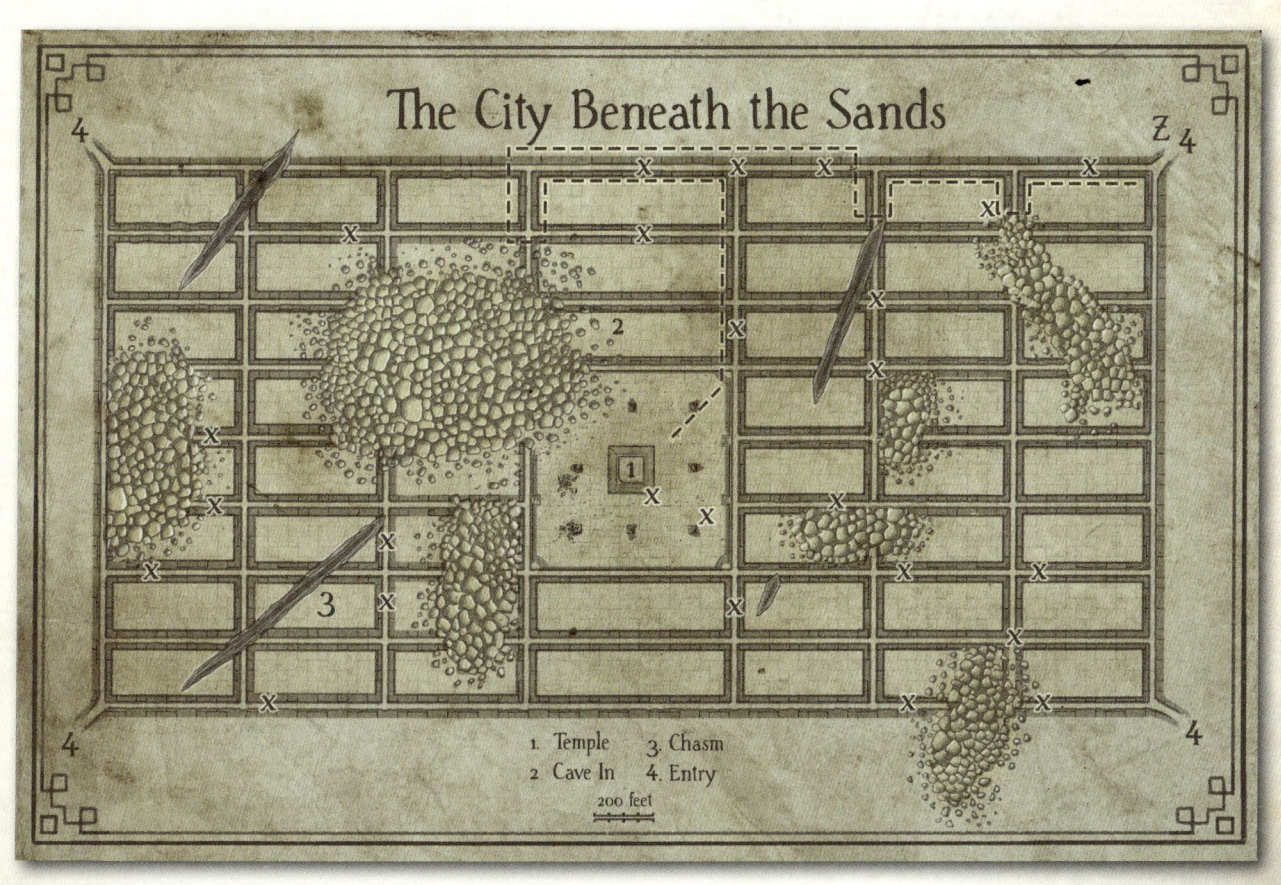

The City Beneath the Sands

1. Temple
2. Cave In
3. Chasm
4. Entry

200 feet

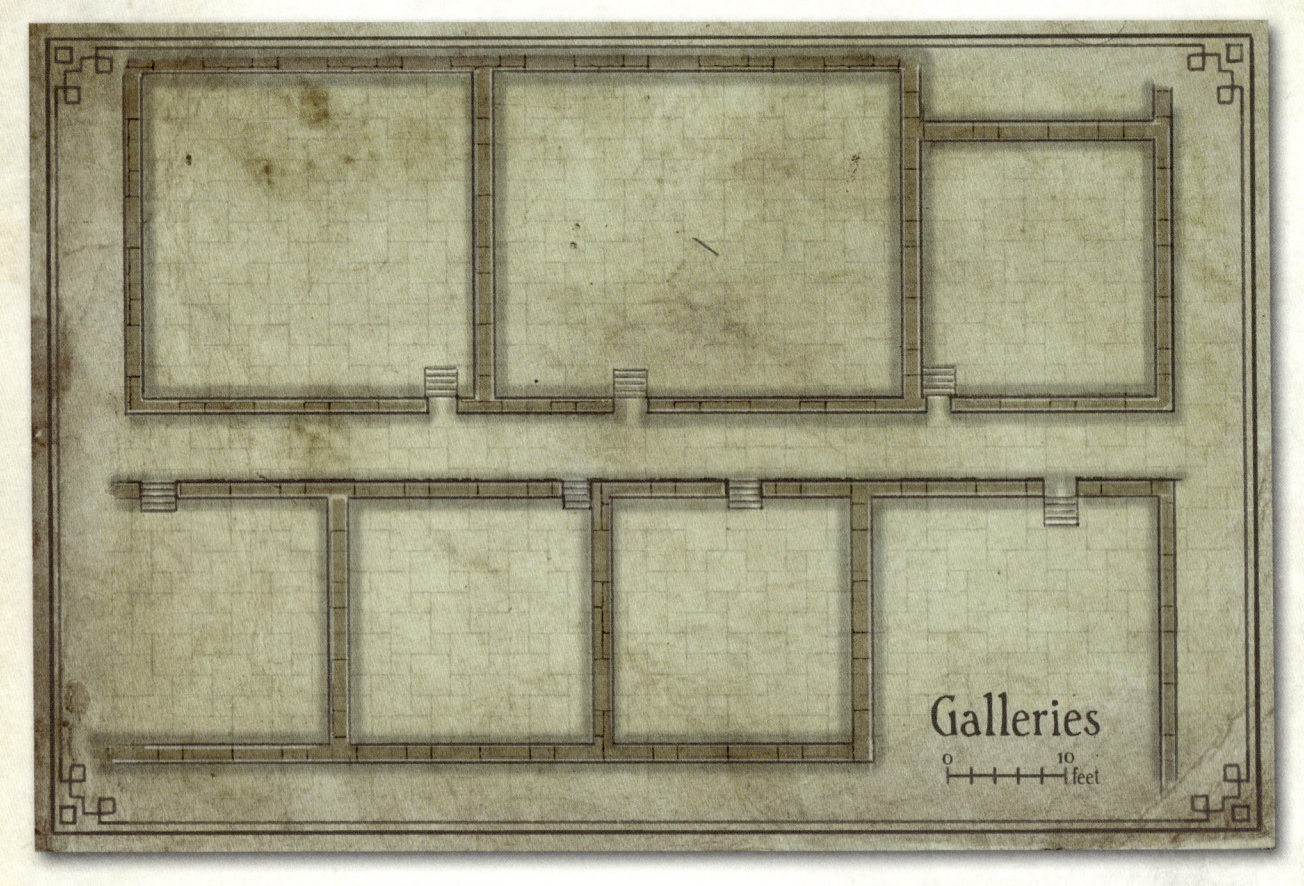

THE GALLERIES

As stated earlier, the "east-west" corridors are the galleries, the residential areas of the buried city. *Map 2: The Galleries* shows a portion of one of these galleries: all of the chambers along the galleries are similar. The residential quarters in the galleries consist of low, doorless entries about five feet high and two and a half feet wide, that open into square or rectangular chambers anywhere from 20 feet square to hundreds of feet square, all with ceilings only six or seven feet high. Some of the living chambers are a few low steps below the level of the outer corridor.

Dust and rubble from chunks that have fallen from the ceiling litter the living chambers. There is little of note or value left after thousands of years spent in dead dry air: scraps of rough fabric, unidentifiable bits of pottery, occasionally a few bones or even skeletons of the degenerate saurians. With a Dire (D4) Observation test desperate player characters may be able to find scraps of cloth or bone with which to fashion crude torches in these places.

As the player characters explore the city, a Challenging (D2) Insight test causes speculation that there must have been thousands of the degenerate reptilian creatures living here long, long ago.

THE CRYPTS

The north-south corridors of the city are of the same dimensions as those in the galleries: about six or seven feet high and of similar width. Here, however, the walls are lined with niches ten feet long, three feet high, and three feet deep. Over ninety percent of these niches each contain the desiccated corpse of one of the long-dead saurian inhabitants of the city, its most prominent and favored "citizens", kept on display within the halls until replaced by the body of another important resident. A given saurian skeleton is armed or decorated as per entry 1–4 in the *Finds* table on page 126.

The seething rage of the saurians makes itself felt in the crypts. Here, rustlings and whispers abound, and anyone succeeding in an Average (D1) Awareness test feels an uncanny sense of loathing, as if the dead reptilian things were watching them with intense hatred. A player character passing into a new crypts section will be attacked by the combined psychic energy of the dead saurians within that section. Passing an intersection along a north-south hallway constitutes entering a new section for these purposes. The gamemaster should look to subject player characters to three tests, made as a group. This attack requires the player characters to attempt a Daunting (D3) Discipline test: if successful it has no effect on the player characters.

THE SEETHERS IN DARKNESS

If the test fails, the target rolls 1+X 🜚, where X equals the number of d20s which failed the test. *For example, if only 1 success was achieved, 2* 🜚 *are rolled. A roll of 1 or 2 on the* 🜚 *indicates that the equivalent number of saurian skeletons are animated and chase after the group.*

The mummified beasts shuffle forth from their tombs and pursue the intruders into the city, dragging their desiccated corpses after their prey, picking up whatever weapons they might find along the way. This can potentially get desperate for the player characters, as there may be dozens of the things crawling after them while their Resolve runs low. Worse, the saurians may coordinate their attacks, surrounding the player characters in the passages or herding them into crypt sections where they can generate more of their vengeful dead.

Once they have encountered the crawling dead things, player characters may decide to start burning the readily combustible skeletons as quickly as they find them. After an hour of this, the gamemaster should call for Challenging (D2) Fortitude tests every subsequent hour, as the smoke and stinking odor of burning bones and reptilian scales chokes the underground like a chimney. Each hour, those who fail their tests take 1 🜚 Fatigue and suffer an additional step of Difficulty to all sight-related skills (including attacks and parries) due to burning eyes. The choking miasma dissipates after they stop torching the dead reptiles, and the smoke will clear after an hour or so. Wiser vandals begin systematically demolishing the skeletons as they are found. Unfortunately, there are just too many of the ragged horrors to destroy quickly enough to prevent their reanimation.

THE TEMPLE

Navigating the corridors of the dead city, the player characters should eventually come to a vast central chamber whose floor is seventy feet below the level of the main corridors. Long stone staircases descend to the floor. In the center of this chamber is a stone building 100 feet long on each side and forty feet high. The building rests twenty feet above the chamber floor, reached by a series of steps which completely surround it. The building's only entrance is a twelve by eight foot doorway in the southwest corner. Bats — some of them giant but harmless — flit and screech about the massive chamber, and their sudden flurry of activity can be used to startle the player characters. There are also crickets the size of a man's fist, centipedes as long as an arm, and spiders the size of pumpkins scuttling about in the corners, amid the rubble, and scrambling through webs — all of these oversized pests are window dressing for effect alone, though the player characters need not know that at first. Should the gamemaster desire, Vermin Swarms are described in the **Conan** corebook on page 332.

Throughout the temple chamber, dozens of long-dead skeletal saurians crouch, bowed as if in prayer. They are armed or adorned as per entry 1–4 on the *Finds* table (page 126). As the player characters approach the temple, each is again attacked once by the psychic energy of the dead saurians. A Daunting (D3) Discipline test is required: if successful, the attack has no effect. Each failure generates a roll of 1+X 🜚, where X equals the number of dice that failed the test. A result of 1 or 2 on the 🜚 indicates that number of saurian skeletons are animated and will come after the group within 2🜚×10 minutes. A result of 6 indicates the player character loses 1 point of Resolve. See page 127 for the degenerate saurian skeletons statistics.

Scattered around the temple are a series of massive twenty-foot high pedestals each topped with a twenty-foot tall stone statue of some terrible creature. A successful Lore test recognizes a few of these statues as depictions of ancient demons or gods, long forgotten by all but the most learned of occult scholars and sorcerers. In the flickering torchlight, player characters that make successful Challenging (D2) Observation tests spy glints of some reflective materials within the features of those statues. The ceiling in the northwestern corner of the temple plaza has caved in, and the three statues nearest this damage have also toppled and shattered across the floor. Player characters successfully searching the ruins of the statues discover 1 Gold's value in small precious stones used to decorate each of the three fallen statues. Generally, these are things such as an eye or other sensory organ, at the tips of tentacles, embedded in a forehead, or in the palm of a hand on the figure's jewelry, etc. Enterprising player characters may wish to climb the pedestals and pilfer the gems from the remaining five statues as well. A Challenging (D2) Thievery or Athletics test is required to scale each pedestal and statue, and separate Daunting (D3) Thievery tests are required to secure each of the 2 Gold worth of stones per statue. The gamemaster may spend up to 1 Doom per statue to add a single step of Difficulty to attempts to pry loose one of the gems. Any failed test indicates the jewel is damaged, halving its value. The first Complication rolled while removing a jewel indicates the fragile stone is shattered into useless shards. If more than one Complication is rolled, the gemstone remains intact and in place but the thief slips from his perch and falls to the stone floor below, incurring 1+2 ⚔ damage.

When the player characters approach the central temple, a successful Challenging (D2) Observation tests allows a player character to hear something large moving, with unlikely care, on the roof. Seconds later, an enormous pale white thing swings down, clutching at the side of the chamber and shrieking at the intruders. This is a cave horror, a ten-foot tall, blind, ape-like thing with a bat-like head (see below). The thing's shriek attack may leave some player characters stunned, and it quickly moves to attack, hanging from the side of the temple while raking with its claw. If the cave horror takes 8 or more points of damage, it flees to the roof of the temple where its shrieks, eventually summoning a second cave horror in a turn or so. When the second creature arrives, both attack the intruders, fighting to the death. On the roof of the temple is a nest of bones and tattered bat corpses containing three hairy, leathery watermelon-sized sacks: the eggs of the cave horrors.

> *"The snake-people were the last to go, yet at last men conquered even them and drove them forth into the waste-lands of the world, there to mate with true snakes until some day, say the sages, the horrid breed shall vanish utterly. Yet the Things returned in crafty guise as men grew soft and degenerate, forgetting ancient wars. Ah, that was a grim and secret war! Among the men of the Younger Earth stole the frightful monsters of the Elder Planet, safeguarded by their horrid wisdom and mysticisms, taking all forms and shapes, doing deeds of horror secretly."*
>
> — Brule the Spear-slayer,
> "The Shadow Kingdom"

CAVE HORROR (TOUGHENED)

Cave horrors are hulking subterranean beasts — twice the height of a man — with powerful ape-like bodies, sharp-taloned paws, and a bizarre, bat-like head. They are blind and eyeless: their large pointed ears extend into where their ocular orbits should be, giving them a heightened sense of hearing. Their nostrils are similarly oversized, so they have an advanced sense of smell as well. The bodies of cave horrors are lightly furred, usually light tan or grey but sometimes shockingly white. These creatures can crawl nimbly along ceilings or walls, often hiding among shadowy recesses in order to ambush their prey.

Cave horrors dwell underground, but sometimes venture out of their lairs for food. They are normally solitary creatures, but a single cave complex may be home to a mated pair and their offspring. Cave horrors reproduce by laying eggs every few years. Said eggs are sacks the size of a watermelon.

ATTRIBUTES

Awareness	Intelligence	Personality	Willpower
8	5	6	8

Agility	Brawn	Coordination
11	14	11

FIELDS OF EXPERTISE

Combat	1	Movement	2
Fortitude	1	Senses	1
Knowledge	—	Social	—

STRESS AND SOAK

- **Stress:** Vigor 14, Resolve 8
- **Soak:** Armor —, Courage 4

ATTACKS

- **Raking Talon (M):** Reach 2, 6 ⚔, Knockdown
- **Bite (M):** Reach 1, 5 ⚔, Vicious

SPECIAL ABILITIES

- **Brachiating:** Cave horrors are capable of moving on walls and ceilings with remarkable agility, easily swinging from ridges and cracks in the surfaces. A cave horror may ignore all Challenging terrain when moving through zones that include trees, and may re-roll any d20 that does not generate a success when making a Movement-related test when climbing or moving across walls.
- **Fear 1**
- **Grappling**
- **Monstrous Creature**

THE SEETHERS IN DARKNESS

> **DOOM SPENDS**
>
> - **Frenzy:** For 2 Doom the cave horror can make an additional attack.
> - **Ear-Splitting Screech:** For 3 Doom, the cave horror can make an ear-splitting screech: Range C, 4 🗲 mental, Area, Stun.

DEEPER INTO THE TEMPLE

Inside the temple are another forty or so dead reptilians, also bowed in eternal prayer and armed with weapons or wearing jewelry, as described above. Once inside the temple, each player character is again attacked once by the psychic energy of the dead saurian. The player character must attempt a Daunting (D3) Discipline test: if successful the attack has no effect. Each failure generates a roll of 1+X 🗲, where X equals the number of dice that failed to score a success. A result of 1 or 2 on the 🗲 indicates that number of saurian skeletons are animated and come after the group within three turns, and any result of 6 indicates the player character suffers 1 point of Despair as well. See *Degenerate Saurian Skeletons* on page 127 for the degenerate saurian skeleton statistics.

The inner walls of the temple are covered with crude carvings depicting the saurian race's history. They are shown digging into the ground and building their subterranean city, going about everyday tasks, worshipping serpent gods and their oversized kings, and the like.

Chunks of the temple ceiling have fallen in, crushing furnishings and skeletons. A central statue of two gigantic twined serpents lies fallen and shattered. Careful examination or an Average (D1) Observation test notes that the statues' eyes are large — fist-sized! — yellowish gems each worth 3 Gold. It requires a Challenging (D2) Thievery test to remove them successfully, with failure halving their value and any Complication destroying them altogether.

One eye is missing from one statue. Entwined stone serpents form an arch over a wide, steep, and dark stairway descending to the crypts below. A successful Average (D1) Observation test or simply descending the steps allows a player character to catch a glimpse of a greenish-amber object glinting on the stairway below. This fist-sized jewel is yellowish, with a deep greenish-black highlight, the whole resembling a serpent's eye. This is the Eye of Sephet! A Daunting (D3) Lore test tells the player characters as much.

> ### THE EYE OF SEPHET
>
> Sephet was one of Set's most powerful priests in ancient times, practically a demi-god himself. The Eyes of Sephet were powerful artifacts sacred to the serpent-folk and their kin, lost for eons untold. The Eyes have several powers usable by whomever carries it, as noted below. Serpent-folk and their kin (including saurians) will do *anything* to reclaim one of the two Eyes, and any human who touched it must be slain for defiling it. Each Eye has the following properties:
>
> - **The Eye has a Willpower 14.** Any Willpower test made by the carrier uses either his own Willpower or the Eye's, whichever is greater.
>
> - **No reptilian creature or monster of Intelligence 6 or less will ever attack the wielder** unless he or she attacks that creature first. Intelligent reptilian races, such as serpent-folk, always attack a non-serpent person who carries the Eye, if they know he has it. The gem is sacred to them, and it is a heresy for a human to possess it.
>
> - **The Eye is a sentient creature hiding in plain sight.** If contact is made via *Astral Wanderings* or similar spell, it may deign to act as a Patron or enter into a Pact. Its demands start off small but steadily grow. It starts off with simple worship costing 1 Gold, 1 Resolve, and 1 Vigor. However, its demands become greater with every Upkeep. The second Upkeep is 3 Gold, 3 Resolve, and 3 Damage. The third Upkeep raises these values to 5, then to 7, etc. The benefit is that the Eye doesn't care where this comes from. The wielder might slay a beast or slave to provide the 5 Damage, induct five others into its cult to provide 1 Resolve each for a total of 5.
>
> - **The Eye counts as a Familiar**, granting +1d20 to all Sorcery tests.
>
> - **THE CURSE OF THE EYE:** The eye has a Doom pool of 2, which it uses to corrupt its non-ophidian wielders. It may spend 1 point of Doom (Repeatable) to grant the wielder +1d20 to any skill test at the cost of 2 🗲 of the wielder's Resolve. If a Trauma is inflicted by this, and the Eye waits till the perfect moment to do this, the wielder becomes convinced that those around them covet the amulet. This Trauma can be undone by giving up the Eye. A Dire (D4) Discipline test is needed to accomplish this, and successfully heals the Trauma as normal.
>
> The whereabouts of the other Eye is unknown, and it may have been long-plundered from the nameless city, or it might be concealed somewhere else within its depths.

The stairs lead down to the crypt of the reptile peoples' kings. Nothing good is likely to venture forth from that dry lair.

THE CRYPT OF KINGS

The rubble-strewn stairway leads over seventy feet down into a room fifty feet square and thirty feet high. Colorful mosaics of the saurians tile the floors, and the three walls without stairs are set with niches six feet wide by six feet deep and ten feet high, with two tiers, one above the other. Each wall has fourteen such niches — seven at ground level, seven more fifteen feet above the floor. Each niche contains the standing skeleton of a man-sized saurian creature, similar to the smaller ones seen throughout the city. These are the ancient kings of the reptile people. Adorned in corroded metal armor, their bony claws clutch battleaxes, broadswords, and spears. Their toothy skulls snarl silently.

Once again, human intruders feel the psychic hate emanating from these long-dead rulers. Each trespasser must make a Dire (D4) Discipline test, which, if successful, has no effect. Each failure generates a roll of 1+X 🦅, where X equals the number of dice which failed to score a success. A roll of 1 or 2 on the die indicates that number of saurian kings are animated and attack the intruders within two turns, and any 6 rolled indicates the player character loses 1 point of Resolve as well. Note that at least one such saurian king animates within three turns of the player characters' arrival here, regardless of these results.

Statistics for the animated skeletons of the degenerate saurians' long-dead kings are found on page 133.

Each of the forty-two saurian kings in this crypt is adorned not only with his arms and armor but with fabulous jewelry (gold breastplates, amulets, and armbands, some studded with uncut rubies and emeralds) worth 5 Gold apiece — a considerable fortune! Unfortunately, any time one of the dead kings is touched or molested in any way, that skeleton immediately animates and gets one free claw attack at the thief. The player characters may have found a fortune, but to collect it all they must slay these reanimated saurian-skeletons! Unless they're bold or foolhardy, the group can more safely make do with the jewelry taken from but a few of the vengeful lizard-kings. If they decide to torch the undead horrors in this relatively small space, not only do the skeletons attack, but the air is filled with poisonous fumes exuded by the long-withered lungs. The damage is X 🦅 with X equaling the number of rounds spent in the chamber.

Worse yet, once the player characters have slain at least one animated saurian king skeleton, one of the other creatures in the upper level of crypts begins a chant: "Hrell-La-Grzz-La-HESS, Hrell-La-Grzz-La-HESS..." Within a few moments, the chant seems to be picked up by the other

The City Beneath The Sands

The Temple
1 Temple
2 Demonic Statues
3 Collapsed Ceiling
4 Stairs
5 Saurian Corpses

100 feet

THE SEETHERS IN DARKNESS

DEGENERATE SAURIAN KING SKELETONS (TOUGHENED)

ATTRIBUTES

Awareness	Intelligence	Personality	Willpower
9	9	8	11
Agility	**Brawn**		**Coordination**
12	12		7

FIELDS OF EXPERTISE

Combat	2	Movement	—
Fortitude	2	Senses	1
Knowledge	—	Social	—

STRESS AND SOAK

- **Stress:** Vigor 12, Resolve 11
- **Soak:** Armor 2 (Corroded Bronze Ceremonial Breastplate), Courage —

ATTACKS

- **Broadsword (M):** Reach 2, 8♦, Unbalanced, Parrying, Fragile
- **Spear (M):** Reach 3, 7♦, Unbalanced, Piercing 1, Fragile
- **Battleaxe (M):** Reach 2, 7♦, Unbalanced, Intense, Vicious 1, Fragile
- **Bony Claws (M):** Reach 1, 5♦, Vicious 1
- **Wrathful Glare (T):** Range C, 3♦, Stun

SPECIAL ABILITIES

- **Fear 1**
- **Night Vision**
- **Unliving**
- **Flammable:** The brittle, dry, scaly hide of the saurian kings burns easily. Attacks with the Burning Quality count as having Vicious 1.

DOOM SPENDS

- **Wrathful Glare:** For 2 Doom a saurian king can make a Threaten attack followed by a weapon attack at the same target within the same turn.

saurian kings, though none move unless tampered with. Within a few turns the entire temple murmurs with the chant, picked up by the psychic residue of other saurians in the city. Then the ground shifts, just a fraction, and a film of dust and debris falls from the ceiling — and the chant is picked up by hundreds of more voices! A Challenging (D2) Lore or Intelligence test may cause one to realize that the dead lizard-people wish to collapse their city on the heads of the intruders. If they don't take the hint, more tremors and ceiling collapses should get the idea across. If the player characters don't leave immediately they'll be crushed when the city collapses within an hour, or as the gamemaster desires. As the group flees, they may still run into other creatures, rouse skeletal saurians, or come across ones awakened earlier. Each player character should also attempt a Daunting (D3) Acrobatics or Athletics test, whichever is greater, during the flight. Failure indicates the player character takes 2♦, Vicious 2 damage from falling rocks and debris. Complications from this test can mean that some or all of the treasure is dropped.

The Inner Temple

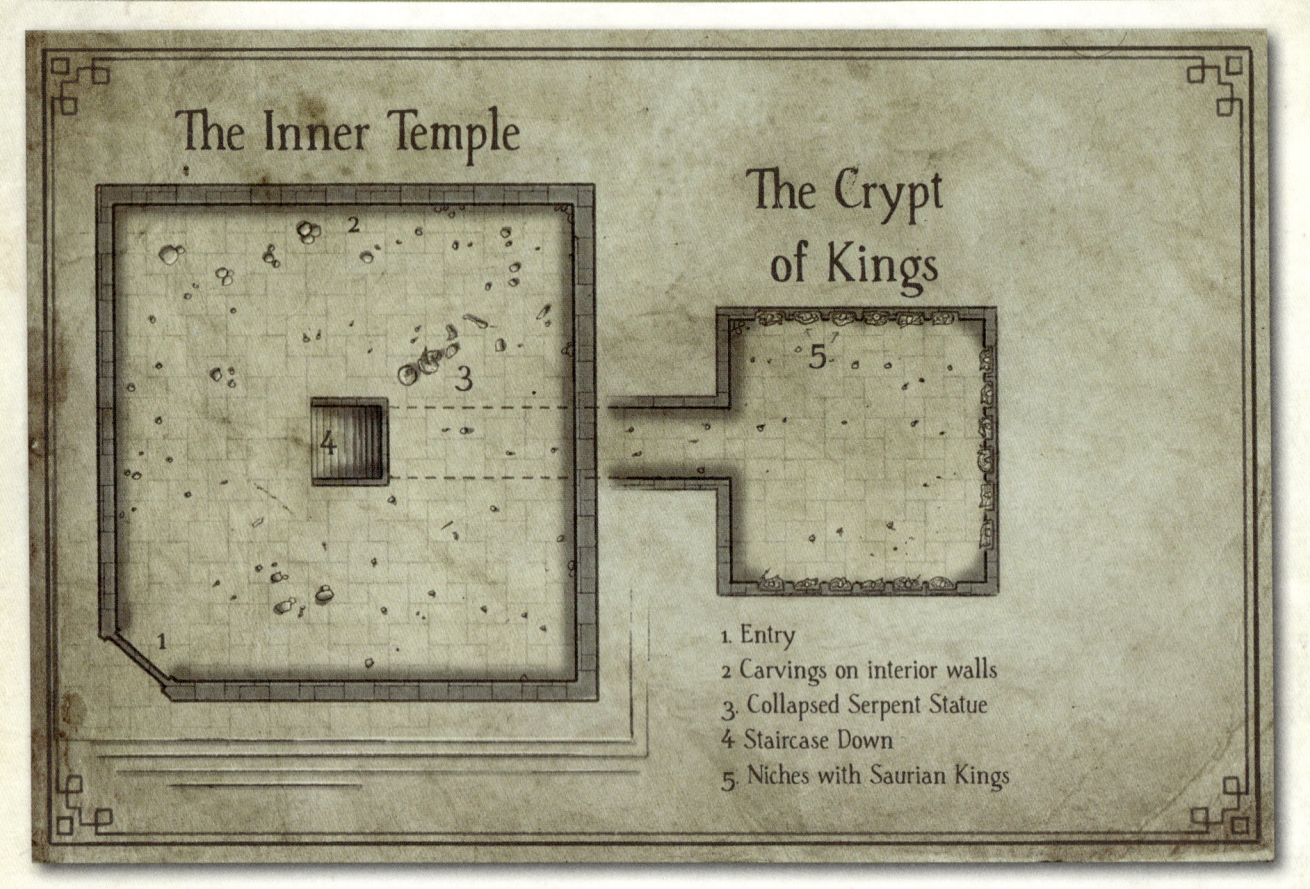

The Crypt of Kings

1. Entry
2. Carvings on interior walls
3. Collapsed Serpent Statue
4. Staircase Down
5. Niches with Saurian Kings

NAVIGATING THE NAMELESS CITY, AND MEETING ITS OTHER RESIDENTS

The player characters begin at the spot marked on *Map 1: The City Beneath the Sands* (see page 127). From there, they must find their own way out. The caved-in areas and chasms are described in *The City Beneath the Sands* section, and the other locations of note are detailed in the preceding sections. There remain a few other points that need to be addressed.

First and most important are the exits from the nameless city. There are three left since the player characters' initial entry point was blocked by a massive cave-in. Each of the exits is located at the end of one of the Galleries. At each point marked "A" on *Map 1: The City Beneath the Sands*, an Average (D1) Observation test reveals what looks like a tiny speck of light far ahead. At the points marked "B", a normal Search test sees the light. Note that if it is night on the surface, this light is not seen. These passages lead to stone staircases that exit into rock outcroppings on the surface, exactly like the one initially found and used by the player characters.

Secondly, if the player characters dealt with the first cave horror quickly and efficiently, its mate still lurks elsewhere in the city, most likely in one of the chasms since its great size (over a dozen feet tall) means it must crawl or move hunchedly through the normal corridors of the city. If player characters stand at the edge of the chasm in which it is wall-crawling, it swings down and attacks, hoping to snag at least one victim for a quick meal. If it takes more than 8 damage, it retreats back into the chasm, perhaps waiting to follow its potential prey. If it was drawn to the cries of its mate in the temple chamber, it lurks in the shadows of the ceiling waiting to pounce and slay.

There are still many galleries and crypts to navigate while attempting to find a way out of the city, and every entry into a new crypts area triggers a psychic attack by the mummified saurians and the possible reanimation of more of the seething horde.

Finally there is the matter of the scholar, Ahmin Seleni. Seleni's progress through the city is discussed above, but if, where, and when the player characters ever meet up with him is left for the gamemaster to decide. It might prove interesting to allow Seleni to escape somehow so that he might return as a recurring villain later in the campaign. Perhaps, if he is killed, his body is lost or unrecoverable, buried beneath tons of rubble or tumbling into a chasm, allowing him the potential of a miraculous recovery, aided by the other Eye of Sephet.

THE SEETHERS IN DARKNESS

ESCAPING THE NAMELESS CITY

The player characters may have to leave the nameless city in a hurry, but they may also have procured a small fortune in gems and jewelry. If they didn't cause the destruction of the city, they may want to return and plunder it again, perhaps with better resources. Unfortunately, within a few days of their leaving the city, the buried metropolis collapses, brought down by its undead saurian kings to avoid further defilement by the surface-worlders. The exit passages may be found, but they too are caved in after a few hundred yards, far from any other signs of the great city. It would take hundreds of workers months — or even years — to excavate the city, highly impractical in this searing hot desert. The group must settle for what they've already pilfered from the ancient city beneath the sands.

AFTERMATH

Hopefully, the player characters escaped to the surface before the city buried itself forever beneath the sands. They may have a few wounds to heal, but they should also have at least a few trinkets and treasures on which to subsist, and to indulge themselves thoroughly. Unfortunately, wealth such as this may draw the unwanted attentions of jealous kings, unscrupulous wizards, and opportunistic thieves and murderers.

If they tell the tales of their adventure in the lost city, the player characters may also draw the attention of scholars wanting to learn more about the city and its residents. The player characters may also find themselves stalked by other disguised serpent-folk and their ilk, angry to learn of the desecration of the city of their ancestors. Their reputation among the reclusive ophidians will not be a positive one. And if they have the Eye of Sephet, it will be much much worse: the serpent-folk will assuredly come for it at some point. But what of the *other* Eye of Sephet?

EXPERIENCE

Avoiding the clawed, skeletal fingers of the long dead saurians, and making it to the surface alive, should be worth 300 experience points for each player character. On top of this, the gamemaster can award 50 or more additional experience points to any player character who was particularly inventive or effective during the adventure. The gamemaster can award these bonuses as she sees fit, but some reasons why extra points might be handed out are given below:

- Revealing Seleni's true nature.

- Killing one of the dreadful cave horrors or performing mighty deeds in the battle with the saurian kings.

- Using the Eye of Sephet without falling prey to its malign influence.

The gamemaster should avoid, if possible, awarding more than 100 bonus experience points to any individual character during the adventure.

CHAPTER 8
SEEDS OF GLORY

> *As for Conan's eventual fate — frankly I can't predict it. In writing these yarns I've always felt less as creating them than as if I were simply chronicling his adventures as he told them to me. That's why they skip about so much, without following a regular order. The average adventurer, telling tales of a wild life at random, seldom follows any ordered plan, but narrates episodes widely separated by space and years, as they occur to him."*
>
> — Robert E. Howard, letter to P. Schuyler Miller

CAMPAIGNS AND JEWELED THRONES

The adventures in *Jeweled Thrones of the Earth* are independent of one another, but it would take little effort for the gamemaster to connect them into a single, continuous campaign. They can be hacked up, played with, moved around and put into bold new shapes and interesting new configurations. Following are different possible approaches to using these adventures as a campaign — as well as a number of different campaign frameworks in which the existing adventures are all linked together, each one leading naturally into the next.

After that are suggestions about how playing with various elements of these adventures provides an opportunity to mix-and-match plot elements from one adventure with the themes of another, perhaps creating a grand, hybrid campaign in which the players will never actually play through one adventure as written, but will instead play all of them in part.

However, this depends on the gamemaster and the preference of the players. Do they want an extended campaign? Do they want something more episodic, like Conan's own career, jumping across the continent with only rough notions of what happened between, sometimes adventures had out of sequence with one another? Or do they want something more linear and deliberate, following up each adventure with specific sequences of travel, upkeep, and perhaps even "filler" adventures based on downtime events, segueing naturally into the next adventure?

Whichever the case is, the ideas presented below may prove useful to any gamemaster and group of players.

FIRST STEPS ON THE ROAD OF KINGS

The world of the Hyborian Age is vast enough to accommodate more than one legend. The continent may have trembled at Conan's footsteps, but he encountered many other remarkable individuals who were equally as notable — characters like Shevatas, Bêlit, Taurus, Hadrathus, Amalric, Strom, Pelias, Zelata, the Devi Yasmina, and others — any one of them equivalent to the stuff player characters are made of.

When beginning a *Conan* game, the gamemaster should consider asking the players themselves what type of campaign they want to be involved in, or even if they want to play in a campaign at all! Do they want to emulate Conan's own saga, beginning as lowly thieves or poor outcastes, and eventually ascending to great stature, perhaps claiming

SEEDS OF GLORY

thrones of their own? And, if so, do they want to do so in the picaresque style with which Howard recorded Conan's adventures — piecemeal, skipping from one period in his life to another, as suited him? Might they not prefer the continuous, gradual accrual of power, skill, and prestige, finally leading to a glorious culmination?

Some players are happy for the thrill of a series of exhilarating adventures, without any overall goal or pattern, while others might feel the need for a solid progression from one exploit to another, seeing how their player characters grow from one experience to the next. This preference is important to know ahead of time, and knowing this, the gamemaster can adjust the ways these adventures are introduced and used to best suit the player expectations, and wring the most out of them.

FROM CHAINS TO CROWNS

This campaign framework is the most straightforward, easily supported by the player characters themselves, with little adjustment. Conan's tale spans his ascent from a rough barbarian to a skilled (if naïve) thief, from his time as a capable mercenary to his years as successful pirate, his sojourn into banditry, exploring the lands of the South and the East, and his return to the border of civilization, a period that ended with him upon a throne. The player characters' sagas can — and perhaps should — be no less broad and far-ranging, and the following outline crafts the adventures in these very pages into just such a story.

The player characters might begin their adventures in the powerless grip of slavery, trapped within the deep, hideous mining shaft described in *The Red Pit* (page 107). From here, should they escape with their lives, almost anything is a step up. Where will they go next? Perhaps one of the few personal treasures one of the player characters managed to retain during their enslavement was an unusual and beautiful amulet. After arriving in the city where *The Thousand Eyes of Aumag-Bel* (page 90) takes place, the amulet is stolen and the player characters must retrieve it.

From there, perhaps they befriend a merchant who offers them what he believes to be well-paid, simple employment, guarding a scholar on a trip into the desert. Except, of course, as the events depicted in *The Seethers in the Sand* (page 121) make clear, this scholar is both more and less than he appears. Escaping the subterranean tomb of the serpent people may be dangerous, but perhaps it all begins to seem worthwhile when the player characters obtain the fragments of a map leading to an abandoned site of ritual, power and wealth.

Unfortunately, this wealth is located atop *The Caves of the Dero* (page 53), its fearsome inhabitants are not keen on allowing the theft of treasure, irrespective of how difficult the player characters' lives might have been up until this point.

The dangers which they have braved and the number of terrifying creatures and events which they have overcome by this point however, has earned the player characters no little prestige and they are approached, or confronted, with the request for help from the borderlands where Picts are massing, threatening to sweep the civilizations of the north away in a tide of slaughter, led by *The Ghost of Thunder River* (page 71). Tracking the true reason for the sudden exodus of the Picts takes the player characters deep into strange, forest and along uncharted rivers. There, secreted away from the world for hundreds of years is a forgotten kingdom of incestuous, warring tribes, plagued by the very *Devil Under Green Stars* (page 5). Fighting their way through generations of mistrust and blood feuds leads the players finally, to a small coastal town where they can purchase a ship home.

However, it is at this point that *The Pact of Xiabalba* (page 35) affects them, smashing the ship to pieces and stranding the player characters on an uninhabited island. Or at least, *almost* uninhabited. For there is one survivor who has a role plotted out for the player characters. Should those player characters emerge, weary and beaten, from this final adventure, there are two ways a gamemaster can seek to resolve the campaign. Either, the alterations which the player characters have made to the fabric of time in *Xiabalba* has left them regents of a renewed island kingdom or leaves them with sufficient gold to return to the mainland wealthy beyond the dreams of princes and merchants.

This, at least, is one way of tying all the adventures together into a coherent whole; while the plot may be loose, each adventure feeds into the next and gives the sense of desperate progression which Conan's career assumes, when read chronologically. But this is just one way of many to use the adventures mentioned above as part of a campaign, designed to plunge your player characters into danger, turmoil and, perhaps, triumph.

RAGS TO RICHES AND RICHES TO RAGS

Of course, for a more unpredictable turn of events, you could start the player characters off in surroundings of relative comfort. Perhaps they aren't wealthy, precisely, but they are employed. Perhaps they are trusted members of the border guard, patrolling the Thunder River. For some time there has been little Pictish activity on the riverbank which borders the wilderness. Until, of course, the player characters stumble into the dreadful events which *The Ghost of Thunder River* recounts. Perhaps, these particular border guards acquit themselves well — well enough in fact to attract the attention of a merchant planning for an expedition… which sends them into the desert and a nameless city.

However, what distinguishes this campaign frame is that, just as the player characters are beginning to feel complacent, they are captured and flung into the Red Pit. It may seem cruel but, well, this is the Hyborian Age. It is a time of savagery and conflict and terrible sorcery. At the time Conan is crucified at the beginning of "A Witch Shall Be Born" he is the captain of the queen's guard, having achieved a rank of great respect. None of this avails him. Instead, it is only his limitless fortitude and strength that enable his survival.

The gamemaster may wish to the characters into just such a situation — depriving them of weapons, armor, gear, and rations, forcing them to reclaim their status as protagonists. It is certain that, when they finally clamber out of the Red Pit, bloodied but still willing to fight, they will have a greater respect for the dangers of the world they are adventuring in — and perhaps the players themselves will have a deeper connection to the characters they play.

It's easy to feel like a hero when butchering whole columns of enemy infantry with a single sweep of a sword. It is a lot harder to feel like that while trying to incite a rebellion in listless, exhausted slaves with arrows zipping past one's ears. This trick can be used, in subtler ways, with other adventures too. If the player characters have become particularly famous and lauded as a result of their deeds, have them stumble into the events of *Devils Under Green Stars*. The inhabitants of that lost city will have no notion of the renown the player characters might have accrued. The same is true of *The Pact of Xiabalba*. However impressive the saga of their past might be, when they are washed ashore on a (virtually) uninhabited island, it doesn't really matter.

Mixing the adventures, and their relationship to one another, can ensure that the player characters are never entirely sure that they are safe or that they fully understand the story they are taking part in. The adventures can form a classic heroic journey, but they can also form a series of, highly unpredictable, peaks and troughs. Both are entertaining: it's all about preference.

DOING THINGS THE OLD FASHIONED WAY

One issue with the player's role in adventuring is that, after 75 years of exposure to sword and sorcery tales, the audience has come to know the formula, to see the connections, to know where things are going. Such stories can, as a result, seem… predictable. Howard's Conan stories were never predictable — or at least, certain elements of them never were, confounding the formula which we think we have identified and digested now.

Readers generally know that Conan — or equivalent heroes — will survive and probably emerge from the tale a little richer and with a few more scars, but for much of the time readers don't know how Conan arrived at the place the adventure begins. The audience certainly doesn't know how Conan will escape from the danger he is about to encounter, any more than the reader can guess what the danger will turn out to be.

This unpredictability is part of what makes the Conan stories so vibrant and so arresting. Where has Conan been before he finds himself in a tavern in the Maul, asking a coarse Kothian precisely what he can tell about the Tower of the Elephant? The reader doesn't know and it doesn't really matter. This is a third way to build a campaign from the adventures in this book, and it is the most typically Howardian. However, it is perhaps the least typical of a conventional roleplaying game, and so it bears a little explanation. Campaigns in roleplaying games often take the forms discussed above — what the two campaign ideas above offer is a continuous story. The conduct of the player characters in one adventure will affect how they arrive at the next — even when the gamemaster is looking to surprise the player characters, to disorient and unsettle their expectations, they are doing so as part of an ongoing plot. It's just a plot with bigger twists.

A more authentically Howardian **Conan** campaign would be to do away with such connections entirely. To eschew a grand, overarching plot and instead concentrate on the adventures as individual episodes, discrete chapters in the growing legend of the player characters. This certainly makes the gamemaster's job a little easier. Instead of agonizing over what experience and rewards should be awarded to the player characters after each adventure — and how that might affect the next adventure — now everything can be resolved immediately.

The carousing which the player characters engage in takes place in the aftermath of their latest triumph, but who is to say what happens between that time and the point at which they stumble into their next escapade? Perhaps they are forced into working as caravan guards as a result of their debt to a merchant and this is how they end up in the city plagued by the insidious presence of Aumag-Bel.

SEEDS OF GLORY

Or perhaps they are simply there already, drinking in the tavern. It doesn't matter.

What matters is that the player characters become embroiled in the series of events which makes up that adventure. The next time something remarkable happens to the player characters might be weeks, months, years later — have they begun to grow old and their skills to dwindle? Or the opposite, have they progressed from the callow men and women they were initially, becoming masters of their weapons and of fighting together as sword-sisters and dog-brothers? This depends upon the whim of the gamemaster or the player characters at the time. And let it be a whim! If an adventure feels like it should be more difficult or taxing, have that adventure take place years in the past, and make appropriate adjustments to each player character's statistics. Of course, it doesn't matter if next adventure sees the player characters withered with age and on one last, desperate attempt to make themselves wealthy, or if the player characters are suddenly in their prime and able to take the fight to the enemy with confidence and skill.

This type of campaign is ideal for running on a more *ad hoc* basis; it allows for the real pulp experience — dramatic, exciting and unconstrained by the need for relentless consistency. It also means that you can pick and choose adventures from this book as and when they appeal to you.

> *"You sit on satin and guzzle wine the people sweat for, and talk of divine rights of sovereignty — bah! I climbed out of the abyss of naked barbarism to the throne and in that climb I spilt my blood as freely as I spilt that of others. If either of us has the right to rule men, by Crom, it is I! How have you proved yourselves my superiors?"*
>
> — Conan, "The Scarlet Citadel"

HACKING IT ALL TO PIECES

Some gamemasters buy adventure books like this for the ideas; the enclosed adventures are not treated as coherent stories more than they are an interesting list of ingredients which can be plucked out and sprinkled elsewhere. This is of course what these adventures are for: mixing and matching elements from different adventures in this book can also provide interesting fodder for a campaign. The gamemaster might take the Pictish foes from The Ghost of Thunder River and replace the antagonists within the other adventures with a cult of Jhebbal-Saag worshippers that have spread, quietly, throughout the major cities of the continent, waiting for the opportunity to incite a mass uprising, crushing the Hyborian kingdoms of Aquilonia, Brythunia, and Nemedia between a force of fanatics from the South and the berserk fury of the true northern Pictish tribes. Or the amulet from *The Thousand Eyes of Aumag-Bel* might become an object of fascination for creatures and foes from outside that lone city. Perhaps this is what the Dero are seeking in the earth beneath the sorcerer's house? Perhaps this is what is being sought in *The Red Pit*, or the amulet has been wrought to house one of the long-lost Eyes of Sephet.

And there's another way of approaching this form of campaign. The gamemaster doesn't need to run an adventure in order to coopt a particular nonplayer character for whatever purpose desired. Perhaps the man who owns and operates the Red Pit, Abdibaal, is intriguing as a potential recurring villain, but the gamemaster would rather avoid having the player characters endure slavery, even briefly. In that case, the player characters might encounter the mine as visitors, accidentally happening upon it maybe, and hack their way to the bottom in search of something — the amulet, maybe, or the only living man who visited the lost city of *Devils Under Green Stars* but has fallen into the bondage. Transplant whole scenes if desired. Perhaps the entrance to Aumag-Bel's under kingdom is *in* the Red Pit? Perhaps when the *Pact of Xiabalba* is finally unmade what appears in its place is the lost city which the player characters can stumble upon in *Devils*! Change endings, change rewards: the gamemaster should feel emboldened to change anything they dammed well please.

Perhaps this seems obvious — certainly, a great many experienced gamemasters will be shaking their heads at this point, thinking *"What else did you expect me to do?"* — but it bears repeating. These adventures are robust enough to be dissected and reassembled into weird, new configurations to suit the kind of game desired. So the gamemaster shouldn't feel constrained or impelled to run things as written because they are written down. Throw elements together and see what happens.

THE (TOWER OF THE) ELEPHANT IN THE ROOM

The above is a series of ideas, possibilities and approaches which is intended to offer a number of different ways that the gamemaster can make the most out of *Jeweled Thrones of the Earth*. Whether a series of one-shots in which the player characters change from session to session, or a linear campaign which documents the rise of a group of battle-hardened mercenaries to the vertiginous heights of political power, this book can help along that path. If desired, the gamemaster can introduce Conan the Cimmerian himself into these adventures — perhaps the player characters are a secret Aquilonian division of his royal guard. It might be that Conan, his hair beginning to grey and his reflexes beginning to slow, dispatches the player characters on dangerous missions throughout the dreaming west and beyond.

Does the campaign, instead, take place when Conan is a young man, only just having left the barbarous steppes of Cimmeria behind? Perhaps in one bustling metropolis, during a chase through the market, the player characters glimpse an towering figure arguing with a guard, before, suddenly splitting the guard's head with a sword drawn at inconceivable speed. Using Conan in these adventures is certainly a possibility and it makes the player characters feel as though they are part, an authentic part, of the Hyborian Age. But the gamemaster is advised to use Conan sparingly — even the most dominant of player characters might be tempted to simply follow in his wake. Who wouldn't?

If the gamemaster wishes to place these adventures within the context of Conan's career, it is advised to be circumspect about it. The last thing the players should want to do is be part of Conan's entourage, watching the doughty Cimmerian solve all their problems for them. Although, perhaps, if the player characters are trapped, beaten and on the verge of death and the dice turn against them… perhaps the unexpected appearance of a battle-scarred warrior with quick eyes and rippling thews might be a perfect surprise addition. Conan is fearlessly loyal to his friends, and perhaps they assisted or fought alongside him at some point in their past (whether they remember it or not!). Perhaps it's a *deus ex machina* too far — the gamemaster should know what will work best for their particular group of players, and trust that instinct.

> *When I began writing the Conan stories a few years ago, I prepared this "history" of his age and the peoples of that age, in order to lend him and his sagas a greater aspect of realness. And I found that by adhering to the "facts" and spirit of that history, in writing the stories, it was easier to visualize (and therefore to present) him as a real flesh-and-blood character rather than a ready-made product.*
>
> *— Introduction to "The Hyborian Age"*

FINAL THOUGHTS

This book is filled with adventures inspired and influenced by the original canon of Conan tales. They are pulp adventures of impossible deeds carried out by implausible people. Making them into a thrilling, whirligig of slaughter and chaos should be easy enough. The gamemaster should remember that the player characters are the heroes of the adventures (especially if choosing to add a soupcon of Conan himself into the mix) and should strive to make their own legends, using these adventures to do just that. Whatever campaign is stitched together from these assorted pieces, it should bloody, bold, and resolute. Players will remember it for years to come, just as the Hyborian Age will speak the names of their characters with the awe and reverence reserved for only the very greatest. If they know what's good for them.

SCATTERED JEWELS…

These fragments are gathered for gamemasters to flesh out into fuller adventures, or they can be broken apart, expanded, or used solely as inspiration for other sojourns into the weird and fantastic world of Conan.

DEMON IN THE IVORY MASK

On an island, in the midst of the Vilayet, there lies a temple. Neither the island, nor the temple, are inscribed on any charts and even the bloodthirstiest pirates sailing those waters refuse to approach it. But, so say those learned in ancient wisdom, the temple contains the effigy of a forgotten king, still wearing the armor in which he was killed. Upon the remains of his face, it is whispered, there is an Ivory Mask. The wearer of that mask can see the future, as clearly as if it were happening before them at that very moment. Who, amongst the kings of the West or the East would not crave such an item, revealing who seeks to kill and usurp them and when the moment is ripe for them to strike for dominion? How many men and women converge on the island even now, swords gleaming and the song of gold in their ears? The real question of course is: what lurks behind the Ivory Mask? Will the visage of the forgotten king reveal precisely why he is referred to in those ancient texts as a Demon Prince? And will any return to tell of it?

THE LAST CHANT OF ACADIUS DELLO

The great priest of Anu, Acadius Dello, died. Hundreds saw his execution by the Mitra-worshipping authorities of Aquilonia. His corpse was burnt. His ashes poured into the sewers. But now there are tales of men, women, and children hearing his last words, filtering through the night air or pervading the breeze as the fields are tilled. The voice calls to them, makes promises of life, wealth,

SEEDS OF GLORY

joy. Already, many have followed the voice's instructions. None have returned. None have been found. Is the spectral voice truly that of Acadius Dello; can the player characters truly be sure he was the beneficent priest of Anu he seemed to be? Or did the robes of his order simply offer a convenient means of hiding his darker intentions? As more men and women vanish and religious tensions between Mitra's worshippers and those of Anu begin to foment, someone must find the truth. No matter how ghastly that truth may prove to be.

AKSEM-SEDDÎN'S RING

The "ring" of Aksem-Seddîn is no magical artifact. It is a gladiator's pit, carefully hidden from the probing eyes of covetous priests, in the middle of the Stygian desert. There, beneath the pulsing sun, men and women are forced to fight to the death for the entertainment of the rich who travel for many miles to enjoy the entertainment which Aksem-Seddîn so lavishly provides. The player characters were caught by Aksem-Seddîn's slave-catchers, while asleep or drunk or both, and are now being prodded into an exposed circle of rock and spear points to fight to the death. Here, among the greed of the wealthy and the viciousness of their fellow combatants, they must fight until they die. But is Aksem-Seddîn all he seems? Can the player characters find a means of escape — through cunning or strength of arms? What are the strange foods which Aksem-Seddîn prepares for his favored fighters, and why do those wealthy patrons of the fighting pit pay such vast sums to enter the tent of Aksem-Seddîn, when they have grown tired of the bloodshed? Surely, the pleasures of the flesh are not worth that much to such jaded palates. Darkness lurks there, but will the player characters survive the trials of the Ring long enough to discover what they are?

BLACK MISTS ON THE MORNING TIDE

A ship arrives at an Argossean port. The crew is dead, save for a single man who gasps a warning — "She comes! She comes! She comes in the mist!" — before dying, his face contorted into a dreadful grimace of pain. The port is thrown into panic — could it be Bêlit, her raids upon merchant shipping finally proving too dull for the Tigress of the Waves? Or could it be something much worse? As morning approaches and the port town reaches hysteria, a creeping black mist begins to seep through the streets, turning the bright morning into an occluded hell, choking out sunlight, sea-wind, and clean air. Horrifying noises echo through the streets, inhuman footsteps stalk those brave few who venture out from behind thrice-bolted doors. There is something, something infernal, in the mists. Who, or what, has created this second night, to bedevil this innocuous sea-trading town? How can it be banished? And, if it is dismissed, its tendrils driven away, what horrors will be revealed?

THE WALLS OF KHORSHEMISH

An army of thousands at the gates — brigands united by an incomprehensible prophecy and a man cruel and savage enough to cow them into submission. The city of Khorshemish stands at the mercy of the unhinged kozak general, Aktillat. Every day the walls strain beneath the dreadful hammering of battering rams; each night, fire arrows deluge the walls, illuminating the rapidly diminishing band of defenders within. The queen of Khorshemish, driven by desperation and her own, furious inability to accept defeat, comes to the player characters, caught within the city walls and previously indifferent to the siege. She knows a way to infiltrate the kozak camp and slay Aktillat under the very noses of his bodyguards; it is written in an old text she has been working to translate. But she will need to guide them herself — no one else can read the words contained in the parchment. Guide a Queen into the very jaws of death, fulfill the fated words of the ancient past, or be crushed beneath the tyrannical heel of a brutal warlord. It's not much of a choice, but it's the one being offered.

THE HOMECOMING OF THE KING

The remnants of the glorious host, armor ripped, weapons notched, have finally turned back. Was the battle lost or won? The crusade completed or abruptly terminated by an enemy better prepared for the attrition of a long campaign? With the player characters rides the king. His personal bodyguard having been decimated by the conflict, he is suddenly vulnerable. Ambush attacks begin in earnest, guerilla raids on the trudging column of tired troops. The player characters are among their number, and know that the king is the intended target. But it also becomes clear that killing the king is not the intention; he is to be taken alive, though, for what reason it is difficult to know. For ransom? For information? Or for some darker perfidy? As the remaining soldiers are picked off in the night, by foes that sometimes seem less than human, things become desperate. The homecoming of the king nears, yes, but has that been the true purpose of these relentless attacks? To ensure that the king arrives home undefended and exposed? What awaits behind the city walls which all have fought so hard to return to? Will the player characters ultimately wish they had died, cleanly, on the battlefield, rather than in the narrow corridors of the palace, with knives at their backs?

SWORDS OF THE LOST LEGION

Many, many years ago, a company of Nemedian knights marched into the deserts of Kush. They never returned. No trace was ever found — no witnesses ever saw them enter the vast wilderness, there were no marks of their passing. It was as if they vanished into the desert entirely. Until one day, they marched out of the desert, three hundred years after they had been thought dead. Possessed by inhuman strength and terrifying speed, this single company of knights has slaughtered its way through a dozen small towns. An army has been sent against them and returned, with stories of unkillable soldiers and arcane weapons of war. What happened to this lost legion in the desert? Did they vanish into the Outer Dark, claimed by some dread entity and now returned, as part of some cosmic joke? Or is the story of the Lost Legion merely a means of concealing a new form of warfare in the clothes of myth and superstition? The sands will likely run red before an answer is found.

THE WHITE HAND OF ASHTORETH

Three aristocrats are dead, along with their households. All of them victims of the assassin known only as the White Hand of Ashtoreth. There is talk of conspiracy abroad, of a coup being carefully orchestrated. A powerful merchant has been known to visit the temple of Ashtoreth to make offerings there, and has been outfitting his hired hands for battle. The king and queen are known to have mistrusted the murdered aristocrats — a preemptive strike? Or is the assassin acting alone? In service to the crown or to their own best interests, the player characters must infiltrate the lowest, most murderous echelons of society, fighting through thieves, cutthroats and leaning on information brokers to track a legendary killer and find the truth. Someone will pay well to know what has caused this madness. Others will pay dearly to make the madness worse. And, for the truly enterprising, perhaps this madness may reveal a means to ascend from the gutters and the blood to the more rarefied, though no less dangerous, upper tiers of the kingdom.

RIDERS OF THE EASTERN WINDS

Kubbalak, the great warlord of the Hyrkanians, was buried almost two centuries ago, in a tomb whose location has never been revealed or committed to paper. All those involved in erecting the tomb and burying it were slaughtered, and it is said that only the true heir of Kubbalak will be able to find the tomb, unearth and acquire its treasures, and finally unite the horse peoples, to wage a war of conquest against the entire world. There is only one problem: the man called Kubbalak never existed. Kubbalak was the creation of a powerful wizard who sought to twist the Hyrkanians to his purpose. Though he died before he could achieve this, such is the power of the myth that Kubbalak is venerated almost as a god. And the tomb has been found — while the man was a fiction, the tomb is a reality — by a band of dangerous mercenaries. Approached by a Hyrkanian shaman who knows the true nature of Kubbalak but is unable to reveal it, such is its cache amongst his people; instead, the player characters are asked to quietly dispose of these mercenaries while maintaining the illusion of Kubbalak's greatness. There is money, respect, and a guarantee of free passage throughout Hyrkania should they succeed. But beware: these mercenaries are potent enemies, now laying claim to the possessions of an ancient sorcerer. The Hyrkanians will not thank the player characters for interfering with what many see as the ultimate destiny of the people of the steppes.

THE FOREST OF FORGOTTEN GODS

In the furthest extremes of Hyperborea, there is a forest. It is covered in the same snow and ice which besets all the barbarian kingdoms of the north, but unlike the other vast forests of the trackless tundra, this forest is filled with statues and idols and relics of a thousand different gods. When the Hyberboreans embark upon their raiding, howling down upon the civilized countries to the south, in amongst the gold and blood they lust for, they also bring back the icons of their enemies' gods. Kidnapping the gods of their inferiors is, the Hyperboreans consider, the ultimate insult and humiliation they can inflict on the weaklings they have bested. Those stolen items are dragged, in triumph, to the forest and dumped there, to molder and be forgotten. But perhaps the player characters have decided to reclaim the images of their chosen deities and restore their honor. Or perhaps they are just after one of the priceless golden statues of Set, Ishtar, or Ibis which can be found there. Braving the wrath of Hyperborean slavers for glory or greed is one thing, but the forest was not chosen at random. It is a favored hunting ground of some horrifying demon-goddess known as Marowit. Just as they player characters hunt the idols of their faith, they too are being hunted. The key difference is that they are hunting for the mere image of a god, while a living god is hunting for them.

EMPIRE OF BLOOD

Acheron never truly died. Its cities fell, its monuments were pulled down, its people butchered. But the empire never ended. It merely fell into desuetude for many years, waiting, waiting to be restored. And now, the remorseless greed of the current inhabitants of the Thurian continent

SEEDS OF GLORY

has brought this restoration one step closer to reality. A scion of the last emperor of Acheron has arisen, his bloodline kept pure by generations of careful inbreeding, the secret ministrations of a deranged cult. An army is being formed, from mercenaries, the desperate, and the true believers, in secret. The player characters learn of the plot, but who can they tell? Who would ever believe them? And the plot grows stranger still. The scion of the last emperor has not so exactingly been bred to rule. He was born to be sacrificed — a bloody ritual will be carried out, in the last temple of Acheron, buried deep beneath the earth, with the aim of restoring the empire to its former glories. Will such a ritual succeed? Has this cult simply been a cruel trick played upon the mad by some dark figure behind the scenes, who plans to use the ritual not to recreate the Acheronian Empire, but instead to gain the favor of the darkest of gods? Either way, a business begun in blood will need blood to end it.

THE HAMMER OF KARNATH

The city of Karnath was destroyed in a single night. Something screamed out of the heavens and pulverized stone, flesh, and civilization, scarring the earth forever more. Whether it was a comet or the whim of a bored god, many have speculated, but none have known. The great pit, formed by the terrible impact of the Hammer of Karnath, is reputed to hold both a surplus of precious gemstones, sticking out from the living rock and waiting to be hewn. The treasures of Karnath are still said to lurk, too, in the remnants of the once-great city — gold lying hidden beneath the powdered fragments of statues and murals. But there are always other treasure hunters, quite willing to kill to ensure the pick of the find. And, when the Hammer of Karnath fell, did it bring something with it? Some malign, alien intelligence which lies, battered and broken, perhaps, in the lowest levels of the crater, merely waiting to be awoken?

… And so the word came southward. The night wind whispered it, the ravens croaked of it as they flew, and the grim bats told it to the owls and the serpents that lurk in hoary ruins. Werewolf and vampire knew, and the ebon-bodied demons that prowl by night. The sleeping Night of the World stirred and shook its heavy mane, and there began a throbbing of drums in deep darkness, and the echoes of far weird cries frightened men who walked by dusk.

— Thutothemes, The Hour of the Dragon

THE HYBORIAN AGE AWAITS YOU

BOOKS COMING SOON

Conan the Thief
Conan the Mercenary
Conan the Pirate
Conan the Brigand
The Book of Skelos
Conan the Wanderer
Conan the Adventurer
Conan the Scout
Conan the King
Nameless Cults
Ancient Ruins & Cursed Cities
Conan Monolith Boardgame Sourcebook
Conan and the Shadow of the Sorcerer
Legendary Beasts & Otherworldly Horrors

ACCESSORIES

Gamemaster Screen
Geomorphic Tile Sets
Doom & Fortune Tokens
Q-Workshop Dice
Card Decks
Stygian Doom Pit
Fabric & Poster Maps
Character Sheet Pad
Conqueror's Bag

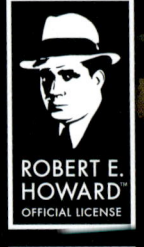

MODIPHIUS ENTERTAINMENT

2D20

CABINET

ROBERT E. HOWARD OFFICIAL LICENSE

HYBORIA

modiphius.com/conan

© 2017 Conan Properties International LLC ("CPI"). CONAN, CONAN THE BARBARIAN, HYBORIA and related logos, characters, names, and distinctive likenesses thereof are trademarks or registered trademarks of CPI. All rights reserved. ROBERT E. HOWARD and related logos, characters, names, and distinctive likenesses thereof are trademarks or registered trademarks of Robert E. Howard Properties Inc. All rights reserved.

The 2d20 system and Modiphius Logos are copyright Modiphius Entertainment Ltd. 2015-2017. All 2D20 SYSTEM text is copyright Modiphius Entertainment Ltd.

EXPLORE NEW WORLDS

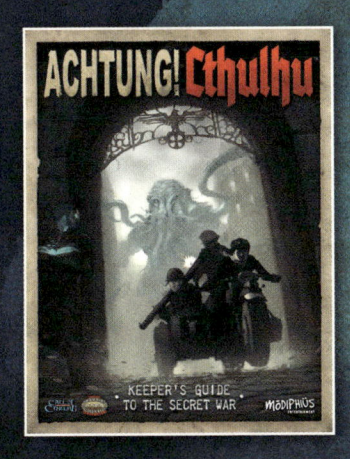

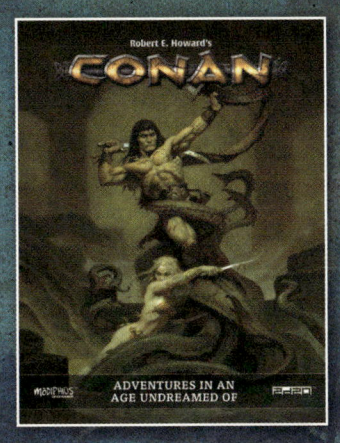

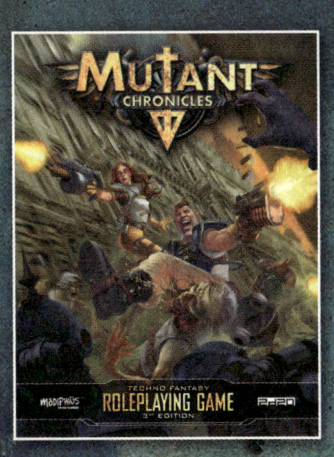

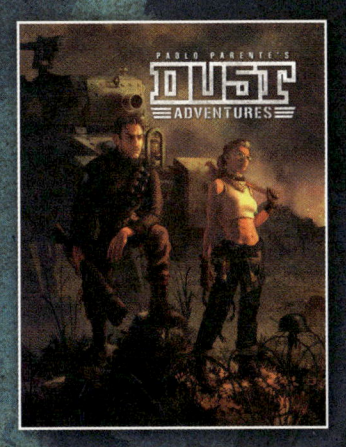

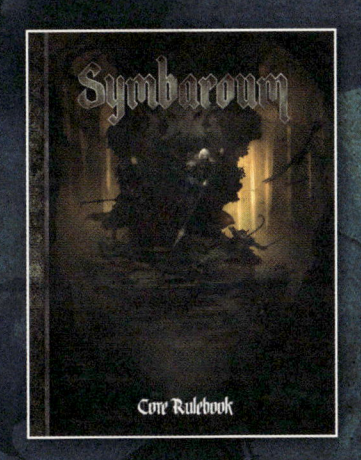

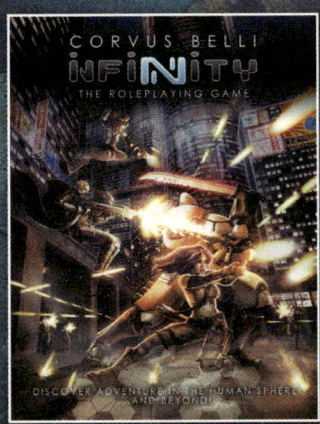

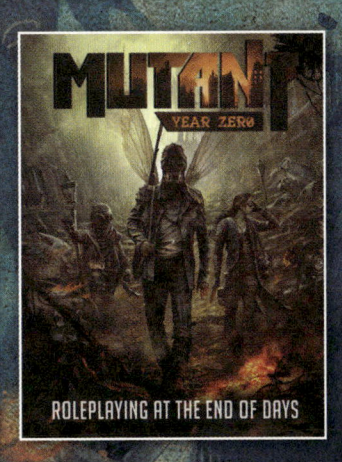

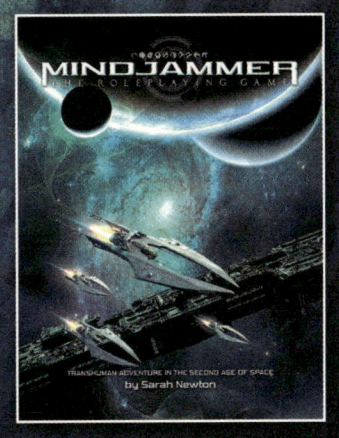

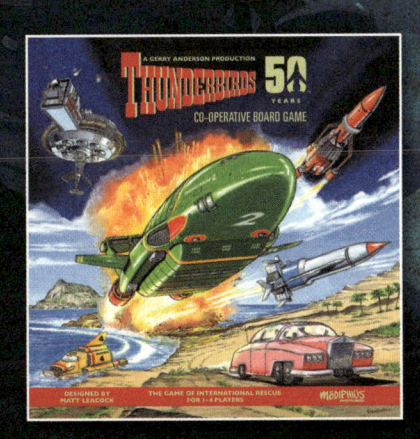

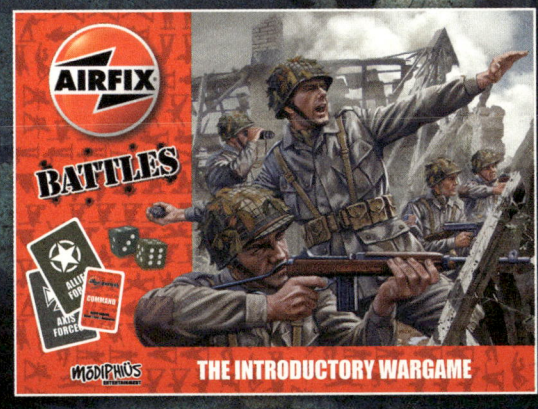

MODIPHIUS™ ENTERTAINMENT

modiphius.com
facebook.com/modiphius